That Better Country

JOHN BARRETT

That Better Country

THE RELIGIOUS ASPECT OF LIFE
IN EASTERN AUSTRALIA, 1835-1850

MELBOURNE UNIVERSITY PRESS

LONDON AND NEW YORK : CAMBRIDGE UNIVERSITY PRESS

First published 1966
Printed and bound in Australia by
Melbourne University Press, Carlton N.3, Victoria
Registered in Australia for transmission
by post as a book

Dewey Decimal Classification Number 279·4

Library of Congress Catalog Card Number 66-12956

Text set in 11 point Georgian type

For Margaret
who read and improved it all
and for
Michael, Susan and Clare
one of whom may some day write
a better book

Our colonists, moreover, unlike the pilgrim fathers of America, have not emigrated to these shores as an asylum from persecution carrying with them their religious ordinances; they have for the most part quitted their native country principally intent on the acquisition of wealth, and with little thought, it is to be feared, of those durable riches, and of that better country, in comparison with which all the possessions of the world are a bauble.

The Eighth Report of the Van Diemen's Land Colonial Missionary and Christian Instruction Society . . . 1843.

ACKNOWLEDGMENTS

This book was made possible by the help I received from many quarters. My mother helped me through my undergraduate years. The Reverend Dr Frank Hambly and my former teachers of history at Adelaide, Professor Hugh Stretton, Mr Noel Adams and Professor Douglas Pike, smoothed my way towards the scholarship which the Australian National University granted and the South Australia Conference of the Methodist Church of Australasia permitted me to take up. I received particular help, in various ways, from Professor Manning Clark, Professor Sir Keith Hancock, Professor K. S. Inglis, Mrs Ann Mozley and Mr Hans Gunther, all of the A.N.U. Very willing co-operation was given by officials of several Churches (including the late Monsignor J. J. McGovern, who vastly preferred the warm history in stone around Parramatta and Windsor to the cold archives of which he had charge) and by the staffs of the Mitchell, Dixson, National and A.N.U. Libraries and of the N.S.W. Archives Authority and the Tasmanian State Archives. I am grateful to all who have permitted me to quote from their works or from sources in their possession, and who helped provide the illustrations. By the courtesy of the Reverend Erwin Vogt, the indulgence of Miss Mary Wright, and the hard work of Miss Beth Cooper and Miss Marlene Rogers, the final typing of the manuscript was done at the Central Methodist Mission, Adelaide: this was yet another C.M.M. service to the needy. Though they may not have realized it, the people of the Naracoorte Methodist Circuit have allowed me to spend a good deal of their time in revising a thesis for publication; I acknowledge it now, with thanks. To all these, and to many others, not least to Sir John Ferguson for his *Bibliography of Australia*, I am deeply indebted.

J.B.

Methodist Manse
Naracoorte, S.A.
1965

CONTENTS

ILLUSTRATIONS

PLATES

FIGURES

xiii

ABBREVIATIONS

A.N.U.	Australian National University, Canberra
B.P.	Papers of W. G. Broughton (microfilm, NL)
B.T. Miss.	Bonwick Transcripts from Documents in London, Missionary Section (Mitchell Library)
Courier	*Hobart Town Courier*
C.S.I.L.	Colonial Secretary, New South Wales, In Letters (N.S.W. Archives Authority)
C.S.O.L.	Colonial Secretary, New South Wales, Out Letters (N.S.W. Archives Authority)
Examiner	*Launceston Examiner*
G.O.	Lieutenant-Governor's Office, Van Diemen's Land, Duplicate Despatches sent to the Colonial Office (TA)
Herald	*Sydney Herald;* from 1 August 1842, *Sydney Morning Herald*
H.R.A.	*Historical Records of Australia,* Series I (unless otherwise indicated)
J.R.A.H.S.	*Journal and Proceedings, Royal Australian Historical Society*
Lowe Committee	Report from the Select Committee on Education, with Appendix, and Minutes of Evidence, 1844, *V. & P. (N.S.W.), 1844*
L.S.D.	Lands and Surveys Department, Van Diemen's Land, Correspondence Records (TA)
Min. of Exec. Coun., N.S.W.	Minutes of the Executive Council of New South Wales (N.S.W. Archives Authority)
Min. of Exec. Coun., V.D.L.	Minutes of the Executive Council of Van Diemen's Land (TA)
ML	Mitchell Library, Sydney
NL	Australian National Library, Canberra

N.S.W. Wes. Dist. Min.	Minutes of the New South Wales District Meeting, Wesleyan Methodist Church (Dixson Collection and Mitchell Library)
P.P. (H.C.)	*Parliamentary Papers, House of Commons*
S.P.C.K.	Society for the Promotion of Christian Knowledge
S.P.G.	Society for the Propagation of the Gospel
TA	Tasmanian State Archives, Hobart
V.D.L. Wes. Dist. Min.	Minutes of the Van Diemen's Land District Meeting, Wesleyan Methodist Church (Wesley Church, Hobart)
V. & P. (N.S.W.)	*Votes and Proceedings of the Legislative Council of New South Wales* (including *Minutes* and *Papers*)
V. & P. (V.D.L.)	*Votes and Proceedings of the Legislative Council of Van Diemen's Land* (including *Minutes* and *Papers*)

INTRODUCTION

In 1788 Botany Bay was simply an extension of England's prison system, a wretched camp of convicts and their guards; but the settlement thus begun was not to be long confined. Food had to be grown, and stock raised; convicts became free, and free men saw opportunities in the new land; the Australian continent beckoned to all who could master her, and many came to compete for her favours. Free migration swelled significantly in the eighteen thirties, and New South Wales and its offshoot, Van Diemen's Land, noticeably increased their rate of development into diversified communities of some sophistication. By 1850 the marks of society were more obvious in eastern Australia than the scars of the penal colonies.

Professor Douglas Pike has aptly described Australia as 'the quiet continent', and it will be argued below that the Australian Churches have had an equally quiet life, changing their real position in the community very little over the years. This, however, does not reduce Australia's history to a monotonous dead-level, without landmarks or turning points. On the contrary, the period from about 1835 to 1850 stands as a prominent watershed between the era of penal colonies proper and the expansion of Australia in the years of gold and of responsible government; it very much helped to determine the form of this later development. In 1840 transportation to New South Wales was abolished. By 1842 New South Welshmen occupying houses valued at £20 a year could elect twenty-four of the thirty-six legislative councillors. In 1850 a £10 franchise was adopted in this colony and for new, similar councils in Van Diemen's Land and Victoria. In the thirties and forties the development of the Churches was unprecedented; the first bishops arrived, the number of the clergy increased by leaps and bounds and churches and chapels appeared throughout the settled areas. There was a vigorous free press, much publication of books and pamphlets, the establishment of new elementary school systems and the opening of the first colleges for secondary education. Water was piped to the city houses, there were steam boats in the harbours, and local manufactures were improving both in quantity and variety. These were crucial years, years of change, years of advance.

I

In the forties a citizen of Sydney could stroll along paved, gas-lit footpaths between gracious Georgian buildings. Shops and inns were there in abundance, and scattered among them were numerous schools, both public and private, a subscription library containing fifteen thousand volumes, a hospital, a legislative council building, the churches of half a dozen denominations, banks and insurance houses, a post office embellished with six Doric columns, a theatre accommodating two thousand persons, and two luxury hotels of three and four storeys. The perambulating citizen, if respectable, might have acknowledged the salute of the mayor—or a physician, a judge, a geologist—whose carriage passed along the macadamized street. He might have resisted overtures from the secretary of a total abstinence society, greeted a prosperous iron manufacturer, succumbed to the plea of the treasurer of a benevolent society, discussed investments with a merchant and land tenure with a squatter, and bowed to a doctor of divinity, before settling himself for speeches arguing the case for a new school system, or for a performance by a choral society. Next day he might have read an account of his evening's entertainment in the *Sydney Morning Herald*. Through it all he might have been little conscious of convictism in the city, though ubiquitous rowdies could have annoyed him in passing, and a glance at a policeman's face might have reminded him of the source whence the constabulary had sprung.

After all, this polite society was still formed upon a base of villainy and ignorance, of debauchery and coarseness. When Sir Richard Bourke, eighth Governor of New South Wales, proposed a radical change in the relation of Church to State (advocating State aid for all denominations), he hoped that thereby would be 'secured to the State good subjects, and to society good men'.[1] Good subjects and good men had to be secured; they did not crowd out to the Australian colonies on every ship, and those who came did not enter a society conspicuous for loyalty, honesty, sobriety or piety. A grand total of over one hundred and fifty thousand convicts landed in New South Wales and Van Diemen's Land. In the mid-thirties convicts constituted over one third of the population of New South Wales, and they still amounted to much the same proportion in Van Diemen's Land in 1850, while there remained in both colonies large numbers of former prisoners and many influences stemming from the worst penal era. Some convicts reformed, some were never criminals in any true sense, and the presence of convicts helped to promote government interest in schools and support of the Churches; but, on the whole, convictism did not foster good subjects and good men. Most of those transported were ignorant and

[1] Bourke to Stanley, 30 September 1833, *H.R.A.*, xvii, pp. 229-30.

brutalized, and those who were Irish had additional reason for despising English law and English religion.

Another part of the problem of developing a decent, orderly society arose from scattered settlement and primitive conditions beyond the main centres. Sydney's streets were macadamized, but it took a bushman to follow safely most of the tracks in the interior. In tiny Van Diemen's Land the difficulties were reduced, but in sprawling New South Wales, where the governors completely failed to confine the spread of settlement, the problem was immense. The theoretical boundaries of settlement were those of the nineteen counties, but men continuously pushed out with their flocks and herds to squat wherever there was grass and water. After 1834, flock owners forced upon the authorities a whole new district, Port Phillip, which soon became a separate colony. The constant expansion caused trouble over ownership of land, made the maintenance of law and order a difficult process, and increased the problem of providing schools and churches—each an important factor in the attempt to produce and preserve good subjects and good men.

Churches and schools were closely connected at this time. Traditionally, the Church of England had been mainly responsible for the elementary schools both in England and in the colonies. The English Dissenters, the Scots and the Irish were also used to schools associated with religious bodies, or conducted according to an agreement between them, and the State had only recently admitted its responsibility to bring education to the masses. The conflict in England between parliament, Anglicans and Dissenters over the control and support of the schools was carried out to the Australian colonies and there made, if possible, even worse by the nature of colonial communities, which were small, scattered and denominationally mixed. How to overcome this problem was one of the most hotly debated questions of the time.

The debate extended to the relative positions of the Churches themselves. In England, rivals and reformers were questioning the position of the established Church, and English colonists brought the challenge to Australia, where it was eagerly espoused by Scots and Irish who clung loyally to their respective national Churches. If the Anglican Church was no Church to the Irish, and if the Presbyterian Church was established by law in Scotland, why should the Church of England alone be supported by colonial authorities? The question was raised fiercely, and had to be answered tactfully. Men like Bourke, with liberal ideas, were not displeased by all its implications, yet they did not find the solution easy. Though it was scarcely practicable, as well as undesirable, in their view, to restrict aid to Anglicanism only, the placing of all denominations upon an equal footing meant braving the wrath of powerful Anglicans and involving the State in enlarged expense. The denominational tangle thus aggravated the problem of using the power of government to build up a good society.

Convict influence, colonial rawness and denominational rivalry were not the only sources of the problem. Much religious ignorance and carelessness in the colonies had first taken root in England, and was simply transplanted. As late as March 1851, the Australian-born formed less than half of the population of New South Wales and just over a quarter of Victoria's. For most people in the colonies, therefore, their British background was directly significant. What that background could mean in the matter of religion, for migrants as well as convicts, was vividly described by a chaplain on an emigrant ship in 1850, when he wrote:

> Now that I am thrown into a mixture of all classes of society, I find with regret, that in this heterogeneous mass there are very very few who seem to have fixed notions of what religion is. There seems to be no rational confession of faith amongst them. They have no idea of the nature of the Sacraments. Some think that religion consists in not being an absolute infidel; others in not being a Papist; others in allowing their neighbour to be of what creed he likes; all their ideas on religious subjects seem to be imbued with a cold vague negative Protestantism, 'that evil spirit of unbelief which departs from the living God'.[2]

Here was the hard core of the problem—English indifference. 'English' is used advisedly, because the Scots were rather more likely to have a religious training and the Irish, for all their hooligan element, were usually ready to confess their sins and assist at the Mass. But vast numbers of Englishmen, from the cities and the lower classes especially, were quite unconnected with either church or chapel at home. The problem had a long history and a wide range, and contemporary witnesses to its existence are numerous and diverse. At the end of the eighteenth century, the evangelical William Wilberforce described even the professed churchmen of the more privileged classes as being 'little acquainted' with Christianity.[3] Some thirty-five years later, the radical William Cobbett answered his own question, 'Does the Establishment conduce to religious instruction?', with a blunt 'No: flatly no'.[4] The unorthodox theist, Thomas Carlyle, saw among the masses

[2] J. D. Mereweather, *Life on Board an Emigrant Ship: Being a Diary of a Voyage to Australia* (London, 1852), p. 64.
[3] W. Wilberforce, *A Practical View of the Prevailing Religious System of Professed Christians in the Higher and Middle Classes in This Country* . . . (London, 8th ed., 1805), p. 7.
[4] W. Cobbett, *Legacy to Parsons* . . . (London, 1947), p. 65. Originally published in 1835.

only the symptoms of the Church's neglect, and among other classes the reduction of God's laws to 'a Greatest-Happiness Principle, a Parliamentary Expediency'.[5] Friedrich Engels, German visitor and embryonic Marxist, produced evidence from which he argued that even farm workers in England had 'to a great extent, broken with the Church' and that, where they outwardly complied, they often inwardly rebelled.[6] No enemy of the Church of England, but one of her bishops, C. J. Blomfield, spoke in 1840 of 'the thousands of miserable destitute souls' living without pastoral care in the Diocese of London alone.'[7] Nor did Dissent or Methodism fill the gap. Dissenters were notoriously middle-class, and usually not missionary minded as far as the working masses about them were concerned. Although the Methodists were supposed to be effective among the poorer classes, with London as one of their strongholds, only about one half of one per cent of that city's population was Methodist in 1815.[8] Even multiplying Methodist numbers several times over, to allow for those influenced but not convinced, gives only a tiny percentage of the people, and many of these were of the middling classes. The idea is quite false that some time after 1738, the year of John Wesley's great religious experience, the English people generally began to attend church or chapel, and retained the habit until the maturing of the generation born in 1859-60, the years of *The Origin of Species* and of *Essays and Reviews*. All too many Englishmen continued throughout this time to grow up neither practising religion nor knowing much about it. When such Englishmen came to Australia, as convicts or as free migrants, they brought their indifference with them, and piled it on the heap of difficulties already made large by isolation and pre-occupation with the business of living, by the breaking of old ties and the early shortage of churches and clergymen.

Colonial authorities recognized the great need for moral and Christian teaching. Public men and newspapers supported religion—at least in the public eye, in a general sense, and as the handmaid of morality and social order, if not from genuine personal piety. Religious provision received the serious attention of government between 1835 and 1850, a heavy expense being borne by the State in giving aid to the Churches,

---

[5] T. Carlyle, *Past and Present* (London, 1899), pp. 136, 146, and 'Chartism', in *Critical and Miscellaneous Essays* (London, 1899), IV, pp. 155-6. These were originally published in 1843 and 1839 respectively.
[6] F. Engels, *The Condition of the Working Class in England* (trans. and ed. by W. O. Henderson and W. H. Chaloner, Oxford, 1958), pp. 303-4. Originally published in 1844.
[7] A. Blomfield, *A Memoir of Charles James Blomfield* . . . (London, 1863), I, pp. 225-6.
[8] Methodist numbers in London (6,350) are taken from M. Edwards, *After Wesley* (London, 1935), p. 163. London's population was well over one million.

and the leading churchmen's ideals for education being allowed to dominate the school systems for years. That this happened was a sign that religion among the nineteenth-century English had another aspect. Though there were millions untouched by religion, there were other millions, especially among the middle and upper classes, who were deeply influenced by Christianity and moral ideals. Evangelicalism, in the broadest sense, achieved its 'maximum influence' about 1840 and showed its 'first signs of decline' about 1870, so that Victorian England was, of civilized countries, 'one of the most religious that the world has known'.[9] What this means is that a society much given to religious observance was developed over the heads of the degraded society composed of the working masses, who had little religion among them: hence the concern of the colonial authorities, and the great unconcern for churches and religious instruction among many of the colonial people. The middle and upper classes were encouraged to take religion seriously by the Oxford Movement, which, beginning in 1833 under the leadership of Keble, Pusey and Newman, went on to inspire and provoke the Christian public by the high church views disseminated through the *Tracts for the Times*. This assertion of the Church as superior to the State, this stress upon sacramental and priestly worship, and the retorts and counter-assertions of fervent low churchmen, brought the claims of Christianity and the duties of the Christian before the eye of the classes who counted socially. On top of this, the middle-class Methodists and Dissenters were increasing in prestige and influence, as well as continuing their effectiveness among their own social groups. Hence many officials and respectable migrants brought religious convictions with them to Australia. This did not mean that they were narrowly pious, for some of the most devout, and all the most dogmatic, churchmen often looked with suspicion and dislike upon the religious opinions of the colonies' leading citizens. The Enlightenment and English Liberalism, as well as Evangelicalism or Tractarianism, had affected the thinking of many colonists, making them inclined to tolerate any creed, and giving them a great faith in purely secular knowledge. This found natural expression in advocacy of State aid to all denominations and in attempts to do away with church schools in favour of broad general systems. To some churchmen such ideas revealed utter carelessness about religious truth, and perhaps it is true to say that these ideas pointed to some degree of religious casualness;[10] yet few of the colonies' influential men were positively

[9] R. C. K. Ensor, *England, 1860-1914* (Oxford, 1952), pp. 140, 137.
[10] It is argued that the 'Authority' which sustained colonial society was not 'traditional Christianity', but 'Moral Liberalism', in Michael Roe, 'Society and Thought in Eastern Australia, 1835-51' (Ph.D. thesis, A.N.U., 1960). Since the preparation of the

averse to Christianity. Their religious beliefs may often have been broad and shallow, but they were held firmly. Religion, indeed, is strikingly apparent in the Legislative Councillors' speeches when they are compared, not with the tongues of angels, but with Australian political debates today. There was, therefore, a weight on the side of religion among colonial people, as well as the heavy weight on the other side. The latter was indeed heavy: after all the debates about State aid to Churches and religious teaching in schools, and after all the practical experiments and the Churches' modest successes, it still had to be acknowledged that many in the colonies retained 'that evil spirit of unbelief which departs from the living God'.

What follows is a study of how the Churches, the State and the people reacted to each other in eastern Australia during the critical years before the gold rushes. The increasing provision of clergymen and places of worship, and the bold granting and speedy restricting of State aid, are discussed in Part One. The second section describes the efforts of the Churches to prevent the introduction of secular systems of education, at first with apparent success, but finally weakening as the forerunners of Australia's modern State schools gathered support. Part Three is an attempt to show the colonists in true perspective, with both the pious and the impious living side by side, and Australia being moulded by the parsons and their laymen as well as by squatters and merchants. Minor themes are developed as the discussion proceeds, and it will not be any accident if the reader gains the general impression that, after all, the differences between that day and our own are not so great. It matters very little how right or wrong are the opinions expressed in this book. Its real purpose is to remind readers that there is a religious aspect to Australian history, and to invite others to look squarely at that aspect for themselves.

---

manuscript for this book Dr Roe has published the substance of his stimulating thesis under the title, *Quest for Authority in Eastern Australia 1835-1851* (Melbourne, 1965).

I

Religious Provision in Eastern Australia

1835–1850

BEFORE THE CHURCH ACTS

The Church Comes to Australia

O N THE SHORES of Botany Bay the first fleet left about a thousand persons, of whom one was a clergyman of the Church of England appointed to the cure of souls. No minister had worse parishioners than had the Reverend Richard Johnson, chaplain to New South Wales in 1788, but he had one advantage over many of his successors: he knew who and where his people were, whereas later clergymen had to cope with much larger numbers scattered over much wider areas. This was a big part of the problem of religious provision in Australia, and neither Church nor State managed to secure chaplains in sufficient numbers to keep pace with the growth and spread of population in the new land; there was always a lag, and always an area farther out where clerical visits were infrequent.

When Johnson resigned his chaplaincy in 1800, the Reverend Samuel Marsden, who had been the assistant chaplain since 1794, was the sole official minister to the four thousand persons in the colony. Limited help was given by the stray clergymen who appeared now and then as convicts or chaplains to the forces, and some good work was done by members of the London Missionary Society who retreated, from time to time, from the perils of Tahiti. In the period 1801-7 regular assistance was given by the Reverend Henry Fulton, an Irish Protestant who had been transported for sedition and who ministered at Norfolk Island after receiving a conditional pardon. The Reverend James Dixon, one of three Catholic priests transported for similar offences, also gained permission to act as chaplain when he was emancipated in 1803; but this provision for the numerous Catholics in the settlements was withdrawn after a rebellion among Irish convicts in the next year. Dixon, who held no faculties anyway, found his position very difficult during the further four years in which he remained in the colony. When Marsden returned to England on leave in 1807, Dixon and Henry Fulton were the only clergymen in New South Wales who were in any sense performing a regular ministry. In 1808 Dixon left the colony and, in the confusion following the Bligh rebellion, Fulton was temporarily suspended from office. William Pascoe Crook, one of the L.M.S. missionaries, was appointed to act in Fulton's place, but he was not ordained and the eight or nine thousand inhabitants of New South Wales were really left without a clergyman until the Reverend William Cowper, another Anglican, arrived in August 1809. The situation was much improved in the next year, when there were four Anglican chaplains, but these men could not banish the results of twenty years' spiritual neglect in the easy way that England banished her criminals to Australia, and they were already having difficulty in reaching those to whom they were supposed to minister. Richard Johnson had initially served his one thousand; they had each to serve more than two and a half thousands by 1810. In the following years, the Anglican clergymen grew in numbers but their chances of performing an effective ministry did not improve. By 1836, the year in which the New South Wales Legislative Council passed a Church Act to step up State aid to religion, there were some four and a half thousand New South Welshmen to each of the seventeen active clergymen in the colony,[1] and the colonists were moving far from Sydney Cove—out to all nineteen surveyed counties, and beyond them to the west, to the south and the future Melbourne, to the north and the future Brisbane. The Reverend Richard Johnson had found his task heart-breaking, but his successors must have been conscious of the one great blessing which had been his.

In Van Diemen's Land, the second Australian colony, a similar process had occurred. In 1804 the four hundred and thirty-three persons in the island settlement had one chaplain among them, but there were almost five thousand persons to each of the nine Church of England clergymen serving there early in 1836.[2] The two colonies suffered another lack of ecclesiastical oversight by being included in the Diocese of Calcutta; no bishop of the Church of England so much as visited Australia until the former Archdeacon of New South Wales, William Grant Broughton, returned to Sydney as Bishop of Australia in June 1836. Two generations had grown up before confirmation, ordination and consecration could be performed properly, as episcopal functions, among Anglicans in Australia.

If Anglicans had lacked a bishop, Catholics had lacked even an official chaplain until 1820—with the exception of James Dixon's single

---

[1] A Census was taken in September, 1836. *Tegg's Almanac*, 1836, p. 52; 1837, p. 118; and *H.R.A.*, xviii, pp. 472-4, are useful guides to the number of clergy.
[2] Arthur to Glenelg, 26 January 1836, *H.R.A.*, xviii, p. 488.

year of office. Even the restricted, unofficial activities of Dixon and a few other priests had covered only about eight of the first thirty-two years. Priests had fruitlessly applied to the British Government for permission to work in New South Wales without pay, and Father Jeremiah O'Flynn actually arrived in the colony in 1817, only to be deported in 1818 because he did not have any authority from the Government. It was an unnecessarily grim situation which does the authorities small credit, for the Catholic population was always from one quarter to one third of the total, and Catholics shrank in horror from Church of England services. Nevertheless, Catholic history is not all a tale of penalties. After the O'Flynn affair, Australian Catholics secured two priests, the Reverend John Joseph Therry and the Reverend Philip Conolly, who were placed on the Government pay roll in 1820, nine years before Catholic emancipation in England, and ten years before formal emancipation was proclaimed in New South Wales. Final assurance that the worst days were over was given in 1835 when the Right Reverend John Bede Polding arrived as bishop—ten months before the Anglican bishop reached Sydney, if that was any consolation. In 1836 there were the bishop, a vicar-general and five priests in New South Wales, and two priests in Van Diemen's Land, all of whom were paid by the State. Their task was formidable enough, for Catholics numbered nearly twenty-two thousand in New South Wales and some two thousand in Van Diemen's Land.[3]

By the mid-thirties several other denominations were securely established in the colonies. The first of these ministers to come to Australia by the express appointment of a religious body was the Reverend Samuel Leigh, who arrived at Sydney in 1815 as the representative of the Wesleyan Methodists, and this denomination was maintaining four ministers in each colony in 1836. Presbyterians were badly served in the first thirty-odd years of the colonies' existence, for ministers did not arrive until 1823, the Reverend Archibald McArthur coming to Hobart in January and the Reverend John Dunmore Lang arriving at Sydney in May. Thereafter the position improved until there were five Presbyterian ministers in both New South Wales and Van Diemen's Land in 1836. The Independent (or Congregational) and Baptist Churches, and the Society of Friends (Quakers), had very restricted early careers. Although Independency came early to the colonies through the visits and, in some cases, the settling of L.M.S. missionaries, and two Quakers, Backhouse and Walker, made a prolonged tour of the colonies between

---

[3] *Tegg's Almanac*, 1836, p. 51; 1837, p. 118; H. N. Birt, *Benedictine Pioneers in Australia* (London, 1911), II, p. 291; *Statistical Returns of Van Diemen's Land, 1824-35* (Hobart, 1836), Table 24.

1832 and 1837, their congregations were slow to expand. Van Diemen's Land was something of an exception to the general rule, for there were three Independent ministers there in 1836; but New South Wales had only one, and there was only one Baptist minister in each colony, while the Friends' representation was small in both.[4] Yet even these minor contributions helped to meet the need for religious instruction in Australia.

Taking all denominations together, the colonists in New South Wales were served by thirty-five ordained ministers of religion in the month of the census in 1836, thus making a ratio of about 2,200 people to each pastor. A total of twenty-three clergymen gave Van Diemen's Land the more favourable ratio of nineteen hundred to one. Some idea of the areas involved and the stationing of the clergy can be gained from Figures 1 and 2, and even the simple arithmetical averages have some use as comparisons with the one thousand persons of mixed creeds who were served by one Anglican chaplain in the Sydney area in 1788. In so far as the major denominations had clerical representatives in 1836, while only one had been represented at the beginning, the provision was much better. But the number of people for which an individual clergyman might be responsible, as well as the area over which they could be scattered, had increased. Anglican and Catholic clergymen, in particular, could expect two or three times the number of parishioners with which the Reverend Richard Johnson had begun, and many of them were still convicts. Because the number of ministers of religion had not increased at the same rate as the population, because convicts still formed a large proportion of that population, and because the area of settlement was becoming enormous, the problem of ministering to the people remained acute.

Churches and chapels were slow to appear on the Australian scene. A Presbyterian congregation formed in New South Wales in 1802 managed to erect a little chapel—Ebenezer, at Portland Head—seven years later. Anglicans on the mainland waited ten years from the foundation of the colony before they saw the foundation stones laid for their first permanent buildings at Parramatta and Sydney, while the foundation stone of St David's, Hobart, was not laid until 1817. After this sluggish start considerable leeway was made up comparatively quickly, so that there were twelve Anglican churches in Van Diemen's Land, and nine churches and eight chapels or schoolrooms used for worship in New South Wales, by the mid-thirties. But only about

[4] *Tegg's Almanac* is again one convenient source for New South Wales ministers. For Van Diemen's Land, see *Van Diemen's Land Annual*, 1836, p. xxii; *Ross's Hobart Town Annual*, 1836, pp. 19-20; V.D.L. Wes. Dist. Min., 11 February 1836 (Wesley Church, Hobart).

fourteen per cent of Van Diemen's Land's total population, and perhaps eight per cent of the people of New South Wales, could have been accommodated in these buildings.[5]

The Presbyterians had several chapels in New South Wales by 1836, and could seat eleven hundred people in Sydney's Scots Church, while some two thousand persons could be accommodated in the southern colony. Catholic accommodation in Van Diemen's Land was hopeless, for there were two thousand Catholics on the island and only one dilapidated chapel seating two hundred. On the mainland the twenty-two thousand Catholics had five churches, accommodating 3,650 persons, and had commenced to build another which was planned to hold one thousand worshippers. The Wesleyan Methodists reported ten chapels in New South Wales, and five in Van Diemen's Land, and must therefore have provided for at least another thousand worshippers, though some of their chapels were extremely crude affairs. Other denominations also provided a few chapels by this time, and the worst was over.[6]

It still was not a happy position. Government statistical returns for Van Diemen's Land showed a grand total of 10,450 seats in church buildings in 1836, which meant that almost a quarter of the population could be accommodated. In New South Wales, however, the thirteen thousand seats provided in the churches and chapels allowed for considerably less than one fifth of the inhabitants. According to the principle accepted by the British Parliament's Church Building Commission, established in 1818, the Church of England, as the Church of the nation, ought to have been offering accommodation for one third of the English population; therefore religious provision in the Australian colonies was falling sadly below the recognized ideal for Great Britain. At the same time, theory was one thing and practice was another even in the old country, where the ideal was not attained any more than in the colonies. Parliament had established the Church Building Commission because of England's failure to provide adequate places of worship, and the position in Australia needs to be compared with the actual situation in the land from which the settlers and convicts had come. When this is done, it appears that many colonials were no worse off in Australia than they would have been at home.

---

[5] *Statistical Returns* . . . , Table 24; W. G. Broughton, *A Charge Delivered to the Clergy* . . . (Sydney, 1841), Appendix A. The sittings in N.S.W. are only an estimate.
[6] Principal sources are: *Statistical Returns* . . . , loc. cit.; P. F. Moran, *History of the Catholic Church in Australasia* (Sydney, n.d.), p. 190; *Report of the Wesleyan Missionary Committee* (London, 1836), pp. 16-17. The poor and temporary nature of some Wesleyan 'chapels' is indicated by the fact that ten were reported here for N.S.W., but only four were given in *Tegg's Almanac*, 1837, p. 118. Hence the compromise figure of seven is shown in Figure 1. Accommodation, of necessity, is only an approximation.

Port
Macquarie

Macquarie (20th county),
1300

Farquhar
Inlet 32°

Macquarie R.

BLIGH 376   BRISBANE 1378   GLOUCESTER 854

DURHAM 3208

PHILLIP 247

HUNTER 808

Port Stephens

WELLINGTON
530

NEWCASTLE

NORTHUM-
BERLAND
5016

ROXBURGH
1980

COOK 2052

CUMBERLAND 39,797

BATHURST 1729

WESTMORELAND
579

SYDNEY

Lachlan R.

GEORGIANA
575

Wollongong

KING 544   ARGYLE
2417   CAMDEN 3161   Illawarra L.

Shoalhaven

Murrumbidgee R.

L. George

MURRAY 1728   ST VINCENT
592

Bateman Bay

0   50
MILES

150   152°

POPULATION OUTSIDE   THE COUNTIES 2,968

Legend:

○   Clergyman (no chapel)

☿   1 clergyman & 1 church or chapel

☿⁴₃   4 clergymen & 3 churches or chapels, etc.

●   Anglican clergyman
○   Catholic clergyman
◇   Presbyterian clergyman
□   Wesleyan clergyman
◆   Independent clergyman
■   Baptist clergyman
+Q   Quaker chapel
+C   Catholic chapel

Figure after each county name is population in that county

Fig. 1   The Nineteen Counties of New South Wales

Population, Clergymen and Churches, 1836

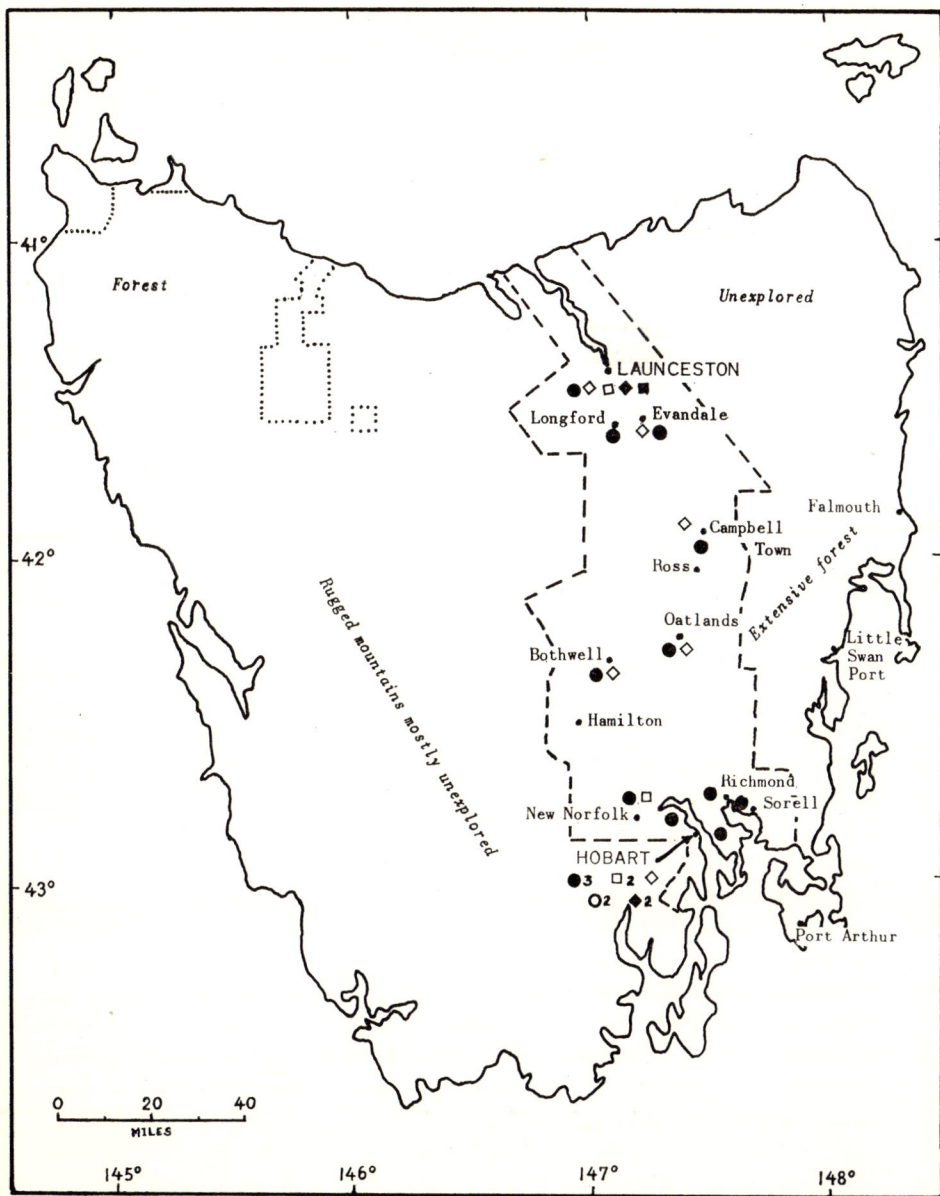

Fig. 2 Van Diemen's Land

Stationing of Clergymen, 1837

The Churches at Home

The Victorian age included so much of the nineteenth century, and Victorian England conjures up such a picture of large families going sedately to church, that it is easy to think of the whole century as static and almost the whole of the English as churchgoers. Some who lived in that century, and who should have known better, seem to have fostered this fond delusion among themselves. Thus the head of the Anglican Church in Australia, the Right Reverend W. G. Broughton, looked distastefully around upon the colonial scene and romantically back upon the English scene. He declared that Australia was totally different from England, where few persons, if they had the proper disposition, could not 'enjoy the benefit of religious instruction and communion'. Even when full weight is given to Broughton's reservation about right inclinations, his statement was hardly realistic, though it must freely be acknowledged that, at first sight, the bishop had grounds for speaking in the way that he did.

For one thing an enormous number could be seated in churches and chapels throughout England and Wales. In 1801, when the population was nearly nine million, fifty-eight per cent could have been accommodated in some place of worship. By 1851, although the population had nearly doubled, seating was available for the same proportion. Clearly, religious provision had received much attention during the intervening years and, judged by the number of sittings only, seems to have been very adequate. This was both a Church of England and a Dissenting achievement, for the 1851 figure was a total of five million seats in Anglican churches and four and a half million seats in Dissenters' chapels.[7] In many places, in fact, non-Anglican provision saved the day. A third of the forty-three thousand people in three working-class wards of Leeds in 1839 could find accommodation in some place of worship, but there were only two and a half thousand seats in the Anglican churches. In 1841 Sheffield Anglicans could accommodate fifteen thousand compared with the Dissenting figure of twenty-five thousand.[8] Whoever provided it, a very large total provision had been made; and from this point of view it could reasonably be said that those who sought to go to church usually could do so. The number of ministers of religion in England was also very great. Towards the end of the thirties there were nearly twelve thousand Anglican clergy-

[7] *P.P.* (H.C.), 1852-3, vol. LXXXIX, p. cxxxi.
[8] J. L. & B. Hammond, *The Age of the Chartists* (London, 1930), p. 230; E. R. Wickham, *Church and People in an Industrial City* (London, 1957), p. 80.

men, including curates, at work in England and Wales.[9] At about the same time there may have been some twelve hundred Independent ministers, fifteen hundred Methodists, nine hundred Baptists and eight hundred Presbyterians.[10] Hence there were well over sixteen thousand ministers of religion working, to some degree, among a total population of fifteen million. At least it can be said that, according to simple averages, the English and Welsh were as well served as New South Wales' first thousand, and considerably better served than Australian colonists in the thirties. W. G. Broughton once implied to a committee of the New South Wales Legislative Council that England had a potent Christian leaven in its rural population. More reliable evidence came from Henry Mayhew, an investigator of the London slum folk in the forties, who found that among Protestants the former countrymen, 'reared in the habit of church-going', went to church most frequently; and parliamentary commissioners, reporting on rural life in the early forties, sometimes came to favourable conclusions on religious observance and clerical attention to the labouring classes in the country.[11]

Thus far, and no farther, is it possible to go with Broughton when he claimed that few in England were unable to enjoy religious instruction and communion. For there are other, and very different, aspects to the matter. One of them stands revealed in the same document which reported favourably on religion in rural Wilts, Dorset and Somerset, for it added that, so far as the clergy's attention went, there was 'the most satisfactory evidence of a great change in this respect having taken place in late years'. Before this there had been a widespread neglect of the rural poor. To take but one example, the Diocese of Lincoln in 1835 included 661 non-resident benefices and there were only 496 curates on these livings, which left 165 of them without a resident clergyman.[12] In many rural parishes the parsonages had been allowed to fall down, so poor had the parsons been, or so long had they been away.[13] Worse still, it spite of the impression of England as a land in which every village has had its spire or tower for centuries, many of the churches also were crumbling with neglect early in the nineteenth century. In not a few villages the church was a 'miserable little hovel', possibly roofed with not much more than the ivy which covered it, being perhaps the place where the beadle hatched out his chickens and the village lads played marbles, and sometimes even

[9] *P.P.* (H.C.), 1840, vol. xxxix, p. 55.
[10] Church officials in England gave assistance with these figures.
[11] H. Mayhew, *London Labour and the London Poor* (London, n.d.), ii, p. 333; *P.P.* (H.C.), 1843, vol. xii, p. 41.　　　　[12] Ibid., 1837, vol. xli, p. 217.
[13] B. A. Bax, *The English Parsonage* (London, 1964), pp. 126-31.

being suffered to tumble down completely.[14] Not surprisingly, other parliamentary commissioners found great ignorance among country people; and the ignorance was of things other than the number of months in a year, for it included total unawareness of the Christian doctrine of life after death.[15] Such was the reality all too often underlying the apparent religious provision in the country; one could always sit underneath the ivy—if the parson turned up. Quite often he had not done this for a long time, and, far from being the leaven in the nation's spiritual life, rural parishioners were sometimes sour dough.

Yet the English countryside was not the real difficulty in the matter of religious provision. The big, new, raw industrial cities formed the hard core of the problem. One contemporary writer dismissed even non-residency of parsons in rural areas as the cause of Anglican ineffectiveness, for, he said, 'its great inefficiency as a national establishment arises from other causes—from the enormous population of the towns, where the minister of the parish *is* generally resident, but utterly incapable of doing the work which he is nominally set to perform'.[16] Between 1821 and 1831 the population of England and Wales as a whole increased by sixteen per cent; but the population of London increased by twenty per cent, Manchester grew by forty-seven, Birmingham by thirty-six, Nottingham by twenty-five per cent, and so on.[17] The increase in the cities was partly by immigration from the country, and the newcomers, together with the offspring of workers already there, were 'dumped down in neglected heaps . . . wholly uncared for by Church or State'.[18] The parsons could do little, even where they wanted to. Sheffield, with a population of over sixty thousand in 1821, was served by eight Anglican clergymen. Before reform in 1844, Leeds had the clergy of only three Anglican churches strictly responsible for the pastoral care of one hundred and fifty thousand people (the other eighteen churches being served by perpetual curates with no pastoral responsibility). In 1836 London had nine parishes with an average of over twelve thousand people per clergyman, four parishes with fifteen thousand and twenty-one parishes with sixteen thousand. A parish elsewhere, with over eleven thousand inhabitants, had no resident clergyman in it at the time of investigation. As the perpetual curate of one industrial town expressed it, with magnificent restraint,

---

[14] Ibid., pp. 111, 125n.; E. Halévy, *History of the English People in the Nineteenth Century* (London, paperback ed., 1961), I, p. 398; W. Cobbett, *Legacy to Parsons . . .* (London, reprinted, 1947), p. 91.   [15] *P.P.* (H.C.), 1843, vol. XII, p. 169.
[16] T. Arnold, *Principles of Church Reform* (ed. by M. J. Jackson and J. Rogan, London, 1962), p. 139. Originally published in 1833.
[17] *P.P.* (H.C.), 1831, vol. XVIII, p. 13.
[18] G. M. Trevelyan, *English Social History* (London, World Books ed., 1948), pp. 479, 481.

'It is quite impossible a clergyman in these populous parishes can properly know his people'.[19]

Neither Catholic priest nor Dissenting minister radically altered the position. The Irish were flooding into English cities, and Mayhew estimated that a hundred Catholic to five Protestant working-class women went to church, with the result that their chapels increased from 346 in 1824 to 574 in 1851 (seating 186,111), and their priests grew in number from 557 to 875 between 1841 and 1853.[20] But Catholics did not change the general pattern of working-class life in the towns. The 'Protestants' were often as little connected with Dissent as with the Establishment. Mayhew reported that more than half of the women street-sellers who attended Dissenting places of worship went to Methodist chapels, but the number who went to any was only a tiny minority. While Methodists were active and highly successful in such working-class areas as Oldham and the mines of Cornwall,[21] they were not reaching even a large minority of the workers as a whole. Less than six per cent of the population attended Methodist meetings in 1821, and 'the Methodists were already tending to become middle class'.[22] And, if this applied to the Methodists, it certainly applied no less to the old Dissenters, the truth about them being revealed in the proud claim by one of their contemporary historians that they generally occupied the 'middle station in society'.[23]

If Methodists and Dissenters were preferring the more prosperous suburbs to the industrial slums, a question mark appears alongside their chapel accommodation. The chapels were still thick in many poor areas, but the congregations were thinning as new buildings were erected in better areas. As the Hammonds suggested long ago, Dissenters had too many chapels after about 1830—not from the aspect of providing for the poor, who tended to ignore them, but from the point of view of keeping up the interest payments on buildings becoming obsolete for that very reason.[24] The practical value of much of the Anglican accommodation must also be questioned, as indeed it was questioned at the time, when the big churches appeared. A Sheffield clergyman declared that one large church was not as effective as several smaller, dispersed chapels might have been, and he freely admitted

[19] E. R. Wickham, op. cit., pp. 70-1; J. L. & B. Hammond, op. cit., p. 229; *P.P.* (H.C.), 1836, vol. xxxvi, p. 1; 1843, vol. xiii, pp. 133, 171.
[20] H. Mayhew, op. cit., I, p. 515; T. E. May, *The Constitutional History of England* (London, 1882), iii, p. 223.
[21] *P.P.* (H.C.), 1842, vol. xv, p. 127; 1843, vol. xiii, pp. 489-90.
[22] K. S. Inglis, 'Churches and Working Classes in Nineteenth Century England', *Historical Studies*, vol. 8, no. 29, p. 45. See also K. S. Inglis, *Churches and the Working Classes in Victorian England* (London, 1963), pp. 9-20.
[23] J. Bennett, quoted in R. G. Cowherd, *The Politics of English Dissent* (London, 1959), p. 15. [24] J. L. & B. Hammond, op. cit., p. 244n.

that the seats for the poor were usually hard, draughty and incon-
venient.[25] The theoretical number of places provided in Anglican
churches bore only slight resemblance to the real provision. For many
years, too, there were no churches, or utterly inadequate buildings, in
area after expanding area. In dozens of parishes the Anglican churches
could hold less than one fifth, and sometimes as few as three or four
per cent, of the inhabitants; and a Midlands mining commissioner
reported that in his area a scarcity of any kind was commonly described
by the phrase 'as few as parish churches'.[26] Household sayings do not
arise, and parliaments do not establish church building commissions
or grant them one and a half million pounds to work with, for no
reason at all.

Although the church builders hoped that the people would come
to worship once they were supplied with a building, their hope was
largely in vain: the new churches usually remained half empty, and
very empty of the workers.[27] This was not just because the working
classes did not find the new buildings congenial; above all it was due
to their tradition of religious indifference. Of many in Smethwick and
Birmingham it could be said that they had been 'always quite heathen',
their forefathers having long lived in ignorance of God. There were
'plenty' of Lancashire coal miners who expected to 'die like a dog, and
then be done wi'',' and were disbelievers because their fathers had been.
At least one third of the lacemakers in Nottingham were described as
being 'kept in restraint only by the strong arm of the law' and as living
'without God in the world'. An assistant curate at Leeds, with duties
among the working classes, found that the majority were quite out
of touch with the Church. The police, for whom some of these people
kept pokers heating in the fire, agreed with the curate when reporting
their success in getting twenty housebreakers transported.[28] People of
this kind, and the absence or inadequacy of religious provision for
them, are as important as any other class or provision in assessing the
real state of affairs in England for comparison with the Australian
colonies. For these were the areas to which the rural workers were
increasingly moving, if they were not moving to the colonies, so that
a majority of the English came at this time to live in the cities; and
these were the people who formed a majority on the convict ships and
in the colonies. Religious provision was good here and there in England,
and for the middle and upper classes almost everywhere; but for the

[25] *P.P.* (H.C.), 1843, vol. xiv, p. 471.
[26] Ibid., 1836, vol. xxxvi, p. 1; 1834, vol. xii, p. 127.
[27] A. Blomfield, *A Memoir of Charles James Blomfield* (London, 1863), i, p. 243;
E. R. Wickham, op. cit., pp. 92, 110-11.
[28] *P.P.* (H.C.), 1843, vol. xiii, pp. 160, 163, 479; vol. xiv, pp. 631, 508-10.

rest it was laughable and laughed at. When a bishop compared religious provision in Australia with that in England, and found the English situation so very much better, he was overlooking many harsh realities and a great mass of the English. When another bishop declared that, of the one hundred and fifty thousand people in Leeds, not three hundred, or even thirty, persons were either as morally wicked or as spiritually ignorant and neglected as colonial convicts, he was either grossly ignorant or wilfully perverse; at any rate, he was being perfectly ridiculous.[29] In practice, men were no farther from a church in the Australian bush than were the general run of working-class people in the English towns. There was, indeed, a greater chance of a clergyman spending a night in a colonial shepherd's hut, than there was of one bedding down in a tenement room in Leeds or London.

For a small minority of the Australian colonials Scotland was the country with which to make comparison; and for a larger minority—about twenty-seven per cent of New South Welshmen in 1836—the homeland was Ireland. There is no reason to suspect that the kirks in the smaller towns and countryside of Scotland were neglected, and provision was not altogether inadequate in the cities. Of the whole population of Edinburgh, twenty-two per cent could be accommodated by the Church of Scotland, and all denominations together could provide for nearly half the population in the mid-thirties.[30] It was certainly said of some of the poor in Scottish cities, 'they cannot tell how they live, nor what they do, so that to ask if they went to Church would be a piece of supererogation',[31] but the Scottish picture of religious provision and observance was brighter than the English, so that any lack of provision in Australia was necessarily more significant for the Scot. In the eyes of most Irish migrants, of course, there was no religious provision unless it was provided by the Catholic Church. At home in the early nineteenth century the Irish were becoming used to more adequate buildings for worship and to a priesthood closer than ever to them in sympathies and habits of living.[32] After Catholic emancipation in 1829 the many Irish migrants to English towns were served all the more by their Church—a devoted priesthood labouring among an extraordinarily devoted people. One instance is provided by Staley Bridge, near Manchester, which grew in forty years from a village of one thousand persons to a market town of fifteen thousand. Some four thousand of these were Irish who had two priests and a chapel with a congregation of over two thousand[33]—a proportion of

[29] F. R. Nixon, *Spiritual Destitution in Van Dieman's [sic] Land* (Leeds, 1843), p. 19.
[30] *P.P.* (H.C.), 1837, vol. XXI, p. 19.   [31] Ibid., p. 55.
[32] See J. A. Reynolds, *The Catholic Emancipation Crisis in Ireland, 1823-9* (Newhaven, 1954), pp. 31, 45-6, 51-2.   [33] *P.P.* (H.C.), 1843, vol. XLV, p. 121.

worshippers to inhabitants which heavily underlined the persistence of the habit of worship among Catholic workers. There was, of course, the problem of drift away from the Church even among the Irish Catholics in England, but it was far less of a problem than the indifference of the English workers, and any lack of priests and chapels in Australia was a serious deprivation for most Irishmen.

As well as the Irish, many of the Scots and the English migrants from upper, middle and some rural classes had less chance of finding adequate church accommodation and ministerial attention in the colonies. Their church and chapel associations could be quite well maintained in the towns and closer settled areas, but they were shattered in the squatting districts. There were enough people in such a situation to make the deficiency in religious provision serious, especially since these were the people who had been the church goers at home. But the poorer people from industrialized England were present in very large numbers. In 1836 between thirty and forty per cent of the people in both colonies were convicts—and convicts came mainly from the towns of the homeland.[34] Of the free migrants in the thirties only a minority came from the towns,[35] but it was still a substantial group, containing many poor persons who needed assisted passages, and the country workers who came to Australia would probably have become English town workers if they had not emigrated, and would have therefore moved into areas badly served by the Churches. When these people came to the colonies, whether to the more populous districts (where most remained) or to the sheep and cattle stations away in the bush, they were not worse off for religious provision than a majority of the English town working classes. If this is only to say that religious provision was very scanty in the colonies, at least it is not to say that migrants necessarily came to worse provision. Indeed, a great many eastern Australians must have found, gladly or indifferently, that the means of grace were more readily available in the colonies than at home.

As Any Race of Heathen

The Reverend Thomas Hassall, Anglican incumbent of Narellan, New South Wales, boasted one chapel within his parish. His other regular services were held in a school, on a house verandah, in a large dairy, in a courthouse, in a log and bark hut, in a private home and

[34] L. L. Robson, 'The Origin and Character of the Convicts Transported to New South Wales and Van Diemen's Land, 1787-1852' (Ph.D. thesis, A.N.U., 1963), pp. 26, 36 and ch. 11. This thesis has since been published as *The Convict Settlers of Australia* (Melbourne, 1965).

[35] R. B. Madgwick, *Immigration into Eastern Australia, 1788-1851* (London, 1937), p. 243.

'in a miserable log building, greatly infested with vermin, formerly used as a School-house'.[36] Work and worship of this kind, which was typical of church life in the colonies, meant that there was a great deal more religious provision than the number of church buildings suggested. In addition, the work of the ordained clergy was augmented by theological students, licentiates, catechists, clergymen who were heads of schools and the ubiquitous lay preachers and pious heads of families. The Wesleyan local preacher, J. J. Walker, took as many as sixteen services a quarter. Presbyterians in New South Wales, Baptists in Hobart and Wesleyans in both colonies did not wait for the arrival of ministers before forming congregations. Catholics assembled in William Davis' cottage, where Father O'Flynn had celebrated Mass, long after he had been deported. W. G. Broughton once described, as no solitary instance, an elderly Church of England minister's visit to an isolated home where he found that the mother had taught her ten or eleven children to repeat the lessons of devotion which he had taught her twenty years earlier in his school on the Hawkesbury. Perseverance in faith, and even religious organization, by no means entirely depended on the presence of clergymen, and the lowly places of worship could be more welcoming than the respectable congregations of England.

All this helped the cause of religion in the colonies, but did not make the colonies religious or religious provision satisfactory. On the contrary, colonial churchmen were depressed by their inadequate means for bringing the gospel to a people who were more often careless than religious. Between 1834 and 1836 Archdeacon Broughton was in England trying to get something done about 'extended and populous districts devoid of Churches, devoid of Clergymen, devoid of Schools', a situation which was leading to a 'visible decline of Religious Principle' and to 'vice and irreligion'.[37] Broughton pleaded for at least nine more chaplains for the colony to which he was returning; but, though he returned a bishop, he returned alone. Australia did not attract the clergy. 'I have really done all that I could to get Chaplains for you; but in vain', the Reverend Charles Simeon, of Cambridge University, had written to the Reverend Samuel Marsden, 'We learn *here* a love of ease and affluence; neither of which are likely to be got by a voyage to Botany Bay'.[38] Therefore Bishop Broughton looked almost in despair towards the wide districts beyond the nineteen counties with their

[36] W. W. Burton, *The State of Religion and Education in New South Wales* (London, 1840), pp. 180-2.
[37] W. G. Broughton, *A Charge Delivered to the Clergy of New South Wales* . . . (Sydney, 1834), p. 20; H.R.A., xviii, pp. 212-13.
[38] Simeon to Marsden, 10 November 1935, Marsden Papers, 1, p. 549 (ML).

wandering population, soon, he feared, to become 'fixed in hopeless unacquaintance with the blessed truths and expectations of the Christian faith'.

> Living in a state of concubinage, frequently promiscuous, without books or means of instruction of any description, the observation of the Sabbath-day totally obliterated among them, their children growing up not only without baptism, but almost in unacquaintance with the name or being of their Creator, these persons . . . are placed in a situation as dreadful to contemplate as that of any race of heathen existing upon this earth.

Yet Broughton did not quite despair. He had been much encouraged while in England by the response of the voluntary societies for the Propagation of the Gospel and for the Promotion of Christian Knowledge in trying to secure chaplains and in raising money. A New South Wales branch was formed soon after the bishop's return, and had contributed thousands of pounds towards the cost of thirty-three churches within a year. When these were built—and only a shortage of tradesmen and labourers delayed a start on many of them—the position was going to be much improved, and Broughton regarded this support as evidence of a proper concern for religion among the 'principal inhabitants'.[39]

The Catholic bishop, J. B. Polding, had similar hopes and fears. He proudly declared in 1836 that an improvement in the moral tone of Sydney was admitted on all sides since the arrival of additional priests, and that many who had been spiritually careless were already reformed. But his clergy were unable to do all that was required. The chaplain at Maitland had to serve also Newcastle, the whole of the William's River, Paterson's Plains, the districts of the Upper Hunter, Patrick's Plains and the Liverpool Plains. In the midst of an increasing Catholic population even the newly enlarged body of priests could do no more than their predecessors, who had been forced to 'run hastily from place to place . . . to supply the most pressing wants of their flocks'. This was bad, since 'passing visits leave only passing impressions', and there were vast areas—the districts of Argyle and Bathurst, 'All the settled country beyond the Blue Mountains', and the penal settlements —for which there were no priests at all. What could be expected, asked Polding, of a people in such a state of neglect? It had been said that no Catholic criminal executed in New South Wales during the previous four years had received the rites of his Church in the colony until he was actually in gaol. How could convicts be reformed without religion? What hope could there be for the free migrant if he were deprived of

[39] *S.P.G. Report* (N.S.W.), 1837, pp. 22-8, 47-51.

pastoral care? And what of the rising generation if the children were only to be 'guided by the depraved example of their parents'? Polding asked for double the number of priests, and quickly.[40]

The dissatisfaction of the two major denominations was reflected in the others. The Presbyterian, J. D. Lang, considered his cause to be suffering for a variety of reasons. First, the influence of the dreadful past had to be overcome. Then there was the official favouring of the Anglican Church and the cold-shouldering of the Presbyterians, so that the Anglicans measured their aid by thousands and the Presbyterians by hundreds of pounds. Thirdly, there was the Church of Scotland's own culpable neglect of colonial religion, and the common ministerial attitude that only a weak brother with no prospects at home would go to a colony.[41] In July 1836 Lang took leave from his duties and went to Scotland in search of more ministers. Lang, who had an opinion and a spate of entertaining words on every subject in the colony, also commented on the disappointing progress of Wesleyan Methodism. This was quite true, for the Wesleyan outreach was very limited. Not until 1839, for instance, did a Wesleyan minister preach in the Illawarra district, and then he was only a visitor. In the same year the Wesleyan superintendent in New South Wales repeated his earlier reports of urgent calls for ministers from various parts of the colony which could not be met. 'We want the labourers,' he told the English committee, 'and we must look to you for them.'[42] Three years earlier, the Van Diemen's Land Methodists had reported the same thing. It was a recurring cry, and a sign of Wesleyan frustration. From Van Diemen's Land, Lieutenant-Governor George Arthur reported that an increase in the number of Anglican pastors was a matter of real and pressing necessity, and that government assistance was needed for every denomination if there was not to remain 'a large class of the community . . . without any religious or moral instruction whatever'.[43] Even the appointment of Bishop Broughton was attacked by a Van Diemen's Land newspaper on the grounds that the colonies could do without expensive prelates but very badly needed humble preachers who could go from house to house in the thinly populated areas.[44] This was not just a figment of an editor's biassed imagination, for the Reverend Joseph Beazley, an Independent itinerating in 1837 with the support of a newly-formed society, found that the Broad Marsh and

[40] Polding to Bourke, 6 May 1836, *V. & P.* (N.S.W.), 1836.
[41] J. D. Lang, *An Historical and Statistical Account of New South Wales* (London, 1834), II, ch. 5.
[42] *Report of Wesleyan Missionary Committee* (London, 1840), p. 28.
[43] Arthur to Glenelg, 26 January 1836, *H.R.A.*, XVIII, pp. 486-95.
[44] *Colonial Times*, 5 July 1836, p. 221.

Green Ponds district was so poorly served that he could make it the centre of his work, and, on visiting Swan Port on the east coast, he was told that there had been only three religious services in the area in nine years.[45]

Perhaps the greatest comfort found by the colonial churchmen in the early thirties was that then as now the majority of the people lived in a few main areas, especially in and around Sydney, Hobart and Launceston. The comparatively small area of some five thousand square miles shown in Figure 2 held virtually all the inhabitants of the island colony as late as 1837. The settled area of New South Wales, by this time including the Port Phillip district, sprawled over perhaps twenty times that area, and itinerating clergymen could be led from one sheep station to another until they were hundreds of miles from home. They might find nothing which could be dignified by the name of a residence, but the stations and the people who manned them were nevertheless there. This was a great part of the problem, yet it did not involve the greater part of the people, not even on the mainland. There were several thousand people known to be living beyond the boundaries of the nineteen counties (see Figure 1), but there were nearly forty thousand people—almost half the total population of New South Wales—living in the county of Cumberland alone. In the neighbouring county of Northumberland, where there were churches and clergymen of three denominations, lived another five thousand persons; and in Bathurst county, another area fairly well served by the Churches, there was a population of nearly two thousand. Hence almost two-thirds of the whole population lived in three counties where they had a fair chance of effective contact with the Churches if they wanted it.

This concentration of the bulk of the population in a few restricted areas was very much in the Churches' favour. Yet it was only a big advantage, not a removal of the problem. Perhaps forty per cent of the people in New South Wales were almost beyond the reach of the clergy. Many who had come to Australia with no interest in religion were being left as they were, and those who had gone to church at home could not retain strong religious connections in the outback. Moral standards were commonly low, and the few travelling clergymen could do little to alter the situation. When zealous churchmen therefore clamoured for assistance, a sympathetic ear was turned by the officers of State, themselves apprehensive of the consequences of neglecting the religious and moral needs of the colonists. The result was an offer of State aid to the Churches through the far-reaching Church Acts of 1836 and 1837.

[45] *Report of the Van Diemen's Land Home Missionary . . . Society* (Hobart, 1838), pp. 8-10.

2

THE PASSING OF THE CHURCH ACTS, 1836-1837

THE INSTITUTIONAL DEVELOPMENT of Christian denominations in eastern Australia owes much to the Church Acts. When the Churches were struggling to grow with the colonies, financial assistance from the State made all the difference. Although it was only a few years—six in the one colony and thirteen in the other—before the Governments imposed restrictions upon the aid they would give, the Churches had by then reaped large benefits and continued to do so for many years. What is more, the Church Acts only applied to the already recognized denominations, thus decreasing the chance of indigenous frontier sects developing. The Churches which are strongest in eastern Australia today are, in fact, those which were strongest, and received most State aid, then. The application of the Acts to a number of Churches, instead of a single denomination, was a particularly important aspect of the legislation, for it committed eastern Australia to the principle of denominational equality. Although small *ad hoc* grants had been made to non-Anglicans before this time, it was still expected in some quarters that only the Church of England was to be duly established; this hope was finally dashed by the Church Acts. Years afterwards, Bishop Broughton remarked bitterly that Australia was a remote quarter favoured as a testing ground for doubtful legislation before it was attempted in England.[1] At any rate, government policy at Westminster and British public opinion vitally influenced the passing of the Church Acts, for parliamentary grants in aid of religion, and the whole question of establishment, were important domestic issues in England at that time.

English Opinion

There were reasons why conservative Anglicans in the colonies hoped for a better deal than the Church Acts gave them. In the early nineteenth century British governments voted some generous grants of money to the Church of England. Alarmed by the upheavals in Europe after the French Revolution, the English upper classes set out to bolster

[1] Broughton to Coleridge, 15 January 1849, B.P.

the Church of England as a safeguard against social, political and religious radicalism. There was also a truly charitable and religious motive behind some of this support. Religious seriousness having begun to increase among both middle and upper classes, many had a high sense of the duty of the established Church. This was the last era in which it was seriously suggested that the national Church ought to provide church-room for the entire population, and, the long years of neglect being admitted, the church extension programme was tremendous. In 1818 Church Building Commissioners were appointed to administer an Act granting one million pounds for the building of Anglican churches in crowded parishes, and a second grant of half a million pounds was made in 1824. By 1836 these commissioners had built two hundred and fourteen churches and chapels—an average of a dozen new churches each year for eighteen years.[2] Upon these grounds alone the Lord Bishop of Australia and his clergy might very well have hoped that the colonial authorities would be instructed to adopt vigorous policies of aid to their Church, and to their Church only.

Yet this aid was already a thing of the past in England. By 1837 the one and a half million pounds had been issued, and for the remaining twenty years of its life the Commission was sorely handicapped by lack of money.[3] The Tories had voted the money, but the Whigs came into power in 1835 and found themselves neither in the same position nor quite of the same mind. The Whigs believed in a firm union of Church and State, but many of them inclined towards an established Church which suited the people rather than the prelates, and was adapted to the present rather than the past. The religion of many a Whig

> seems to have been a blend of the classical precepts of morality and the moral sense of the Scottish philosophers, improved by Christ's special injunctions to toleration and forbearance, and substituting for the dreamy ambition of establishing Christ's kingdom on earth, the nearer but no less desirable objective of the Reign of Liberty.[4]

On top of this, the cold facts of practical politics and public finance did not permit the continuation of large ecclesiastical grants. A Tory cabinet entered office in 1841, but no new grant was forthcoming, partly because of difficulties over the budget. The practical politics included the strong criticism of the Church of England coming from several

[2] *P.P.* (H.C.), 1836, vol. xxxvi, p. 173.

[3] Ibid., 1837, vol. xxi, p. 8; M. H. Port, *Six Hundred New Churches* (London, 1961), pp. 95, 115-22.

[4] G. F. A. Best, 'The Whigs and the Church Establishment in the Age of Grey and Holland', *History*, vol. xLv, p. 107.

quarters. The Church was widely unpopular, and talk of disestablishment was particularly loud and frantic, until certain reforms were effected after 1835; and, even then, while the mobs and demagogues became less important, there were steadier ideas and groups set against establishment. Not least among them were the Dissenters, from whom all direct penalties were being removed and to whom much political power was passing. Lord Sidmouth's defeat in 1811, when he had to give up a bill aimed at Methodist and other preachers, was not due only to Liberal peers but was very much a consequence of Methodist and Dissenting outcry. Even the 1818 'Million Act' was opposed by Lord Holland because it said to Dissenters, 'You, gentlemen, who pay for yourselves . . . shall also contribute to the creation of those churches in which you have no interest whatever'.[5] Throughout the following years battles on similar grounds were waged against church rates and establishment generally. The middle-class Dissenters, with their belief in individual freedom and in the liberty of conscience, often found themselves in line with the aristocratic Whigs who also maintained a tradition of civil and religious liberty; and both contributed to that curious hotchpotch of ideas described as English Liberalism, a stream which flowed very strongly at this time. The Philosophic Radicals, also to be classed among the Liberals, had a marked influence upon English thinking in these years, and they condemned established Churches. Their leader, Jeremy Bentham, said emphatically, 'No power of Government ought to be employed in the endeavour to establish any system or article of belief on the subject of religion'.[6] The broad churchman, Arnold of Rugby, argued for the extinction of Dissent by comprehension within the Church of England, and proposed a re-organization which almost amounted to the extinction of the Church of England.[7]

At the other extreme from the broad churchmen, the Tractarians were emerging to point the Church of England to the Catholic elements in its faith and to elevate the Church over the State until even State aid for church building was considered to be an indefensible intrusion into Church affairs. This put Tory statesmen in a dilemma; if some of the churchmen were denouncing votes of money, others of their constituents would be no less severe on any attempt to increase and restore Church endowments, which was what the Tractarians believed to be the Church's right. Tories, too, were affected by some of the liberal ideas of their time. One of them, Sir George Murray told Parliament in 1832 that England had an obligation to provide the

[5] Quoted in A. W. Dale, *History of English Congregationalism* (London, 1907), p. 583.
[6] See A. Bullock & M. S. Shock (ed.), *The Liberal Tradition* (London, 1956), p. 44.
[7] T. Arnold, *Principles of Church Reform* (London, reprinted 1962), pp. 87, 109-40. Originally published in 1833.

means of religious instruction for the colonies, but that it would be '*bad* and *dangerous*' to establish only one denomination.[8] The Tory party was also obliged to deal with the Catholic question in a 'Liberal' manner. Peel told the King in August 1828 that to withhold Catholic emancipation would 'imperil the royal authority in Ireland, and the King's reputation in Europe'. The ministry was helpless, and the Tories had to act on this advice or immediately wreck their party. The Catholic Emancipation Act of 1829 was the result.[9] This was practical politics coming into line with the confident tolerance of the Liberal notion that, in an age of enlightenment and of extensive and rapid change, Catholics were being affected as much as anyone, and that religious differences would come to an end.[10]

When English opinion was in such a state of flux, and liberal ideas opposed to exclusive establishment of one denomination were so prominent in men's thinking, it is not in the least surprising that the Australian colonies should be allowed to pass Church Acts which helped other denominations, not just the Church of England.

A Church Act for New South Wales

Church history in New South Wales from its foundation to the passing of the Church Acts has an allegory in the story of the Anglican cathedral at Sydney. In the time of Governor Lachlan Macquarie the foundations, and only the foundations, were solidly laid for St Andrew's. But later, in 1837,

> from the imperfect manner in which the plan of the Town was at first designed, the line of George-street was found actually to intersect one of the angles. To the Town itself it must ever have proved a source of deformity, not of ornament. There was, therefore, no hesitation in removing the entire foundation, and His Excellency the Governor, Lieutenant-General Sir Richard Bourke, was pleased on the 16th of May, to lay the first stone of the proposed new building.[11]

The time of Macquarie was the time of Anglican ascendency, when every other denomination had to get around the solid Church of England authority. Wesleyans were reprimanded when they trespassed on what were regarded as Anglican preserves of time and town in holding services. Schoolmasters were threatened with loss of their government salaries for allowing W. P. Crook to preach as an Indepen-

---

[8] Quoted in J. West, *The History of Tasmania* (Launceston, 1852), I, p. 198n.
[9] J. A. Reynolds, *The Catholic Emancipation Crisis in Ireland, 1823-9* (Newhaven, 1954), pp. 161-2.
[10] G. F. A. Best, op. cit., pp. 109-10.
[11] A compressed and slightly paraphrased version of the account in *S.P.G. Report* (N.S.W.), 1837, pp. 23-4.

dent in the school buildings. Not only was Father O'Flynn bundled off home soon after he arrived in 1818, but even the two approved priests, Therry and Conolly, were warned by Macquarie against prose-lytizing and were forbidden to interfere with Catholic children in Church of England orphanages. Dr Lang, the Presbyterian, complained of the possibility in 1825 of penalties under the 'Rogues-and-Vagabonds' Act for ministers of religion who did not send a return of baptisms, marriages and burials to the Anglican minister of the 'parish'. In 1825, indeed, Anglican privilege seemed assured by the royal charter which established the Church and School Corporation, which was to hold one seventh of the land in each county, and to use the income derived from it for the maintenance of the schools and clergy of the Church of England.

But Anglican supremacy had reached its highest point, and was soon to decline. Neither in New South Wales nor in Van Diemen's Land, where large tracts of land were also to be set aside for the Church of England, did the promised endowments bear much fruit. Survey difficulties, antagonistic land interests and the granting of land in areas where sale or rent was difficult, hacked down the benefits en-visaged. Quite soon the Van Diemen's Land grants were withdrawn from the hands of the Church, while the New South Wales Church and School Corporation's charter was suspended in 1829 and finally revoked (after Broughton had found a technical fault which rendered the suspension illegal) in 1833. The Anglican Church secured only a fraction of the expected aid and its supremacy was likewise being whittled down. The State was unwilling to lose so much land revenue for the benefit of one Church when other denominations were becoming bitterly vocal against its favoured treatment.

The Governor of New South Wales in 1833 was Sir Richard Bourke, an Anglican, but also an Irishman with Catholic relatives, and a man with his full share of liberal opinions. When news was received of the order in council dissolving the Corporation, Bourke was not at all dismayed. On the contrary, he was as pleased to get the establishment of one denomination out of the way as he was a little later to get the foundations of St Andrew's out of George Street. Encouraged by the implications of the order, Bourke advised the British Government as to what needed to be done about the Churches in the colony. He insisted that New South Wales was not like England and Scotland, where Anglicanism could be established in the one area and Presby-terianism in the other, for the different denominations were well re-presented in all parts of the colony. Many of the most respectable free migrants were Protestant Dissenters, and Catholics formed a significant proportion of the inhabitants. The unequal aid given by the Government to the various Churches had been justly petitioned against, and Bourke recommended that support be allowed for 'every one of the three grand divisions of Christians indifferently'—Anglicans, Presbyterians and Catholics—and that provision also be made for other denominations which might require aid.[12] Amid changes of government, the Colonial Office took some years to decide about the thorny proposal, but in the end full permission was given for Bourke to go ahead. He wasted no time and the Legislative Council wasted none. On 22 July 1836 the Governor laid on the Council table a Bill to promote the building of churches and chapels, and to provide for the maintenance of ministers of religion. Seven days later it became an Act—the famous Church Act, a product of land interests, a new religious tolerance, a spirit of reform, the colonial denominational mixture and the desire to improve colonial society. The Treasury was to grant sums up to £1,000 equal to the amounts privately raised for the building of any church, chapel or clergyman's dwelling, provided that a minimum of £300 had been raised at the time of application. A scale of State-paid stipends was fixed for 'duly appointed' clergymen, which varied according to the number of adult residents who declared their desire to attend the places of worship under each clergyman's charge. In areas where it was impractical to build a church, payment was to be made equal to the amount voluntarily subscribed towards a minister's support. In the regulations under the Act, the Church of England, the Presbytery of the Church of Scotland and the Roman Catholic Church were specifically named as the Churches which would participate, and there was a clause authorizing the granting of aid to 'any denomination of Christians not named in these regulations'.[13]

This was an Act of tremendous significance. It forbade Anglicans a monopoly of State aid, placing Presbyterianism and Catholicism on an equal footing with the Church of England and opening the door wide for Wesleyans and others to secure support. So much was it in accord with majority opinion in the colonies (and not the Australian colonies only, for Canada was faced with a similar situation) that the legislation was accepted with scarcely a breath of public criticism.

There was in fact some strong opposition to the measure, though it was largely veiled from public view. Bishop Broughton, for instance, had declared frankly to Lord Glenelg that he could not work with Bourke in a scheme of aid to 'three separate forms of Religion, and

12 Bourke to Stanley, 30 September 1833, *H.R.A.*, XVII, pp. 224-30.
13 For the Act, 7 William IV, no. 3, see *The Acts and Ordinances of the Governor and Council of New South Wales*, 1836, pp. 719-23. For the Regulations, see *N.S.W. Government Gazette*, 12 October 1836, pp. 762-4.

possibly to every congregation of Dissenters and Jews upon the same principle', and he had delayed his acceptance of the bishopric until he had made this plain. After returning to the colony, Broughton let Bourke know, both in conversation and by letter, that he thought the Act to be iniquitous and impolitic.[14] Yet the bishop seems to have hardly expressed his disapproval to the colony at large. This could have been only a tactical silence, adopted for three reasons. First, he considered it more important to form alliances and wage war against the proposals for education which Bourke was putting forward at the same time. Secondly, the Anglicans were still expected to get the lion's share of State aid, because their numbers and wealth would enable them more easily to qualify for the subsidies. This, in fact, is what happened, and Broughton must have realized the value of the promised aid far too clearly to allow himself to be over-drastic in his opposition. In the following years the Bishop was to be heard both condemning the Church Act, as basically wrong, and also fighting to preserve it, for he needed the money it produced for his Church. The third tactical reason for Broughton's comparative silence in 1836 was simply that the measure had overwhelming support among the colonists. The *Sydney Herald*, no lover of Bourke and his policies, and extremely critical of the educational proposals which the Governor considered to be the complement to the Church Act, congratulated the colonists on the latter, adding that there appeared to be 'no dissenting voice on this subject'. [15] The *Colonist* was also strongly opposed to Bourke's plan for education, and indignant at the general standard of legislation passed in the 1836 session, but it hailed Bourke's recommendations about the Churches, and Glenelg's approval of them, as 'the *Magna Charta* of the Religious Liberty of this infant Empire', and excepted the Church Act from censure.[16] Bourke, therefore, had good reason to report that, if opposition could have been aroused, the Bishop of Australia would have brought it up 'in array', but, as it was, the measure had met with 'the sincere and grateful acquiescence of all classes'.[17] Broughton was never intimidated, but he could be wise enough to choose his time and method, and sometimes even to admit defeat.

Part of the popular support was born of a union of prudence and charity. As Bourke's successor, Sir George Gipps, was to tell the Legislative Council, the numerous churches in progress showed a very satisfactory desire to 'supply moral and religious instruction to the

[14] Broughton to Glenelg, 3 December 1835; Bourke to Glenelg, 8 August 1836; *H.R.A.*, xviii,, pp. 700, 476.
[15] *Herald*, 4 July 1836, p. 2.
[16] *Colonist*, 16, 30 June, 25 August 1836.
[17] Bourke to Glenelg, 14 September 1836, *H.R.A.*, xviii, p. 537.

people', although much remained to be done before the bad impressions of the colony could be dissipated in quarters where it was desirable to 'maintain a good repute'.[18] The whole flux of opinion about the established Church in Britain was transmitted to the colonies also. Very often the colonists cared as much for common decency as for any brand of faith, and even sturdy supporters of the Anglican Church were very much influenced by the century's tolerance, or were at least able to see that they could not expect State aid if it were denied to others. The major non-Anglican denominations were delighted with the Act. The Presbytery of New South Wales expressed 'unmingled feelings of gratitude and joy'.[19] When Bourke left the colony, the Catholics presented a farewell address which referred to his adoption of 'that happy medium . . . best and fittest for the wants of the colony'.[20] The Wesleyans, anticipating their own inclusion with the big three, welcomed Governor Gipps with an expression of pleasure at the 'enlightened and liberal policy' which was granting them 'express recognition of their religious rights and immunities'.[21]

There were some conscientious objectors to government aid. From the first day of its publication (1 January 1835) J. D. Lang's *Colonist* had disapproved the principle of State aid, as distinct from the principle of equality to be observed if aid was to continue, and there might have been much more criticism if the colony had been less occupied with the school question, or if the Independents had been stronger. Yet Lang accepted State aid when it came, and even the Baptists and Congregationalists were not unmoved by the scramble for assistance, being guilty of some aberrations from the principle they usually upheld, for applications for government aid came from the trustees of the Bathurst Street Baptist chapel and from the Independents at South Head.[22] Conservative Anglicans who, like their bishop, deplored the Church Act in their hearts, said little; no less than any other denomination, they needed State aid in their difficult task of building up institutional religion from the stump-strewn ground. It was far more important to get aid for themselves than to deny it to any other, far better to share it than to lose it altogether. Denominational attacks were to be made on the Church Act after 1836, but were usually aimed at getting more aid or a greater share of existing aid. Only occasionally, as in the case of Lang's final rejection of government assistance, was the principle of

[18] *V. & P.* (N.S.W.), 1838.

[19] Presbytery to Glenelg, 27 July 1837, quoted in W. E. Gladstone, *The State in its Relations with the Church* (London, 1838), p. 271.

[20] P. F. Moran, *History of the Catholic Church in Australasia* (Sydney, n.d.), pp. 191-2.

[21] *N.S.W. Government Gazette*, 28 March 1838, p. 226.

[22] Min. of Exec. Coun., N.S.W., 23 Feb. 1839, 4/1520 (ML).

State aid denounced by churchmen; and even less criticized was the principle of denominational equality accepted in the Church Act. That could no more be altered than the laws of the Medes and Persians.

The Van Diemen's Land Church Act

Twelve months after the passing of the Church Act in New South Wales, a similar Act came into force in Van Diemen's Land. Colonel George Arthur had been sent a copy of Glenelg's despatch to Bourke, with instructions to take similar steps in his colony. Arthur was in full agreement with the proposals, but his term of office was drawing to a close and he had to leave the task to his successor. Yet he had helped push the legislation along by his own policy of *ad hoc* aid to non-Anglican denominations, a policy which had been opposed by such Anglicans as Chief Justice Pedder, but which had the continuing support of the Legislative Council as a whole. Indeed, the Council, by nine votes to four, favoured the placing of Presbyterian ministers on the same footing as Anglican chaplains after their people had petitioned for it in 1836.[23] The ground was therefore well prepared for the new Lieutenant-Governor, Sir John Franklin, who set out to extend and systematize aid to the Churches in 1837.

The Bill for a Church Act in Van Diemen's Land, in contrast to that of New South Wales, took time to win acceptance; it was laid on the table on 10 July 1837 but passed the third reading only on 27 November. The Act finally produced[24] was also more stringent than its mainland counterpart. The Treasury in Van Diemen's Land was to grant sums equal to the amount privately subscribed for the erection of churches to an upper limit of £700, and two hundred free bona fide members of the denomination were required to live within ten miles of the proposed church if it were to be built in Hobart or Launceston. The New South Wales Act granted up to £1,000; it did not make Sydney a special case; it required only one hundred adult persons, living 'within a reasonable distance', to express their intention to attend; and it explicitly directed that convict servants could be included in the number. The southern colony's requirement of only eighty persons to form a congregation in places outside the two main towns did not give much in, since these eighty still had to be free persons and bona fide members of the denomination. Stipends were not permitted to be as low in Van Diemen's Land as in New South Wales. On the mainland the rate was £100 per annum if there were one hundred persons associated with the church, £150 if there were two hundred, and £200 if there were five hundred.

[23] *Courier*, 12 August 1836, p. 2.
[24] 1 Vict., no. 16, *Hobart Town Gazette*, 8 December 1837, pp. 1305-11.

The lowest sum could also be granted where there were less than one hundred people in the congregation, if circumstances warranted it; and, where no place of worship could be built, but the scattered population desired the services of a minister, the Government was prepared to pay between £50 and £100 per annum in amounts equal to voluntary subscription. The normal stipend of £200 fixed by the Van Diemen's Land Act was the only item more generous than the New South Wales provision—and even this might have been more apparent than real because of the higher cost of living in the island colony. The Van Diemen's Land Act was stricter, too, in requiring ministers' appointments to be confirmed by the Crown and reason for dismissal to be submitted to the Lieutenant-Governor. In contrast, the New South Wales Act only asked for an annual declaration that the clergy were performing their duties well enough to justify the continuation of their stipends.

As in New South Wales, only the Anglicans, Presbyterians and Catholics were included in the Church Act of the sister colony. Any benefits the Wesleyans and other minor denominations received were to be by special annual votes, and they were not considered part of the 'Establishment'. This was not because officialdom was unappreciative of their role. Arthur, who had proposed a yearly grant of £400 in a lump-sum for the Wesleyans, had been emphatic in his approval of the Wesleyans and Dissenters, and Franklin was no less so. The annual grant was duly approved for the Wesleyans, and was later increased to £500, while the Independent minister at Hobart, the Reverend Frederick Miller, was offered a 'gratuity' of £200 a year. There may have been some doubts, born of ignorance and a minor dispute, about the Wesleyans having a 'recognized governing body', and the Methodists may have been strangely scrupulous about claiming all their adherents as persons 'in communion' with them; but, of all the possible reasons why they were not brought properly under the Act, the most likely is that they simply lacked a confident, aggressive spokesman. The Dissenters were excluded by their own principles as much as anything else, for the proffered gratuity was refused by Frederick Miller, though Dissenters accepted assistance whenever colonial necessity and denominational rivalry caused them to compromise their ideals. Grants were made towards the cost of building a number of their chapels—including Miller's own—and the Reverend Henry Dowling, the Baptist minister at Launceston, justified his State stipend on the grounds that he worked among convicts. No recognized denomination was excluded from government benefits if they were asked for, and the acceptance of this principle of religious equality was probably more important to the colonial community than the aid itself. All the Churches were accepted, not just tolerated.

In the discussion of the Church Act in the island, where the measure was very well aired for over four months, there were constant appeals to the principle of equality. When, for instance, the Legislative Council set out to clarify a section of the Act dealing with appointments to Anglican churches, the Colonial Treasurer dissented from the resolutions because they seemed to deny the principle of 'the absence of all distinction whatever between the three Churches', a sentiment which was echoed by the *Tasmanian* in an editorial.[25] Captain Forster objected similarly to one special allowance to the Wesleyans, since he understood the whole object of the legislation was 'to sink all sectarian differences'.[26] A suggestion that people in thinly populated districts would be better served if various denominations were allowed to go in together to get a church built was opposed by two Protestants, Matthew Forster and the Colonial Secretary, who thought this would be unfair to Catholics, who could not unite with others.[27] Catholics were benignly regarded in Van Diemen's Land, in contrast to the virulent anti-Catholicism which was made plain in the education debates in New South Wales. There were fewer Catholics in the island, and their Church was weak, so that many thought that there was little to fear from them. They even called forth a genuine sympathy in the editorial columns of the pro-Anglican *Courier*. In a biting passage the paper said, 'Because the Roman Catholic religion is the prevalent one in Ireland, the misrule, the anarchy, the discontent, and starvation pervading that country, are to be ascribed to *it,* and British neglect, or injustice, is to be accounted as nothing'.[28] Tolerance was very much to the fore.

Yet the Act was not accepted quickly and quietly like the mainland's legislation; it took nearly five months compared with seven days in New South Wales. There was not much serious doubt about the Act being passed, but, while the Council bickered over details, the Anglican clergy rose up in a body to protest vehemently against the measure. They could do this for a number of reasons which did not apply in New South Wales. First, the lack of a large block of Catholics, which reduced sectarian bitterness, also reduced the challenge to Anglican claims. Secondly, Van Diemen's Land had no equivalent in 1837 to the education controversy which smothered debate of the Church Act on the mainland. Finally, the matter of providing churches for a spreading

[25] *V. & P.* (V.D.L.), 1837 (29 November); *Tasmanian,* 1 December 1837, p. 386
[26] *Courier,* 28 July 1837, p. 4.
[27] Ibid., 1 December 1837, p. 2.
[28] Ibid., 5 September (supplement to 8 September) 1837, p. 1.

population was not so urgent in Van Diemen's land, and less urgency
left room for more criticism. This the Anglican clergy indulged in long
and loudly, arguing that the measure would support error as well as
truth, thus confusing men all the more and assisting the steady attacks
on Anglicanism by 'Romanism, aided by worldliness and infidelity'.[29]
Here anti-Catholicism appeared, and here religious toleration was
equated with religious indifference; but such sentiments were not
accepted by most colonists. Even the *Courier*, usually the paper most
inclined to support the Church of England, published plenty of news
items about church rates controversies and pleas for reform of the
established Church in England and came out against the Anglican
clergy in the colony at this point. It protested that the Legislative
Council could not be a court of cardinals and pronounce upon doctrine,
and it claimed to have 'canvassed the sentiments of all classes' and
to have found that the principles of the Church Act were 'heartily
concurred in'.[30] With the Anglican clergy glaringly excepted, the newspaper was certainly right. The Governor and Legislative Council had
no need to fear that the Church Act would be widely opposed.

Questions of detail, not of principle, were the real subjects of debate
and the cause of delay in the Council. Let two or more sects combine
in the erection of a place of worship, said Mr McLachlan. Reduce the
minimum sum to be raised voluntarily to £150, urged Mr Kerr. Their
proposals were countered in various ways: a congregationally divided
group could give too little security; it was not intended to cover the
country with 'twopence half-penny chapels'; the measure should not
encourage carelessness about denominational loyalty (that would be
indifference, not liberality); and there would be quarrels—the Quakers
not liking to be kept waiting in the rain because a Presbyterian preached
too long.[31] This was typical of the debates. On principles nearly all the
councillors agreed: they wanted the greatest benefit to the community,
by the equalization of the status of the different Churches and by a
happy compromise between State support and congregational maintenance. The *Courier* supported the Church Act because of 'the combination in it of a modified voluntaryism, with secured provision, on a
frugal scale, to the clergy'; increased government aid was unquestion-
ably needed, in this paper's opinion, and this was the best way of
giving it.[32] The *Colonial Times*, admiring Frederick Miller's refusal of

[29] 'A Member of the Church of England' [Archdeacon Hutchins], *An Appeal to the Members of the Legislative Council of Van Diemen's Land, against the "Church Act"* . . . (Launceston, 1837), and a petition from the Anglican Clergy, *Courier*, 24 November 1837, p. 2.
[30] *Courier*, 14 April 1837, p. 4; 5 September 1837, p. 1.
[31] Ibid., 28 July 1837, p. 4.
[32] Ibid., 26 May (p. 4), 28 July (p. 2), 29 September (p. 2), 1837.

a government salary and wishing that the bishop's salary had been used instead to enable humble preachers to go from hut to hut in the interior, was at least unruffled by the Act. The Council itself was well satisfied: it passed the Church Act on 27 November 1837 by ten votes to one.

The Immediate Aftermath

Religious equality was embodied in the Church Acts because tolerance was already a part of the typical colonist's outlook. The Acts acknowledged and reflected a belief, rather than gave rise to one. Therefore, while the writing of religious equality into the colonies' statutes was truly significant, theoretical rights were not the main point of these measures. They were meant to be practical, to get churches built and clergymen stationed among the Australian settlers. And immensely practical they were.

They could not, of course, change the religious scene everywhere and all at once. Two years after the New South Wales Act was passed, stockowners still spoke of a great want of churches in the remoter areas and pointed to continuing difficulties of church building. The Committee on Immigration was told by these men that they could give nothing towards churches in certain areas until their new purchases of land began to pay their way; that it was quite impractical to build a church in some districts because the people were so scattered; and that entire counties still lacked even a clergymen.[33] Two years later still, an Anglican society spoke in similar terms. The county of Bathurst had only one Church of England minister, while the Liverpool Plains, many parts of the Hunter River district, the county of St Vincent and other areas were either 'entirely destitute' or lacked 'all regular and certain administration of the ordinances of religion'. Broughton was becoming caustic about this, and pointed out that the Church Act failed to provide for such areas where the minimum of £300 was unavailable.[34] Even from little Van Diemen's Land came cries of the period being critical and of the 'scantiness of the means of grace'.[35] The Port Phillip District was also the subject of a report, signed by C. J. La Trobe, in which it was said that some three thousand white settlers were 'almost destitute' and over five thousand were 'entirely destitute of religious ordinances'.[36] The Church Acts were not

[33] Report from the Committee on Immigration, with the Minutes of Evidence, pp. 814-16, 857-8, *V. & P.* (N.S.W.), 1838.

[34] *S.P.G. Report* (N.S.W.), 1840, p. 43.

[35] *S.P.G. Report* (V.D.L.), 1841, pp. 6-8.

[36] *Report of Church of England Lay Association, New South Wales, for 1844-5*, pp. 62-4.

proving entirely satisfactory for the Churches' needs, and they had worked no miracles.

Yet they had worked: there had been much improvement and there was real hope of more. The squatters knew that as soon as their properties showed a profit, and they could donate money for a church, the Government would back them pound for pound and also contribute to the minister's stipend. When they gave evidence before the Immigration Committee they expressed a confidence that clergymen could be supported in many places, and actually reported the commencement of a church building here, and the arrival of a clergyman there, for the first time. The same S.P.G. reports also gave vivid glimpses of this other side. Van Diemen's Land had two additional clergymen, three churches about to be started and nine in the course of erection—most, if not all, benefiting by the Church Act.[37] The New South Wales report referred to a growing seriousness about religion, the immediate taking up of all the sittings in the new churches, and the arrival of ten Anglican ministers. Speaking for the Wesleyans, the Reverend John McKenny said in 1839 that the previous two years had seen 'a wonderful change', because the migrants had included a 'great number of religious persons' and the 'late stir . . . respecting the religious interests of the convict population' had increased the attention given to spiritual matters.[38] Not least in 'the late stir' had been the passing of the Church Act.

The Anglican report of progress in New South Wales from the beginning of 1837 to October 1841 included eight consecrated churches, four churches opened by licence, fifteen churches in progress, twelve parsonages completed and eight in the course of being built. Up to the end of 1836 only ten churches and five parsonages had been erected, so the Church Act was having a good effect—particularly since the new buildings were as far out as East and West Maitland, Goulburn, Limestone Plains, Paterson, Mudgee and Melbourne.[39] The Catholic Church took advantage of the Church Act 'without delay', so that in 1841 they had nine churches completed and six in the course of erection, as well as some 'small chapels' either built or being built—twenty-five churches and chapels in all, which was a big advance from the 1836 total of five places of worship. They were concentrated in the most densely populated areas, but some were fairly well out—at Goulburn, Bathurst,

---

[37] By no means exhaustive reference to Min. of Exec. Coun. from 30 July to 4 December 1838 (EC 2/6 TA) revealed that at least seven of the nine had received aid under the Church Act.
[38] *Report of Wesleyan Missionary Committee* (London, 1840), pp. 28-9.
[39] W. G. Broughton, *A Charge Delivered to the Clergy of New South Wales . . .* (Sydney, 1841), Appendix A.

Hartley and Paterson—and a church was being built at Melbourne.[40] At Port Phillip the Churches received considerable help under the New South Wales Church Act. By 1840, when there were nearly six thousand people in the settlement, the denominations were well on the way towards proper organization. The Presbyterian minister and an Anglican clergyman were both being paid by the Treasury, and a permanent Anglican church was being erected under the Church Act. One of the Catholic priests was paid by the Government and, while the Wesleyans had received nothing from the State towards their brick chapel, they were helped by a £500 annual grant for their Buntingdale aboriginal mission. The Independents excepted, the Churches were receiving valuable assistance from the Government.[41] Presbyterian progress is indicated by the fact that their five ministers serving in New South Wales in 1836 had been increased to eighteen ministers and eight licentiates in 1841.[42] There were also in the colony about forty-four Anglican priests and deacons, of whom twenty-nine had been appointed under the Church Act, twenty-four Catholic priests, eight Wesleyan ministers (excluding two missionaries to the aborigines), a Baptist and an Independent minister. In round figures there were about one hundred clergymen and probationary ministers in New South Wales in 1841.[43] The census of that year returned nearly one hundred and thirty-one thousand people, so that there was an approximate ratio of one clergyman for every thirteen hundred people. This was the best ratio since the first few years of the colony's existence. The Church Act—and, in the case of the Anglicans, the splendid assistance of the S.P.G.—had been highly effective.

In Van Diemen's Land there had been about thirty ministers of religion in 1837, but by 1841 the number had grown to fifty, of whom thirty-five received full State support, as distinct from the annual grants to the Wesleyans and the Baptist, Henry Dowling.[44] With some fifty-one and a half thousand people in the colony, there was a minister for every ten or eleven hundred persons—a marked improvement on the nineteen hundred to one in 1836. The provision of churches on the island had increased from thirty-two in 1838 to fifty-five in 1841, so that church building was sixty-four per cent greater in these three years

40 J. Kenny, *A History of the Commencement and Progress of Catholicity in Australia, up to the year 1840* (Sydney, 1886), p. 185; P. F. Moran, op. cit., pp. 240, 229-30.
41 R. D. Boys, *First Years at Port Phillip, 1834-42* (Melbourne, 2nd ed., 1959), pp. 100-2.
42 *Minutes of the Synod of Australia, October 1841* (Sydney, 1841), p. 40.
43 *Tegg's Almanac*, 1841, pp. 188-93. See also Gipps to Russell, 1 May 1840, *H.R.A.*, xx, p. 605.
44 V.D.L. Blue Book, 1841, pp. 293-311; V.D.L. Wes Dist. Min., 1841, Q. 6; Melville's *Van Diemen's Land Annual*, 1828, p. 16; *Third Report of Van Diemen's Land Home Missionary . . . Society, 1838* (Hobart, 1839), pp. 8, 12.

following the Church Act than it had been in the previous three years, and nearly thirty-nine per cent of the fifty-one thousand people in the colony in 1841 could be accommodated, compared with thirty-one per cent of the forty-six thousand living there in 1838.[45]

Governor Gipps's favourable comments upon the working of the Church Act in New South Wales could, therefore, have been equally well applied to the other colony. Gipps considered that the legislation had succeeded in its objects: the means of religious instruction had been increased 'in a very remarkable manner' and the Church of England itself, while receiving great financial benefit, had also gained by being no longer an object 'of envy or hatred to dissenters'.[46] These essentially practical Acts were eminently successful, and advanced the principle of religious equality as well as the extension of the Churches. But they were already proving too successful when viewed from the angle of government finance. In the two eastern Australian colonies the Governors and their councillors were becoming worried men.

[45] *Statistics of Van Diemen's Land, 1824-39* (Hobart, 1839), Table 24; ibid., 1838-41 (Hobart, 1843), Table 37.
[46] Gipps to Russell, 8 February 1841, *H.R.A.*, xxi, pp. 218-19.

3

THE GOVERNMENTS REPENT

Treasuries at Bay

THE SHEER COST of the Church Acts to the colonial Governments quickly caused them concern. Aid had to be kept within limits, but the Councils were not sure how this could be done. An early hope was that the aid would be temporary, and that the Churches would stand on their own feet after being helped over the initial stages of development. In the 1833 despatch which began it all, Sir Richard Bourke had vaguely predicted that, in time, a system of aid depending on the amounts raised by the Churches themselves would relieve the Treasury of a considerable charge. In less guarded language, he once said that he anticipated the day when the Churches would 'roll off State support like saturated leeches'.[1] But such optimism quite under-estimated the extent of the Churches' growth and the constancy of their demands. Far more realistic were those who saw at once that the Treasuries could easily get into difficulties over State aid.

The cautious included many members of the Legislative Council in Van Diemen's Land, who repeatedly emphasized the need to safeguard government funds. Their uneasiness was completely justified, and the entertaining *Colonial Times* was not merely indulging in hyperbole when it hoped that 'the famished people' would not be taxed 'in order to procure turtle and port for the over-fed preacher', for Van Diemen's Land was feeling the effects of economic depression. The basic causes were falling wool prices, small land sales, a shortage of coin and an adverse balance of payments; but, these being allowed their proper place, the contemporary historian, John West, had a valid point when he claimed that the demands of the Churches soon threatened the Government with serious difficulties. Deriving its income from customs and land sales, the Legislative Council had seriously reduced resources and did not find it easy to meet the new demands of the Churches.[2]

[1] Quoted in J. S. Gregory, 'Church and State, and Education in Victoria to 1872', *Melbourne Studies in Education, 1958-1959* (Melbourne, 1960), p. 12.
[2] *Courier*, 28 July 1837, p. 4; 1 December 1837, p. 2; *Colonial Times*, 6 September

45

New South Wales soon had similar difficulties. The Church Act was introduced in auspicious years, with wool coming into its own, private capital flowing into the colony, a tremendous demand for land, and boom conditions all round; but in 1841 this came to an end—dramatically illustrated by a fall in land sales receipts from £316,626 in 1840 to £90,388 in 1841 and £14,575 in 1842. It was 1845 before the depression released the colony from its stifling grip.[3] Even before this slump, Sir George Gipps had been deeply concerned about the cost of the ecclesiastical establishment. He acted strictly on the principle that Downing Street looked with a favourable eye only upon Governors who balanced their budgets, and, being a chronic worrier about deficits, he was mightily alarmed when faced with one amounting to £102,365 in 1839. He did better, despite his annual pessimism, in 1840 and 1841, when he had surpluses; but, to keep him nervous, wool prices were falling after 1836, a severe drought began in 1838 and the demand for government services of all kinds was increasing. The Governor was opposed neither to the Churches nor to State aid. He was driven, he said, 'by the consideration alone of the state of our finances' to protest against the amount of aid given to religion.[4] Soon after his arrival in the colony, he had tried to do something about this by rashly reporting that there was 'no want . . . of Clergymen of any denomination',[5] with the result that the S.P.G. was told by the British Government that expenditure could not be increased and clergymen might not even be replaced when vacancies occurred, and all denominations were warned that they must look for future support to the people themselves. The final result, however, was in favour of the Churches rather than the Treasury. Bishop Broughton protested strongly against this violation of the Church Act, by-passing Gipps in writing to deny his statement that the number of clergy was adequate. The Governor was subsequently told that, although the funds of the colony might have to be spared temporarily, it was clear that there was need for an even larger measure of religious instruction, and that he must make the utmost effort to meet the cost. The Catholics also acted quickly and managed to get more priests approved and appointed.[6] The victory remained with the Churches, and the problem with the Government.

The Governors, however, continued to speak their minds. Gipps complained when more than four per cent of the total government

1836, p. 311; J. West, *The History of Tasmania* (Launceston, 1852), I, pp. 209, 219. On the economic situation, see R. M. Hartwell, *The Economic Development of Van Diemen's Land, 1820-1850* (Melbourne, 1954), pp. 190, 205-9.
[3] B. Fitzpatrick, *The British Empire in Australia* (Melbourne, 1949), pp. 31, 55, 71.
[4] Gipps to Normanby, 3 December 1839, *H.R.A.*, xx, pp. 408-9.
[5] Gipps to Glenelg, 9 November 1838, ibid., xix, p. 656.
[6] The relevant documents are in ibid., xx.

expenditure in 1838 went to the Churches, and he continued to complain as it rose to about eight per cent in 1841. The amount in the latter year was £33,600—a big rise on the £26,574 spent in 1840, and an alarming increase on the £13,242 spent in the palmy days of 1834.[7] In the mid-forties Gipps asked again for relief, recommending that no more clergymen be sent to the colony, but the British authorities only asked more questions when applications for appointments were made; they did not stop additional clergymen from coming. Lieutenant-Governor John Franklin was equally concerned in the southern colony, where, between 1837 and 1842, the claims of the Churches increased from about £12,000 to over £15,000 annually because of 'contributions under the Act' and 'additional clergy and erection of churches'.[8] What particularly worried both Governors was that they could not restrict the expenditure in any way. 'At present', said Gipps, 'the Government is called upon to provide Salaries for Clergymen, without having the smallest power of setting limits to their numbers.'[9] Proposing £2,000 one year in aid of churches and parsonages under the Act, Franklin added that this large sum had to be granted to those who applied because the law put the amounts 'beyond the control of the Government'.[10] The Governments were seeing what they had not seen clearly enough at the time of the passing of the Church Acts: they were committed to meeting increasing claims without any safeguards or powers to restrict them. Somehow they had to regain control over their own creations.

New South Wales Limits Its Church Act

Control of its Church Act was secured by the New South Wales Government when the Imperial Government granted the colony a new constitution in 1842. The Constitution Act, together with Schedule C annexed to it, fixed £30,000 as the figure to be voted annually for public worship.[11] The colonial Act was not formally amended, and applications and grants were still made according to its regulations, but the Government was not obliged to grant more money once £30,000 had been paid out in any year. The Church Act might as well have been radically amended, because, in choosing to work within the limit laid down in the Imperial legislation, the colonial authorities were ignoring the fact that the measure which remained in the colony's own statute book was an indefinite appropriation Act. Formal amend-

[7] Minutes on Finance and Abstracts of Revenue and Appropriation, *V. & P.* (N.S.W.), 1839, 1841, and 1842.
[8] Duplicate Blue Books, C.S.O. 50/? (unnumbered addition to file) to 50/6 (TA).
[9] Minute on Ways and Means, *V. & P.* (N.S.W.), 1839.
[10] Finance Minute, *V. & P.* (V.D.L.), 1842.
[11] 5 & 6 Vict., c. 76, *Statutes At Large*, xvi.

ment probably would have been made if the New South Wales Attorney-General, J. H. Plunkett, had not confused the issue in the mind of the Secretary of State. Plunkett first advised against any amendment before the elections under the new constitution because he feared that any direct interference with this popular Act might cause a religious outcry. Then, clearly sharing his Government's concern over the cost of State aid, he studied the legislation again and, lawyer-like, discovered a loop-hole. The Act had an introductory clause which enabled the money to be granted 'with the advice of the Executive Council', and the Attorney-General realized that it might be possible to render it inoperative by persuading the Executive Council to vote against additional grants of money. Made wary by all this advice, however, Lord Stanley was content to provide a way out in the Constitution Act and let the colonial Government grasp the nettle of the Church Act itself.[12] The depression of 1841-4 cleared the way even more, for the Churches could not raise enough by voluntary subscription to push their demands beyond the £30,000 limit. In 1843, the year in which the Constitution Act came into force, the Estimates for 1844 included £36,000 to cover expected claims under the Church Act. The Legislative Council flatly refused to pass this amount, but it did not matter in the end, for the Churches were unable to claim the sum. Private contributions having fallen off, there was an actual surplus of £4,000 from the £30,000 allowed.[13] The same thing happened in 1845, and this played right into the hands of the Government, seeking to accustom the Churches and the community to the upper limit.

One problem posed by allotting a fixed sum to the Churches as a whole was how to allocate it among the various Churches when their united demands finally exceeded the limit. There had to be some way of sharing it other than giving most to those who applied earliest. The Catholics pressed Gipps in 1844 to re-allocate the money according to the numerical proportions of the various denominations shown in the 1841 census, rather than basing it merely on the average amount of money privately subscribed. The Catholics wanted it this way, of course, because they were numerous but comparatively poor, and such a division would have benefited them by some three and a half thousand pounds annually. At first both the colonial Government and the Secretary of State resisted the suggestion, preferring to determine the new allocation by reference to previous claims, but in 1845 Gipps and his Executive Council decided to adopt the Catholic proposal. Though the denomina-

---

[12] Stanley to Gipps, 24 August 1844, and enclosures, *H.R.A.*, xxiii, pp. 732-8.
[13] Gipps to Stanley, 21 January 1844, ibid., p. 348; Gipps to Stanley, 7 August 1845, ibid., xxiv, pp. 442-3.

tions still had to apply according to the Church Act's regulations to receive their quotas, that Act was less than ever what it appeared, and had been intended, to be. The Government of New South Wales was now well secured against the embarrassing demands which would have come as church development got back into full stride.

The colonists were well aware of what the Government was doing, but most of them were either too indifferent or too alarmed about the Government's financial difficulties to protest. The allocation of the fixed sum according to the number of adherents actually won wide approval,[14] but some objections were made. The Wesleyans challenged the accuracy of the 1841 census, claiming that many were served by their Church who had not described themselves as Wesleyans in the returns. They set out to educate their adherents in time for the 1846 census and to convince the Governor that their claims were correct and that the division should be made according to the new census. When taken it certainly proved their point. The colonial Government was seeking a stable allocation to avoid the inconvenience of adjustments every few years, and resisted the Wesleyan claim. Lord Grey, however, instructed FitzRoy to make a special grant to the Methodists, and the Government would not so easily have made the transition from one scheme to the next if the Wesleyans themselves had not magnanimously decided 'to suffer the loss of a few hundreds annually rather than disturb the religious peace of the colony'.[15]

It was not all as easy as this. There was a more significant and less relenting opposition than that of the Wesleyan Methodists, for the Right Reverend W. G. Broughton, bishop of a Church with larger responsibilities and closer connection with the State, was not so ready to submit. His patience had been strained to breaking point by government policy ever since the Church Act came into force. He had found in 1836 that no part of the allowance could be used to buy more than an acre for a church site, or one and a half acres for a house and garden; his arguments that land was cheap, and that a clergyman had to keep a horse, were met by the blunt statement that to grant more would be to go farther than the Church Act contemplated. A little later he proposed to erect some cheap wooden chapels, but could get no government aid because they were not the kind of building envisaged in the Act.[16] The bishop also complained about the refusal of

[14] Reported, with irritation, in Broughton to Coleridge, 3 January 1844, B.P.
[15] FitzRoy to Grey, 27 February 1847, and enclosures, *H.R.A.*, xxv, pp. 376-87; Grey to FitzRoy, 8 October 1847, and W. B. Boyce to Colonial Secretary, 3 June 1848, ibid., xxvi, pp. 3, 539.
[16] W. Pridden, *Australia, its History and Present Condition* . . . (London, 1843), pp. 351-2.

assistance where the £300 could not be raised because of the scattered nature of settlement and, all too often, the settlers' contempt for religion.[17] On top of this had come the 'direct departure' from the Act itself by the fixing of the £30,000 limit and by making available to each denomination a fixed proportion according to numbers. Broughton opposed this from the beginning. The Church Act had made provision for 'a perpetual appropriation of an indefinite portion of the General Revenue' which depended not on numbers, but on complying with the provisions of the Act; to go back on this legislation was to favour Catholics and injure Anglicans. So Broughton had argued at the time of the Catholic petition and the Legislative Council's refusal to vote the full Estimates, and he made similarly strong and bitter claims during the course of the Executive Council's discussion in August 1845.[18] Soon after the decision went against the bishop, he resigned his seat.

This did not mean that Broughton had given up. The problem of the bush kept troubling him, and he kept troubling the authorities. The revision of the system of selling crown land between 1844 and 1847 gave him an opportunity to press the Church's claims on the Government, and he seized the chance with characteristic vigour. The Church Act was 'vitally defective in principle, and the most absurd and mischievous example of Legislature in the annals of the world' because it failed to give much help to areas where the squatters would not even improve their 'own' land while they lacked security of tenure, let alone contribute to church building. For once, and at one point, the bishop's desire to see the land securely held, having been bought at a price which would provide funds for government support of the Church, brought him into agreement with Governor Gipps; but Broughton, trying to remedy both policy and situation, continued to paint a dark picture of the effects of government practice. In April 1845, five of his clergymen were responsible for an area containing two counties and eight districts beyond the boundaries—an enormous tract of country stretching from Moreton Bay to Portland Bay. Ten other districts beyond the boundaries were 'altogether destitute', yet within all eighteen districts there were at least fourteen thousand people, and only occasional visits by Catholic and Presbyterian clergymen added any spiritual oversight to that of the five Anglicans. Since the Government had spent a total of about £400 on religious provision in the area, while spending £15,000 annually for civil purposes there, and drawing an

[17] *S.P.G. Report* (N.S.W.), 1840, pp. 33-9.
[18] Broughton to Gipps, 18 January 1844, *H.R.A.*, XXIII, pp. 351-2; 'Copy of a Paper entered on the Minutes of the Executive Council . . . 4 August, 1845', P.R.O. Copies of Missing Enclosures to Despatches, 1845, pp. 3312-15 (ML).

even greater annual revenue from it, it seemed to the bishop that government policy was to encourage 'the Establishment of the dominion of Atheism'.[19] Broughton managed to get the Archbishop of Canterbury and the S.P.G. to press his claims upon Imperial authorities, so that the Secretary of State told Gipps to try to make provision from land sales revenue; but nothing came of it. Gipps's suggestion that something to this effect be included in a House of Commons Bill then being prepared to amend the Act regulating the sale of waste land in the colonies was ignored in despatches, the amending Act and the regulations under it. Broughton fought to the end, but lost.

He won only minor skirmishes, one of which was the continuation of a grant of £450 annually to clergymen who ministered to convicts in remote parts. Governor FitzRoy proposed to discontinue this upon the break up of the convict establishment, but Broughton successfully protested, so that the sum was allowed—in the proportions of £300 to Anglicans, £100 to Catholics and £50 to Presbyterians—until early in 1850.[20] Some help was also given to destitute areas and to clergymen beyond the boundaries from the surpluses remaining from the annual vote of £30,000 in years when the Churches could not claim the full amounts allowed; in 1847, for instance, contributions were made from this money to such remote projects as an Anglican parsonage at Cooma and a Catholic church on the Darling Downs.[21] But this was not aid on a scale which satisfied the Churches as they recovered from the bad years and set out to supply the increasing population. If even the Bishop of Sydney could not pry open the door of the Treasury, the new Bishop of Melbourne, appointed in 1847 to relieve Broughton of part of his huge diocese, was certainly not going to receive the help he badly needed from the New South Wales Government. The Right Reverend Charles Perry was in a desperately unhappy financial position when he entered into his charge; the Anglican allocation under Schedule C was completely exhausted after he and three of his clergy had been paid, and the rest of his men—approaching a score—had to be supported by voluntary giving, the help of the S.P.G. and other uncertain sources.[22] The Legislative Council was not going to create additional

[19] Broughton to S.P.G., 22 June 1844; Broughton to a private friend in England, 17 February 1846; Broughton to S.P.G., 3 April 1845; *H.R.A.*, xxiv, pp. 496, 782, 494-5.
[20] FitzRoy to Grey, 12 February 1848, and enclosure; Grey to FitzRoy, 10 November 1848; ibid., xxvi, pp. 229, 675.
[21] FitzRoy to Gladstone, 29 September 1846, ibid., xxv, pp. 199-200; Statements of Expenditure . . . for . . . Purposes Specified in Schedule C, 1846 and 1847, *V. & P.* (N.S.W). 1847 and 1848.
[22] Statement of Expenditure . . . 1850, ibid., 1851 (First Session); Perry to Broughton, 4 June 1850 (Separate), B.P.; *The Church in the Colonies, No. XXIV, A letter from the Lord Bishop of Melbourne . . . November, 1849* (London, 1850), p. 15.

difficulties for its Treasury just after it had managed to reduce the embarrassment of its Church Act. While the Council had itself evaded the letter of that law, its officers dealt with applications for aid very much according to the regulations. When Presbyterians at Bathurst asked for £57 towards the erection of a church tower, they were refused it on the ground that more than three years had elapsed since their previous request for aid; up to £200 would have been available (the Presbyterian quota permitting) if application had been made within the three years.[23] The Government was giving nothing away which could be kept.

This is not to say that the Churches were receiving little assistance from the State. The Government's annual grant for religious purposes was far from negligible, and the New South Wales Churches continued to share their £30,000 each year until aid was abolished in 1862. The new colony of Victoria secured its own Constitution Act in 1851, to which was appended a Schedule B allowing an annual grant of £6,000 towards 'Public Worship',[24] an amount which was increased to £30,000 in 1853 and was continued until 1870. Thus the spirit of the original Church Act in New South Wales had by no means been lost to the colonies; yet there was a different spirit abroad. The Victorian Government was initially committed to a very small sum, and the increase in 1853 (after gold had brought new wealth) actually resulted from an attempt to abolish aid.[25] There was considerable addition here to the writing which had appeared on the wall of the elder colony's chamber in the mid-forties, when New South Wales imposed a firm restriction upon the Church Act. Within ten years of the passing of that measure, though aid went on, it was widely accepted that all State aid to religion must eventually cease. This opinion was not the same as Bourke's optimistic expectation that the Churches, once afloat, would happily hoist their own sails; it was the sterner resolve that, for the sake of government finance, the Churches must be cut adrift and left to make their own way whether they liked it or not. Most influential colonists were essentially practical men, practical before they were pious. It was not that they were impious; they had their religion, and they liked to see the Churches at work in the community; but they had as ready an eye for other things, and were strangers to the zeal which would have built churches and spread the gospel whatever else had to suffer because of it. This had been true down the years, and it continued to be the principle by which leading Australians conducted the nation's affairs.

[23] Memos, 17 and 20 September, on W. Stewart to Col. Sec., 18 August 1847, C.S.I.L. 2/1717 (ML).
[24] 13 & 14 Vict., c. 59, *Statutes At Large*, xx, pp. 180-90.
[25] See J. S. Gregory, op. cit., p. 33.

Once they were securely established, they had begun to do something to make up for their neglect of religious provision. The Church Act was meant to give practical assistance to the Churches, providing they asked nothing unreasonable. When that aid began to cause practical difficulties for the Treasury, it was quickly limited. Later it was abolished altogether—on practical grounds, not in a spirit of rejecting the Christian heritage. The Churches have been welcome in Australia, when and where they could be fitted in.

The Problem in Van Diemen's Land

Definite limits to the Church Act did not come so quickly in Van Diemen's Land, but the Legislative Council there tried very early to find safeguards. Its Act was amended three times between 1838 and 1841, once to allow a slight increase in aid, a second time to significantly tighten the Government's control over the whole Act, and a third time to restrict the possibilities allowed by the first amendment.[26] Of the three, the 1840 amendment was the most important. This gave the Governor and Executive Council power to refuse aid, even when an application conformed with the requirements of the Church Act, if they considered that the church or minister's dwelling was not strictly necessary. The New South Wales Act had, from the beginning, contained the saving clause 'with the advice of the Executive Council', so the Van Diemen's Land amendment was not as radical an innovation as it might appear. Yet there was this significant difference between the two colonies: whereas one clause had been formally included in the New South Wales Act and largely overlooked, the Van Diemen's Land change was deliberately made two years before the mainland remembered and appealed to the clause in question. What is more, the various claims for aid were very closely watched in the southern colony. The Executive Council recommended in 1838 that forage for horses be allowed only to ministers in country areas; applications for aid in church building were repeatedly refused or delayed because all the requirements of the Act had not been met; and, in 1843, the Audit Office advised the Colonial Secretary to insist that detailed contractors' bills be included with all applications for assistance.[27] Clearly the southern colony was bent on securing a way of escape from exorbitant demands.

Yet the Churches were still supported by the Government at a large

[26] 2 Vict., no. 17 (1838), 4 Vict., no. 16 (1840), 5 Vict., no. 9 (1841). See *Hobart Town Gazette*, 7 December 1838, pp. 1125-6; *Acts of the Lieutenant-Governor and Legislative Council* (V.D.L.), 1840 and 1841.
[27] Min. of Exec. Coun., 15 June, 10 October 1838, 8 January, 17, 29 April, 8 May, 2 July 1839, E.C. 2/6 (TA); C.S.O. 8/85/1943 (TA).

and increasing cost, and this was quite as significant as the attempt to limit aid. Here was another Government in a dilemma. It agreed that the Churches should be given substantial aid, but realized that the ever-growing drain on colonial funds had to be checked. It may even be said that, for a time, the Churches' needs were put first. The 1840 amendment was mild, and a sign of support for religion, when compared with the immediately preceding proposal of Charles Swanston that the Church Act be repealed altogether because of the 'enormous and increasing' cost to the Treasury. Seen from this angle, the actual amendment was not even a true compromise; it was a clear decision in the Churches' favour in spite of the Treasury's difficulties. Thus have pious sentiments sometimes won a round in practical Australia.

There were still the difficulties, and they were many and serious. In the forties Van Diemen's Land was carrying the cost of police and gaols, previously met by Great Britain, while receiving nearly all the convicts sent to Australia. A change in policy denied settlers the convicts' cheap labour, increased Government expenses in maintaining the new probation gangs, and sometimes involved colonists in further loss when the gangs' agricultural produce was dumped on the market. The colony was also involved in an expensive and immediately harmful immigration programme, due to fears of a labour shortage following the non-assignment of convicts and to the unrealistic economic theory that an increased labour supply would lower wages and raise profits. Commissariat expenditure (by England, for the garrisons) helped the position, but did not help enough; the proceeds from the sales of Crown lands fell off to nothing, private and public money both being in short supply. The worst was over by 1846, but not before a crisis in the Legislative Council when the six non-official members resigned, and not at once giving place to great prosperity. Eardley-Wilmot declared that his Government's contribution towards religious instruction was more liberal than practical, and that the time was fast approaching when the State would have to stop paying any clerical stipends; but the old dilemma appeared once more in his finance committee's comment that it would be a reproach to the decent citizens in the convict colony if the Government withdrew from the field of State aid, and the same policy was continued, with a few minor reductions such as disallowing forage for clergymen's horses.[28]

As a matter of fact, the continuation of transportation to Van Diemen's Land not only made State aid desirable but also helped to make it possible. The Imperial Government gave assistance by paying both

[28] Governor's Minute, 23 July, *V. & P.* (V.D.L.), 1844; Address on Estimates, 21 October, and Report of Finance Committee, ibid., 1845.

'Convict Chaplains', appointed specifically for work among convict gangs, and 'Missionary Chaplains', who ministered to convicts and ticket-of-leave men dispersed throughout the community. What is more, the Colonial Office accepted the practice of their 'Missionary Chaplains' being responsible for the free, as well as the convict, population in their areas. This was a large saving of the colony's funds. In 1849 the colonial Treasury paid out £7,904 for the support of Anglican ministers and the British Government added another £4,355. Ten of the thirteen Catholic priests in the island were also attached to the Convict Department, and the British Government was responsible for £2,322 annually, compared with only £1,328 paid by the colony.[29] Yet there was a penalty to be paid which was perhaps greater than the bonus received by Van Diemen's Land remaining a penal colony. No new constitution was granted; and therefore there was no equivalent to New South Wales' Schedule C and no limit imposed upon the amount of money to be granted to the Churches. The Legislative Councillors, denied an easy way out, and being practical men at heart, began to try to force a way. Informed in 1846 that four additional Anglican chaplains were being allowed for in the Estimates by direction of the British Government, the Council reacted strongly and passed a resolution refusing to pay any additional clergymen of any denomination until the financial affairs of the colony were in better shape. The temper of the Council was made plain in the passing of this resolution by ten votes to four. Another time the Council rejected the Governor's estimates *in toto* to emphasize its angry dissatisfaction with the trends in colonial expenditure. Despite these flashes in the pan, however, neither the Council nor the Lieutenant-Governor was able to do much to reduce the amount which went out annually to the Churches. In the closing years of the decade the actual expenditure was usually less than the estimates, but the latter continued to rise and the expenditure on State aid rose with the rest. The £13,435 estimated for Church needs in 1849 became £16,125 in 1850 and £15,925 in 1851. The result was that, when Van Diemen's Land at last secured a limit on State aid, the figure was still a high one—£15,000.

Aid continued on this scale from 1850, when the limit was set down in the third part of Schedule C attached to the Imperial Act for the Government of Her Majesty's Australian Colonies, until 1869, when State aid was commuted by the payment of one lump-sum to the Churches.[30] Therefore the Van Diemen's Land Government could not

[29] Report of Committee on Convict Expenditure, ibid., 1848; Denison to Grey, 26 August 1848, 4 November 1848, G.O. 33/63, 33/65 (TA); *Statistics of Van Diemen's Land for 1849*, Tables 44, 46.
[30] 13 & 14 Vict., c. 59, *Statutes at Large*, xx, pp. 180-90. The Church Act was dis-

be accused of indifference to religious provision. Financial reasons lay
behind its restiveness under its commitments, and there was considerable reluctance to stop all State aid. Extreme suggestions to this effect
were rejected. As elsewhere, the Churches were not of overriding importance to this Government, but they were far from unimportant.
Like their New South Wales counterparts, these Councillors were
simply practical men, neither saints nor unbelievers, who tried to
balance Church claims with other demands when balancing their
budget. Nevertheless the trend away from the Church-State connection
was evident. In Van Diemen's Land, no less than on the mainland, the
continuation of government assistance to the Churches was in doubt
before 1850.

A Cargo of Bishops, and a Problem of Command

Bishops, those expensive prelates, were not always regarded with
favour by the colonial press, the preference being for humble men
with homely manners and small stipends. 'Free institutions are demanded by the Colonists,' grumbled one editor, 'and behold by the
first opportunity, a cargo of bishops, priests and archdeacons are [*sic*]
sent out.'[31] The bishops arrived, and were followed by others; the
Churches which had their representatives in the colonies introduced
also their full ecclesiastical systems; and the hard-pressed Governments
did their best to meet the cost and to interfere as little as possible
with the control and organization of the denominations. This was
another aspect of the relations between Church and State which
showed the colonial Governments' tolerance and tact, and possibly
their sympathy for the Churches.

By the middle of 1836 there were two Australian bishops, W. G.
Broughton of the Church of England and J. B. Polding of the Catholic
Church, both resident in Sydney and both receiving from the Government considerably more than the average chaplain. The latter might
have got his £200 annually, but Polding received £500 and Broughton
£2,000. Francis Russell Nixon was consecrated Bishop of Tasmania in
1842, an appointment which was made possible by a fund raised in
England for the establishment of additional bishoprics in the colonies,
but towards which the Van Diemen's Land Government at once
allocated £800 per annum. Bishop Broughton, after years of toil in his
vast diocese, offered to reduce his salary by half if two additional
bishops were appointed, but the New South Wales Government only

posed of by 26 Vict., no. 17 (1862), which divided the £15,000 among the Churches (and
Jews) in a fixed annual proportion. The abolition of State aid came with 32 Vict., no. 30
(1869), when a lump sum of £100,000 was divided among the denominations.
[31] *Colonial Times*, 5 July 1836, p. 221.

cut it by one quarter while agreeing to pay an annual stipend of £500 each to William Tyrrell, Bishop of Newcastle, and Charles Perry, Bishop of Melbourne, both of whom arrived at the beginning of 1848. This did not mean that the Governments suddenly became unexpectedly generous and allowed large additional grants. They had to find ways and means from within the existing resources. Bishop Nixon's stipend came from earlier provision allowed for a previous archdeacon, and the mainland bishops' salaries were met from unexpended money in the 'Building Fund' (one sixth of the £30,000 allowed by Schedule C), it being expected that the full sixth would again become available for building upon the retirement of some early appointees who drew abnormally high salaries. Similarly, the bishops' residences were paid for from money being held in another fund—the old Church and School Land estate.[32] In this way the Governments juggled their finances so that, with the help from private donations (such as £330 annually for both Tyrrell and Perry from the Colonial Bishoprics' Fund), the new Anglican bishops were allowed for in the ecclesiastical department. It is significant that the Governments bothered; they could so easily have refused to adapt their means to the Church's need.

The Catholic Church also increased the number of its bishops and received State aid for them. What is more, they were permitted to proceed with the erection of the Hierarchy in Australia in 1842, when Bishop Polding became the archbishop, and Robert William Willson, of Nottingham, was consecrated Bishop of Hobart. Willson arrived in 1844, and four years later C. H. Davis arrived in Sydney as Bishop of Maitland and Coadjutor of the Archbishop, and J. A. Goold, a priest aged only thirty-five, who had been in the colony since 1838, was consecrated Bishop of Melbourne. Polding continued to receive his £500 annually; Willson in 1850 was receiving £400 and £100 house allowance as well as extras for forage and a grant 'in lieu of fencing glebe'; and in 1849 Davis and Goold received £250 each from the Government, although their existence was not acknowledged in the *Votes and Proceedings* for 1851 and 1852— presumably because all the money under Schedule C had been used up. Sometimes the Governments' severely limited resources could be called on no more, but all in all the Catholic prelates received much assistance from the Treasuries.

As might be expected, the landing of the 'cargo of bishops' produced some clashes between civil and ecclesiastical authorities over their respective jurisdictions; but the more remarkable thing, yet another sign of the civil authorities' readiness to co-operate with the Churches, was

[32] FitzRoy to Grey, 31 March 1849, and enclosures; Grey to FitzRoy, 30 September 1848; *H.R.A.*, xxvi, pp. 310-14, 619.

that these collisions were comparatively rare. The seed of potential conflict was sown when the Reverend Richard Johnson was instructed to obey orders from the Governor or other superior officers according to the rules and discipline of war. Later chaplains were similarly commissioned and were nominated to chaplaincies by the Governors. In 1810 Macquarie omitted the military clause from the commissions and vested immediate control and superintendence of the clergy in the Principal Chaplain. Upon the appointment of an archdeacon in 1824, control of the chaplains passed from the Governor to Archdeacon Scott. The Governor retained a formal right to appoint and suspend, but only upon the archdeacon's recommendation, and the ultimate decision lay with the bishop of the diocese, who lived far across the sea. When Australia was erected into a self-contained diocese, and the bishop was resident within it, the Letters Patent gave him full power according to the ecclesiastical laws of England, and the Governor was commanded to assist him to carry out his functions. Somehow, through all these years, the gradual changeover was effected without much trouble.

In the forties the most dangerous challenges in New South Wales came from an individual member of the Legislative Council, Robert Lowe, and a group of low church (and possibly no church) citizens who were opposed to Bishop Broughton and his ecclesiastical ideals. In 1846 Lowe proposed a Bill to confer on Anglican clergymen a freehold in their benefices and invest control of each benefice in a lay committee. This would have struck at the root of the bishop's power, but Broughton secured permission to address the Council and the Bill was subsequently 'cast to the moles and to the bats'.[33] In 1849, after the bishop had suspended the licences of two deacons, F. T. C. Russell and P. T. Beamish, Lowe again attempted to get the Council to intervene.[34] But the Bishop of Sydney and the Government of New South Wales were not to be drawn into this conflict; if the Government was of no direct help to Broughton in matters relating to his Consistorial Court, it was not actively obstructive. The Church of England was to look after its own affairs.

In Van Diemen's Land, however, a serious collision occurred in this period between the Governors and Bishop Nixon. Convict chaplains and religious instructors, the latter usually hoping to be ordained, had been placed under the direction of the Comptroller-General of Convicts, and were thus removed from the control of the bishop. He, in retort, refused to ordain any of these men, even though some of them were

[33] Broughton to Coleridge, 3 October 1846, B.P.
[34] See K. J. Cable, 'Religious Controversies in New South Wales in the Mid-nineteenth Century', *J.R.A.H.S.*, vol. 49, pt. 1, pp. 66-7.

already deacons and convict stations had been known to call upon a
Catholic priest to administer the last rites because the Anglican instructor was not qualified. In 1844 he despatched Archdeacon Marriott
to England to get this matter—and others—put to rights.[35] Marriott
blundered. He personally accepted the new appointment of 'Superintendent of Convict Chaplains', although in so doing he became 'essentially a civil officer, appointed by the Crown . . . and removable by the
Crown', and the control denied the bishop was vested in the bishop's
archdeacon.[36] This was the last straw, and Nixon left for England in
1846 to plead his case. The result was that the office of superintendent
was abolished and the bishop gained the right to station the 'colonial
chaplains', though the Lieutenant-Governor retained the power to
station 'convict chaplains'.[37] Negotiation with Sir William Denison
after the bishop's return resulted in a still more amicable arrangement,[38] and the air cleared after some years of great unpleasantness.
Though this was one of the worst clashes which occurred between the
rival authorities of Church and State, it was born of administrative
blunder rather than any deliberate attempt to interfere with the Church
of England.

The Governments were anxious to avoid meddling with the internal
affairs of any Church, just as they were reluctant to favour one at the
expense of another. Typical examples of government policy, one large
and the other small, are the permitting of a Catholic Hierarchy in
New South Wales (the first actually to be erected in British dominions
since the Reformation) and the payment of ministers of the Presbyterian
Synod of New South Wales in spite of protests from the other section
of that denomination. The Churches had to decide their own affairs,
and the State wanted to be tolerant rather than to take sides. It was
argued at the time by men like Broughton and Nixon that government
policy revealed no positive virtue, but only a negative approach to
religion. As bishops of a Church solely established and once exclusively
tolerated in England, and as Christian men convinced that their own
creed embodied the maximum of truth and the minimum of error,
their view was reasonable. In some senses they were probably right.
From certain aspects, however, government policy could not be called
negative. It showed a positive respect for the right of every body of
Christians to their creeds and their internal organization. It stood on

[35] Wilmot to Stanley, 29 January 1845, G.O. 25/11 (TA); A. Nixon to C. Woodcock,
3 April 1844, N. Nixon (ed.), *The Pioneer Bishop in Van Diemen's Land, 1843-63*
(Hobart, 1953), p. 24.
[36] F. R. Nixon, *A Charge delivered to the Clergy . . . April xxiii, MDCCCXLVI.*
(London, 2nd ed., 1848), pp. 43-9.
[37] Grey to Denison, 16 December 1847, G.O. 1/67 (TA).
[38] Denison to Grey, 26 August 1848, G.O. 33/63 (TA).

the side of Christianity in its broad sense, and the colonists would not have permitted it to stand for any narrower definition. And it resulted in some very positive financial aid, for the Churches received over half a million pounds under the Church Acts between 1836 and 1850. At the end the Governments were certainly preparing to rest on their laurels; but they had made, and were for a time still to make, a solid contribution to religious provision in the colonies. At the half-way mark in the century their repentance was not so much over the granting of aid, as over the original passing of indefinite appropriation Acts.

4

PUBLIC CRITICISM AND SUPPORT

Later Reactions to the Church Acts

THE COLONIAL GOVERNMENTS kept wary eyes not only on their finances, but also on the popularity of the Church Acts. These were not democratic days, but they were still days in which the pressure of public opinion could be decisive. The authorities, both in the colonies and in England, took seriously the attitudes of press and people in Australia. Within a few years of the passing of the Church Acts, the official purse-watchers were detecting some reassuring signs, for public opinion became increasingly divergent over the measures. If the Governments' attitude was an amalgam of two conflicting aims (to support religion and to relieve government finances), public opinion was no less so. There was growing public criticism of the effects of the Acts, though very much use continued to be made of them, and general support for them was not withdrawn.

How much they continued to be publicly esteemed was revealed in the comment and warning of J. H. Plunkett, six years after the enactment of the New South Wales Church Act, that it was still the most popular of all colonial Acts, and that direct interference with it could result in an uproar. All sorts of reasons—selfish, practical, moral and religious—combined to keep the Acts popular in certain quarters in both colonies. The number of convicts, together with their propensity to crime and their religious ignorance, still weighed heavily in the scales on the side of government support of religion. James Macarthur dismissed legal reforms, the provision of police and the emphasis upon punishment, as negative approaches to the problem; he insisted that Australia needed 'the provision of pastoral religious instruction, and the means of religious observances, for its entire adult population'.[1] The people of Van Diemen's Land were described as being 'generally anxious for some form of worship, both as a moral agency and from its tendency to raise the respectability of a township'.[2] Clergy-

[1] J. Macarthur and E. Edwards, *New South Wales, Its Present State and Future Prospects* . . . (London, 1837), pp. 211-12.
[2] J. West, *The History of Tasmania* (Launceston, 1852), I, p. 208.

men were usually welcomed and generously entertained in the interior of New South Wales—if not necessarily because of their calling, at least because any traveller was welcome who had 'even the slightest appearance of being respectable'.[3] Even lower motives were alleged to prevail at times in support of the Church Acts' provisions. 'It would appear', scoffed a journalist, in discussing one application for aid,

> that the ready zeal with which they attached their signatures proceeded more from the prospects of gain, which the building of a church seemed to diffuse so suddenly among them, added to the prolonged vision of a steady stipend to be consumed by the resident clergyman, rather than any abstract love or devotion to the Presbyterian faith, to which they hesitated not to announce themselves such unflinching adherents.[4]

There were many reasons for continuing to support the Church Acts and hence they retained favour with many people.

Church people themselves, being zealous for the spread of the gospel, or jealous of the spread of other denominations, used the Acts to the full. At one time, applications for assistance in building new churches were coming into the Van Diemen's Land Executive Council at the rate of one every other week.[5] New South Wales Wesleyans were very anxious to participate, not only because of Anglican and Presbyterian activity, but also because the Catholics were doing so much that the people were in danger of being 'consigned to the awful and destructive errors of Popery'.[6] Bishop Broughton reported, fifteen months after the Act was passed, that contributions had been made towards nearly forty Anglican churches; and, a few years later, he raged about the effect the 'most nonsensical church-law' was having:

> In almost every paltry little town (for example in one which I noticed lately containing 70 houses) you see the Church of England, the Roman Catholic, the Wesleyan and Presbyterian meeting-houses all perched in a row.[7]

Behind the bishop's caricature lay the reality of intense competitive activity among the Churches. This did not always have bad results, even for the Right Reverend W. G. Broughton. Picture him conducting Divine Service at Braidwood in May 1840. Consider the reason for his face being especially set and stern, and for the service being held at the house of Dr Wilson, outside the town. After the Court House had

---

[3] J. O. Balfour, *A Sketch of New South Wales* (London, 1845), pp. 80-1; D. Mackenzie, *The Emigrant's Guide . . .* (London, 1845), p. 49.
[4] *Courier*, 24 May 1839, p. 2.
[5] E.C. 2/6, pp. 225-365 (TA) show nine applications in four months of 1838.
[6] N.S.W. Wes. Dist. Min., January 1839, Q. 27.
[7] Broughton to Coleridge, 19 October 1837; 2 April 1844, B.P.

been prepared for the Anglican service it was taken possession of by a Catholic priest! Yet, trumpeted the bishop, the only effect would be to make the members of his communion 'more zealous and determined to possess a church of their own'. As his report was going to press, he was able to add, 'In proof of the correctness of this persuasion, I have this day (2nd July) received information that the full amount has been raised'.[8] How much longer, one wonders, would this have taken if a bishop and a priest—and an imp?—had not visited Braidwood on the same hilarious day?

Very often, however, denominational rivalry and congregational jealousies lowered the Churches in the public estimation and further jeopardized the continuation of State aid. One reason for the amendment of the Church Act in Van Diemen's Land in 1840, so that aid depended upon the discretion of the Government, was a tendency for dissident groups in congregations to come out, 'leave their late pastors to their salaries and their solitude', and apply for aid towards other churches and pastors—as is reputed to have happened in both the Presbyterian and Anglican churches in Launceston.[9] Denominational rivalry in the smaller communities, with two Churches trying to claim the allegiance of the same persons, or splitting a group which had previously worshipped together, sometimes led to serious discord in the neighbourhood and to contesting claims before the Executive Council.[10] After details were announced of the new Constitution Act for New South Wales, including its Schedule C, the *Colonial Observer* prophesied complete voluntaryism among Presbyterians within ten years, and a Presbyterian minister, the Reverend Dr John McGarvie, doubted whether the principle of State aid was still worth contending for, the public mind being so unsettled by a veritable crusade against establishment.[11] In Van Diemen's Land, the Presbyterian-aligned *Launceston Examiner* spoke caustically of the State aid question:

> Rival sects display the temper of mastiffs over a bone; and instead of one taking the blade, and the other the shank, they quarrel about possession. Nor will the conflict cease till religion is left to its own resources.[12]

The *Courier,* despite its clear sympathies with the Church of England, was outspoken against the 'expensive habit of placing two or three ministers unnecessarily in every village', and condemned the 'ungodly

---

[8] *S.P.G. Report* (N.S.W.), 1840, pp. 34-5.
[9] *Courier*, 28 August 1840, p. 4.
[10] J. West, op. cit., 1, p. 208; *Courier*, 24 May 1839, p. 2; E.C. 2/6, pp. 544, 599-600, 611 (TA).
[11] *Colonial Observer*, 12, 22 October 1842; J. McGarvie, Diary 1843-7, 2-6 January 1843 (MS. ML).
[12] *Examiner,* 3 July 1844, p. 419.

strife' and 'indecent race'. Once it was provoked into declaring, 'The Church Act should be repealed'.[13]

Nevertheless, this strong and repeated criticism in the newspapers did not amount to a true campaign against State aid. When these papers really took up a matter, they devoted columns of print to it in issue after issue, but it was not so in this case. The amending Acts in Van Diemen's Land, for instance, were passed over with the briefest of mentions in the press. Opposition to State aid being continued was not irrevocable or even consistent. Although predicting the end of all government subsidies, the *Colonial Times* directed its real attack against abnormally large salaries.[14] The *Courier,* asking for the repeal of the Church Act at the end of one month, had asked at the beginning of the same month for the Wesleyans to be put on an equal footing with other denominations under the Act.[15] Thus public opinion was not only divided, but was often uncertain of its own mind, and was torn between two ideals. On the whole, government assistance for religion was desired; but it was very strongly felt, too, that State aid should be limited for prudent financial reasons. And any apparent abuses were quickly resented.

Governments, watching the public reaction, could be sure that their efforts to restrict aid would be supported; but they could not yet feel that abolition of all aid would be approved by a sufficient number of the influential people. The Churches themselves were becoming increasingly aware that they must make the best use they could of an aid which was only temporarily assured, and that time was not on their side. Public opinion was slowly but definitely hardening against State aid.

Church Support Among the People

Fairness to the Churches requires the plain statement that none of them were just living off the State, or dissipating their energies in futile rivalries. On the contrary, all the major denominations did a great deal to help themselves, receiving a large sum from private donors, as they pushed farther out with the settlements. By 1843 non-Anglican Protestants in Van Diemen's Land were not far behind the Church of England in providing sittings in their churches, of which the largest proportion had been built chiefly at their own expense.[16] Furthermore, no church was built without the same sum being raised by voluntary contribution as was granted by the Government; so the bigger part of

[13] *Courier*, 24 May 1839, p. 2; 28 August 1840, p. 2.
[14] *Colonial Times*, 13 August 1844, p. 2.   [15] *Courier*, 7 August 1840, p. 2.
[16] Ibid., 17 November 1843, p. 3; *Statistics of Van Diemen's Land, 1842-4* (Hobart, 1845), Table 36.

the cost of all eighty-three churches and chapels in the island had been borne privately. In a longer period, between 1842 and 1848, no less than twenty Anglican chapels, costing over £36,000, were built in the colony without calling on government aid—an impressive achievement by the denomination most inclined to look to the State for support.[17]

In the Church of England, indeed, the need for self-support was being increasingly stressed. Late in 1843, Bishop Nixon announced his intention of restoring the weekly offertory, a practice which had fallen into disuse, 'in the hope of eventually making the Church provide more and more for Herself, and of teaching Her to rely less upon the Government for Her support'. This was not done without opposition. The bishop's wife reported that bad times were dinned into her ears by wealthy members who could spend lavishly on entertainments, even if they could not contribute towards a schoolroom, and from the other end of the colony came complaints that the offertory was a Tractarian innovation—which was as good an excuse as any.[18] The offertory, however, was restored and it remained. In New South Wales Broughton did the same. He secured editorial support from the *Herald*, but had differences with some of his low church clergy and people (Tractarianism again being called in as reason for resisting its re-introduction). The *Atlas*, edited by Robert Lowe, blossomed into verse against 'Will G. Australia'.

> I'm Pope Bill! Here's my system voluntary,
>   For Schedule C can't cram us all.
> Of *raising* money you're so cursed chary,
>   I now insist you'll let it *fall*.

But Broughton won the day, and the offertory was taken up in most Anglican churches.[19]

The need for voluntary support was far greater than the mere adoption of the offertory could meet. The exhaustion of various English funds and the restriction of government aid called for large private efforts, and these were often made. The depression of 1841-4 caused the suspension of many churches and parsonages which were in the

[17] Account of Churches . . . built by Members of the Church of England . . . without any contribution from Colonial Funds, enclosure, Denison to Grey, 4 November 1848, G.O. 33/65 (TA).
[18] Nixon to Woodcock, 24 February 1844, A. Nixon to Woodcock, 30 December 1844, in N. Nixon (ed.), *The Pioneer Bishop in Van Diemen's Land, 1843-63* (Hobart, 1953), pp. 23, 17; R. R. Davies, *"The Offertory" not an innovation: A Sermon* . . . (Launceston, 1845), Appendix A.
[19] Broughton to Coleridge, 15 August 1844, B.P.; *Herald*, 29 February 1848, p. 2; *Atlas*, 6 May 1848, p. 223; W. G. Broughton, *A Letter to Henry Osborne* . . . , Sydney, 1848.

course of being built. We are in danger,' wrote Broughton, 'of losing much of the advantage we have acquired during the past seven years.' But by the beginning of 1846 the churches unfinished in 1842-3 were nearly all completed and about twenty more had been commenced, and Broughton was saying that there was 'a very earnest desire on the part of the people everywhere to have churches' and that they usually did their best to build them.[20] Difficulties remained a little longer in the southern colony, where, for example, the Wesleyans soon changed from expressions of pleasure at the continued generosity of their people despite the unparalleled commercial distress, to reports of chapels heavily encumbered with debt, burdensome interest rates, the inability to raise a stipend for an additional minister, and serious losses through the removal of their members to the 'more prosperous' colonies of South Australia and Port Phillip. But by 1847 they were able to write about an 'encouraging share of temporal and spiritual prosperity'.[21] Church leaders found plenty of cause for worry in the depressed years, but a significant number of private citizens continued to give well to the Churches' funds. Chapel building in the colonies was by no means due only to paternalistic Governments; it was a project in which the people themselves played a large and enthusiastic part.

A most important contribution was made by the 'middling classes' in the community—the prosperous tradesmen and shopkeepers-turned-merchants. Presbyterians and Independents tended towards the higher income brackets, and even the Methodists found most support coming from the 'respectable' people: as the Reverend John McKenny once asserted, 'There are more shopkeepers and mechanics amongst us than there are of the lower orders'.[22] From the Church of England, which included the widest range of classes in its membership, as well as contributing more than any other Church to the upper classes, there emerges some evidence that the financial support given by the colonial middle classes may have been greater than that given by those holding the more important offices or the most land.

The classes, as always, are impossible to define neatly, but it is possible to make several generalizations. First, it was easier in the mid-thirties to distinguish between the men whose main interest was in land and sheep, and those mainly concerned with trade and manufactures, than it had been earlier; by this time, a man tended to be either in one camp or the other. Secondly, the big landholders were usually higher on the social scale than the urban manufacturers and

[20] Broughton to S.P.G., 5 May, 3 July 1843; Broughton to Coleridge, 20 January, 12 June 1846, B.P.
[21] V.D.L. Wes. Dist. Min., 1841-7.
[22] Lowe Committee, Evidence, p. 112.

merchants, for land gave prestige which mere money did not, and the origins of the prosperous townsmen were more likely to have been in humble ranks—among tradesmen and shopkeepers. Therefore it is not inappropriate (though it is only approximate) to describe those with land interests as upper class, and the merchant-manufacturers as middle class. Thirdly, it may be permissible to lump together the men with land and, for convenience's sake, call them all 'squatters'. There was, actually, an important distinction, which reflected different values and caused clashes of interest, between the 'gentry' who first acquired land by grant or purchase, and the squatters proper who got their land, very simply and almost entirely, by putting stock on the crown land beyond the boundaries.[23] Yet this division, which was never complete, became more blurred in the forties when the landowners had to become squatters if they were to survive, so that Governor Gipps remarked that 'almost everybody, who has any property at all, is a Squatter'.[24] In the following discussion, therefore, 'squatter' is a blanket term to cover all men with large interests in land and consequent social prestige; while 'middle classes' is used for men with mainly urban interests, who were making money but not usually the social register.

Bishop Broughton claimed that it was not the squatters and their upper-class allies, but the middle classes who were giving him financial support. In 1846, £1,600 was collected towards the cathedral, but relatively few contributions had come from men who had 'the entree at Government House, or any of the tokens of colonial rank or distinction'. Earlier, when he had called a meeting to try to clear a church debt, the only 'person of station' present was the Chief Justice, while half the debt (of £3,000) had been wiped off at the meeting itself by an ironmonger, an auctioneer, a linen draper, a brewer and a customs agent. Two years earlier the same lack of support by 'the influential people' had been reported by one 'in the middle class of life' himself.[25] In 1847 Charles Kemp was rejoicing in two things: first, that from working in a carpenter's shop for fourteen shillings a week, he had advanced to the editorship and joint-proprietorship of the *Sydney Morning Herald;* and, secondly, that by his exertions and personal gift of £250 an Anglican school had been erected in Trinity Parish.[26] An Anglican clergyman, who commenced his ministry in 1848, recalled that, when collecting money for schools and religious purposes, he might 'get a pound from the shepherd and ten shillings from the station

[23] See M. Roe, 'Society and Thought in Eastern Australia, 1835-51' (Ph.D. thesis, A.N.U., 1960), pp. 80, 159.   [24] Gipps to Stanley, 3 April 1844, *H.R.A.*, XXIII, p. 518.
[25] Broughton to Coleridge, 3 October 1846; J. W. Jones to Coleridge, 26 October 1844, B.P. The Chief Justice was Alfred Stephen.
[26] C. Kemp, Diary 1847-8, 2 June, 19 July 1847 (MS. ML).

owner'.[27] Religious inertia among 'those . . . called *squatters*' (according to Broughton) was such that, unless they could be recalled to a sense of duty, the squatting districts would 'speedily become one vast continuity of flagrant infidelity'. The bishop was not very hopeful of success in that quarter. As he said:

> there is something which does absorb all the anxieties and faculties in one intense effort to grasp unbounded acres and uncountable flocks; and attending on this, is an appalling remissness and indifference as to how the fear and worship of God, or belief in Christ, or the sacred institution of his Church, are to be introduced and upheld among the (in that point of view) unhappy dwellers in those solitary places.

His consolation, he repeated, was in the 'very singular' fact that among 'the middle classes' there was 'a visible *in*crease of religious earnestness'.[28]

Men whose wealth was almost entirely invested in land had a special excuse during the depression years, for Broughton himself was ready to admit that persons of property could not raise money. Nor was this difficulty confined to the depression. Shortage of cash continued to be the chronic complaint of many squatters, particularly as opportunities for true squatting became less, and outright purchase at increasingly high prices was forced upon them. The Joyce brothers of Victoria bought a run of fifty thousand acres in 1851 for £2,000 (exclusive of the sheep) which had been bought from the original owner in 1845 for £25 (or, actually, for one hundred ewes). They had bought their own first station in 1844 for £50. There was a vast potential of wealth in their hands, but not much ready money, and they had been forced to wait for years before accumulating the cash to buy their second station.[29] This commonplace difficulty needs to be understood when considering the landowners and their giving or not giving to the Churches.

The squattocracy may also have been less disposed to build churches because of their antagonism towards Bishop Broughton over his support of Governor Gipps on the land question. The squatters wanted to secure their land for as little as possible. Gipps, though not objecting to the squatters' free use of crown land, did not want it to pass permanently into their hands at a price based on its immediate value as unimproved grazing land. On the contrary, he insisted upon maintaining a high price for actual purchases, and upon costlier licences and more stringent regulations generally. The primitive standard of housing,

[27] J. S. Hassall, *In Old Australia* (Brisbane, 1902), p. 73.
[28] Broughton to Coleridge, 9 January, 6 March 1847, B.P.
[29] G. F. James (ed.), *A Homestead History, the Reminiscences and Letters of Alfred Joyce . . . 1843-64* (Melbourne, 1949), pp. 123-5.

and the lack of facilities for education, worship and the maintenance of law and order in the squatting districts made him all the more convinced. Here he came into line with the opinions of the bishop. Broughton wanted to see the squatters given security of tenure to facilitate the development of holdings and the building of proper homesteads—and Anglican schools and churches; but he did not want the formation of 'a monstrous pretty oligarchy' by selling too much land too cheaply to too few. High prices, and hence a revenue which would assist the introduction of more people and more religious provision into the area, were what he argued for.[30] In so far, however, as the opinion of Broughton coincided with that of Gipps, squatter resentment—and finally successful squatter resistance—would not advance the bishop's aims for increased support of the Church of England. The bishop was, in fact, attacked by Robert Lowe in bitter and biting words.

> When we find him fighting side by side with the Governor, in the endeavour to counterwork the laws of nature, and concentrate the population of this Colony, we find him embarked in a cause which he well knows is injurious to its material interests. . . . But he also knows that the policy, though ruinous to the State, is beneficial to the Church. Concentration may depress the Colony, but it will elevate the hierarchy.[31]

Much of this feeling must have been common among the squatters. It possibly contributed to a long persisting outback opinion that all clergymen are 'on the make'.[32] Certainly it helps explain why Broughton found at the time that his best support was coming from urban middle classes.

If there was this tendency for the squatters to withhold their support from the Churches, it must not be erected into a cast-iron law. There were far too many exceptions. George and Edward Cox were the main contributors to the Anglican Church at Mulgoa (where they lived), and George Cox enabled a church to be built at Mudgee (where he had a station). E. C. Close built a handsome brick church at Morpeth. On the lower Hawkesbury, gifts of Wiseman land and money made one Anglican church possible. St Paul's Church at Cobbitty was erected largely through the liberality of Charles Cowper. The Church of St John,

---

[30] Broughton to Coleridge, 18 May 1844, B.P.; Broughton to a private friend in England, 17 February 1846, *H.R.A.*, xxiv, p. 780. On the question of Broughton entering a positive compact with Gipps on this issue, see J. Barrett, 'The Gipps-Broughton Alliance, 1844: A Denial Based on the Letters of Broughton to Edward Coleridge', *Historical Studies*, vol. 11, no. 41, pp. 54-60.   [31] *Atlas*, 10 May 1845, p. 277.

[32] 'I don't know what you parsons want to come round this back-country for at all. . . . You only come about once in seven years, and you wouldn't come then if there wasn't money in it. You're all on the make, the whole - - - lot of you, and for all the good you do when you do come, you might just as well stop at 'ome.'—C. H. S. Matthews, *A Parson in the Australian Bush* (London, 1908), p. 16.

Camden, was built at the expense of the Macarthurs. It was chiefly through the exertions of William Dumaresq that a church was secured for Scone. St John's, Limestone Plains, was made possible by a gift of £300 and one hundred acres of land for the support of a clergyman from Robert Campbell (in his land-owning phase). In the provision of an Anglican school at Peel—a project always second only to church-building in Broughton's eyes—the name of W. H. Suttor was most prominent. These instances range through the late thirties and forties, and feature men with squatting interests.[33] All the churches mentioned were within the boundaries, and the donors were 'gentry' rather than upstart squatters; but this only suggests two important factors in determining squatter contribution or non-contribution; how much real money the squatter had, and how many people were in any district.

The evidence of James Bowman before the New South Wales Committee on Immigration may be called on in this connection. Bowman was willing to give £200 towards building a church near his established property, and he thought that as the population increased his neighbouring proprietors would also help to provide a house for a resident minister, and, as soon as his new purchases began to pay their way, he would be willing to consider giving money towards churches in their vicinity. The next witness, John Coghill, wanted a clergyman in his district if he would itinerate and not be bound to a particular place of worship, for no other arrangement would be practicable.[34] Such factors contributed to the squatters' unreadiness to give money for churches. When they were securely established, and their districts became more settled, they were often willing enough to build places of worship. In one area in the Western District of Victoria the Presbyterian squatters long considered it impossible to establish a clergyman (let alone build a church) in their midst; but later, in 1847, the squatters took the initiative in calling the Reverend William Hamilton to Kilnoorat, and undertook to pay him £200 a year and to build a manse. By the end of the forties the situation had so improved that it could be described in these words:

> The different churches and their ministers though situated in towns were in fact usually adjuncts of the neighbouring homesteads, for in traditional style as lords of the colonial manor the Western District squatters supported their chosen churches.[35]

The squatters had to become secure and established, little colonial lords

---

[33] One convenient source is the annual reports of the N.S.W. branch of the S.P.G.
[34] Immigration Committee, Minutes of Evidence, pp. 814-16, *V. & P.* (N.S.W.), 1838.
[35] M. Kiddle, *Men of Yesterday* (Melbourne, 1961), pp. 110, 172, 300. See also C. S. Ross, *Colonization and Church Work in Victoria* (Melbourne, 1891), pp. 183-4.

(with their ladies at their elbows), before they could be expected to give of their largesse. This may cast some doubts upon the depth of their religion, but it also casts some coolly practical doubts upon the charge of gross irreligion among them.

The noticeable increase in middle-class support for the Church of England was described by Broughton in 1847 as 'very singular'. Had he forgotten that he had deliberately set out in 1839 to woo them? Cautiously, after much thought, he decided to propose the inclusion in his management of the Diocesan Committee of the S.P.G. 'a class of persons not heretofore held in sufficient account to be admitted: that is of the better description of tradesmen'. He gave his reasons. Many tradesmen were wealthy and respectable. They had influence, and the bishop thought that they were favourably disposed towards the Church of England, but they had not found 'any medium of positive or personal communication with it', and therefore could not show their goodwill. Since the Church had not been 'enabled to operate on them', they and their families were lured away, and went 'to swell the torrent of dissent'.[36] Ten years later, the Bishop of Melbourne, for precisely the same reasons, set out on the same hopeful quest for the middle classes.[37] Besides the conscious wooing by the bishops, there is here more than a hint of the old story of men supporting the denomination in which they could count, and of moving up the denominational scale when increased income brought greater respectability. The normal squatter of the forties was often more secure socially than financially; before giving to the Church he could wait a few years. The man emerging, through wealth, from the ranks of the tradesmen was socially insecure; he could both satisfy his religious feelings and become better accepted in society by donating large sums to the Churches—and if to the Church of England, so much the better for his social status. A combination of social and financial influences of this kind affected very much the pattern of public support for the Churches in the forties. Contributions from the colonial upper classes, among whom the squatters were prominent, were large and important, but were often slow in coming. In total, the donations from the middle classes, including many who were newly respectable and prosperous, may not have been any larger, or even as great; but they must have been more numerous and were, apparently, given more willingly and steadi'y through years of financial difficulty for both squatters and Churches. It is not impossible, indeed, that the middle-class support was actually greater than the colonial gentlemen's in these years.

[36] Broughton to Coleridge, 14 October 1839, B.P.
[37] *First Report of the Melbourne Diocesan Society* . . . (Melbourne, 1849), p. 7.

These economic and class factors help to explain the history of the Churches; but they do not, in themselves, constitute an interpretation. The bishop who cut his salary by £500 to make other bishops possible, and who was forced to get into a cheaper house and not keep his own horses, is hard to fit into any popular idea of the materialistic interpretation of history. When a glimpse is given of the same bishop, as late as 1849, holding confirmation at Montefiores in a church of slabs and then moving on to preach at an inn, his concern about money was clearly justified. The truly religious motive can be clearly and continuously seen in the people's support of the Churches. Prominent in the *Appeal to the Public* made by Anglican laymen in 1844 was their genuine horror at the thought of wide districts getting only an odd visit from a clergyman whom the settlers would probably never see again and could not send for 'in the hour of misfortune and death'.[38] It was religion pure and simple which brought out the Wesleyan layman John Fidler, when he heard of spiritual neglect in New South Wales; he thought he 'could manage to get a living and preach about . . . on Sundays', and he always managed to get congregations and to have chapels erected, then enlarged, as he moved from place to place in the colony.[39] The Reverend William Waterfield, an Independent who worked along the north-west coast of Van Diemen's Land, found that his ignorant hearers had nothing to give but 'their good wishes and their attention', and was kept there by their response in beginning to read the Bible, to keep the Sabbath and to legalize their *de facto* marriages.[40] In 1848, when Catholics were granted a Jubilee at the accession of Pope Pius IX, so many penitents presented themselves in Sydney that the archbishop was compelled to call in the assistance of priests from the country.[41] In place after place, time after time, significant numbers responded to Christian teaching.

Bishop Broughton could complain of lack of support among the squatters. All Christian men looked with apprehension and pity on the areas where religious observance, and religion itself, was almost non-existent. Some support of religion was undoubtedly due to the poor motives of personal prestige or public respectability (when is it not so?), and much has to be said about the prevalence of irreligion among the people, especially the lower classes. But none of these facts, nor all of them together, can be presented as the whole truth. It was the people's demand for churches which threatened to make the

[38] *Report of the Church of England Lay Association for New South Wales, 1844-5* (Sydney, 1846), pp. 162-4.
[39] John Fidler, 'Recollections of Methodism in Illawarra', Methodist Church Papers, Uncat. MSS. Set 197, Item 4 (ML).   [40] *Colonial Times*, 28 May 1844, p. 3.
[41] H. N. Birt, *The Benedictine Pioneers in Australia* (London, 1911), II, p. 174.

Church Acts more than the Governments could cope with, and, even where the Acts applied, heavy private contribution was also called for. On top of this were the numerous chapels built entirely by voluntary giving, and, behind these, revealed repeatedly in private journals and letters and in such lives as that of John Fidler, lay much religious feeling which was true and tenacious. Not all the people, not even a majority of the people, were really concerned about spiritual things; but a large minority were concerned and, by their concern, helped to mould Australian life.

5

RELIGIOUS PROVISION IN 1850

VERY SELDOM do Churches have the resources or the flexibility to work in the best way in every area; normally there are churches and clergymen in places where there could be retrenchment, and none in new areas which urgently require them. In this sense, religious provision is hardly ever adequate, and the eastern Australian colonies were no exception to the rule, for there were some areas very well supplied, and other areas very badly neglected, right up to 1850. Yet, by that time, the public and private efforts made since 1836 to provide adequate religious provision had borne much fruit. The great majority of the people could call in a clergyman without undue delay, and attend a service of worship with reasonable regularity, so that it cannot be said that the Australian character and outlook were for long, or in large measure, formed in the absence of ministers of religion and of churches. Colonists may have been often absent from church, but, the remotest settlements excepted, the Church was not absent from them.

In New South Wales church buildings had increased to the extent of accommodating about sixty thousand persons—most room being provided by Anglicans (between fifteen and sixteen thousand seats), Catholics (twelve thousand) and Wesleyans (ten thousand). The total was four and a half times the number accommodated in 1836, while the population had grown only one and a half times (to 187,000), so that almost one third of the people, instead of one sixth, could find room in the churches. Cumberland County, with eighty-one thousand people and thirty thousand sittings, and the other 'settled districts', having twenty-nine thousand sittings for seventy-nine thousand people, could seat about thirty-seven per cent of the people living in them, thus achieving in practice the ideal at which the Church Building Commissioners aimed in England. Closer analysis, distinguishing the favoured centres like Sydney and Maitland from the many smaller settlements without churches, would take some of the comfort from these averages; but, on the other hand, there was large additional accommodation in temporary chapels and other meeting places. The

Free Presbyterians offered more seats (1,700) in such buildings than in their churches, which seated 1,650. The Anglicans at Braidwood (where the church, though subscribed for, was only about to be built) held service for forty-five persons in the court house, and for three hundred and fifteen people in nine other preaching places in the district. As well as their ten thousand sittings in sixty-three chapels, the Wesleyans had two and a half thousand sittings in seventy-six additional preaching places. In many settlements Divine Service was regularly held in irregular buildings, and the people could worship if they wanted to.[1]

The problem was still in the squatting districts beyond the county boundaries. In 1850 more than twenty-seven thousand people lived in these outback areas, and they were almost entirely without churches. To the churchman who believed it desirable, even essential, that people should be able to assemble regularly in the company of other Christians for the ministry of the Word and the Sacraments, these neglected station-folk were a grievous worry. It was no relief for him to know that, more often than not, it was simply impractical to build churches, and that out there lived less than fifteen per cent of the total population. But it is important for an appreciation of the development of Australian religious habits to realize how small this percentage was, and to know that by 1850 a large majority of the people in New South Wales had churches in their towns and districts. If it is true that the mateship of the bushman proper was widely adopted as a substitute for the fellowship of the Churches, his influence was disproportionate indeed. It seems better to say that the Churches had to face the task of winning men from an indifference bred in various quarters—in the bush, the convict system and the British social and urban background.[2] In any case, whatever the sociologist of religion may decide about the Churches' success or failure, and wherever he may allot the most influence, the simple fact remains that churches were within the reach of most New South Welshmen by the middle of the nineteenth century.

The colonists in the Port Phillip District were not so fortunate. This region had much the same population in 1850 as New South Wales had in 1836—about seventy-seven thousand; but it had acquired this number of people in sixteen years, whereas New South Wales had taken nearly fifty years to do it. The rapidity of the migrant intake, plus the handicap of inferior 'District' status, inevitably meant that church-

---

[1] Return of Number of Churches, Livings, etc., N.S.W. Blue Book, 1850, p. 611 ff. Population figures here and in the following pages have been taken from the censuses of N.S.W., Vic., and V.D.L. in March 1851 (i.e., close to the end of 1850, and before the gold rushes).

[2] Russel Ward, while emphasizing the first, by no means overlooks the other influences; see *The Australian Legend* (Melbourne, 1958), pp. 84, 169, 209.

building in the Port Phillip area lagged. The position was far from hopeless, for thirteen per cent of the inhabitants could be accommodated in the churches, which had over ten thousand sittings (more than half of them in Anglican and Wesleyan buildings), and, as always in Australia, the bulk of the people were in a few main centres—over fifty-four thousand living in the three districts of Melbourne, Bourke (immediately to the north) and Grant (Geelong), where the churches were also concentrated.[3] Still, church accommodation was seriously inadequate, and the churchmen were worried, acknowledging the 'fearful lesson' of England, where it seemed that recent efforts to provide more adequate church-room were failing to overcome many generations of neglect.[4] The gold rushes of the next year were greatly to aggravate the problem, flooding new migrants into the land and throwing the Churches into confusion, before new-found wealth, new colonial status and increased State aid improved the situation.[5]

The position in the Port Phillip District in 1850 suggests a further point for the sociologist's consideration: Australian religious habits may well have been influenced, strongly and permanently, by the lag which usually occurred between the settlement of an area and the possibility of getting a church built. Men who had got along without a church for years would be very conscious of the eventual building of one, and would be likely to react strongly. They might determine to stay out of it; they might welcome its advent with an eagerness whetted by the years of denial; they might deliberately steer a middle course; but none was likely to watch unmoved the erection of a church in his neighbourhood. When two churches were erected in a small community the divisive effect upon the locality was often obvious to both the zealot and the more detached, and gave food for thought. Many in England grew up within sight of an old church spire which was part of the scenery; but it was very different in Australia, where a church building was a new, or still recent, achievement. Attitudes to the Churches were more likely to be jolted in the colonies than at home.

Compared with the mainland, there was a slow increase in population in Van Diemen's Land. Its seventy thousand people at the end of 1850 were only sixty per cent greater than the number in the mid-thirties, and were seven thousand less than the Port Phillip District's mid-century population. The smaller population growth and the limited area of the island made the provision of church-room easier. Conse-

[3] *Statistics of the Port Phillip District . . . 1850* (Melbourne, 1852), p. 6.
[4] *First Report of the Melbourne Diocesan Society* (Melbourne, 1849), pp. 19-20.
[5] Note W. L. Blamires and J. B. Smith, *The Early Story of the Wesleyan Methodist Church in Victoria* (Melbourne, 1886), pp. 56-60.

quently there were seats (twenty-eight thousand, over sixteen thousand of them in Anglican churches) for forty per cent of the people by 1850.[6] This compared more than favourably with both the twenty-four per cent accommodation in 1836 and with the accepted minimum standard of provision. Nor was there the same problem, in this more compact colony, of the man outback. The situation in particular localities was, of course, sometimes bad; and the locality did not have to be in the remoter settlements—the minister of St John Baptist's parish in Hobart published two sermons in 1851, advertising that the profits, if any, would be devoted to the erection of a church in the parish which then had only a licensed school-room.[7] But the position generally was good in Van Diemen's Land. Indeed, in the colonies as a whole, the provision of churches had vastly improved since the mid-thirties, and was suffi-cient for the needs of the people in many places. The religious zeal of private citizens (and the calculating motives of personal advantage!), allied to the Church Acts, had battled with an enormous problem with considerable success.

The number of clergymen in the colonies had also increased greatly by 1850. There were about one hundred and fifty ministers of religion working in New South Wales—seventy-two Anglican, twenty-nine Cath-olic, twenty-eight Presbyterian, fourteen Wesleyan, four Independent and three Baptist.[8] The ratio of clergymen to people was, therefore, one to 1,250—which may be compared with one to 2,200 in 1836, or one to 1,125 as recently as 1961.[9] The improved position in 1850 did not mean an ideal situation. Twelve hundred and fifty people—say three hundred families—can keep a clergyman fairly busy under the best of circumstances; and the circumstances in New South Wales were not the best. In 1848, Bishop Broughton wrote to a friend in England in a vein which well illustrates some of the difficulties.

The day after tomorrow I am to start again to the district of Illawarra; where I have two Churches to consecrate, confirmations to hold, and other duties to discharge. How to get there is more than I can tell at present. Roads there are none; and I am not like Parson Adams and the Bishop of New Zealand who prefer 'the pedestrian expedition'. It has been raining two days incessantly and seems likely to continue six days longer: so that the country will be all in a flood. And as to the Steamer, she is such a tub that I verily believe if overtaken by a southerly gale

[6] *Statistical Returns for Van Diemen's Land, 1849* (Hobart, 1850), pp. 27-32.
[7] F. H. Cox, *Perseverance and Endurance . . . Two Sermons . . .* (Hobart, 1851).
[8] N.S.W. Blue Book, 1850, p. 612 ff.
[9] Population approximately 3,920,000. Preliminary estimate of clergymen (Occu-pational Code 055), 3,484.

she would not hesitate to go to the bottom even with the whole bench of bishops on board. However we do in the Colonies contrive to manage these things in a way which would be more wonderful than agreeable to you who live in a country of railroads.[10]

But the people of Illawarra were lucky: they had churches to be consecrated, and clergymen to prepare candidates for confirmation. Beyond the boundaries of location were at least ten thousand persons without a clergyman stationed among them or anywhere near them. Some twenty-thousand persons beyond the boundaries (excluding those in Stanley and Moreton) had a grand total of only seven clergymen actually stationed within their sprawling districts, and even one of the counties—Georgiana, with over fifteen hundred inhabitants—lacked a resident minister of any denomination. (See Figure 3.) The Churches could have used many more clergymen, not simply to ease the burden on those they had, but to supply people who had no ministerial attention whatever, or had only occasional visits from itinerating chaplains.

Once more, however, it must be stressed that most New South Welshmen were concentrated in a few areas. Over forty per cent lived in Cumberland County alone, over sixty per cent in the five counties of Cumberland, Northumberland, Camden, Argyle and Bathurst, and the clergy were stationed at fairly close intervals among them. Mitigating the effects of too few parochial clergymen were people such as two Anglican ministers who were heads of schools, three Presbyterian ministers who were 'professors' at the Australian College, three Wesleyan catechists at Camden, Wollongong and Scone (as well as their ninety-four local, or lay, preachers) and a Baptist 'deacon' ministering at Goulburn. A minority of the colonists were well beyond the normal reach of clergymen, but the majority had ordained men within reasonable riding distance as well as the sprinkling of lay and part-time pastors in their midst.

In Port Phillip, between 1848 and 1851, the number of ministers suddenly expanded. Bishop Perry arrived to find only three men stationed in his diocese, but he had twenty under him in 1850. In addition to the Anglicans, there were fifteen Presbyterians, eight Catholics, five Independents and four Wesleyans—a total of fifty-three clergymen in active work in the District.[11] Among seventy-seven thousand people, this meant a clergyman for every 1,453 persons, a remarkably good ratio when compared with the New South Wales figure at that time, or with the present-day Victorian ratio of one to

10 Broughton to Coleridge, 5 January 1848, B.P.
11 N.S.W. Blue Book, 1850, p. 642 ff, plus such supplementary sources as N.S.W. Wes. Dist. Min., 1850; Registrar's Book, Diocese of Melbourne; P. F. Moran, *History of the Catholic Church in Australasia* (Sydney, n.d.), p. 730.

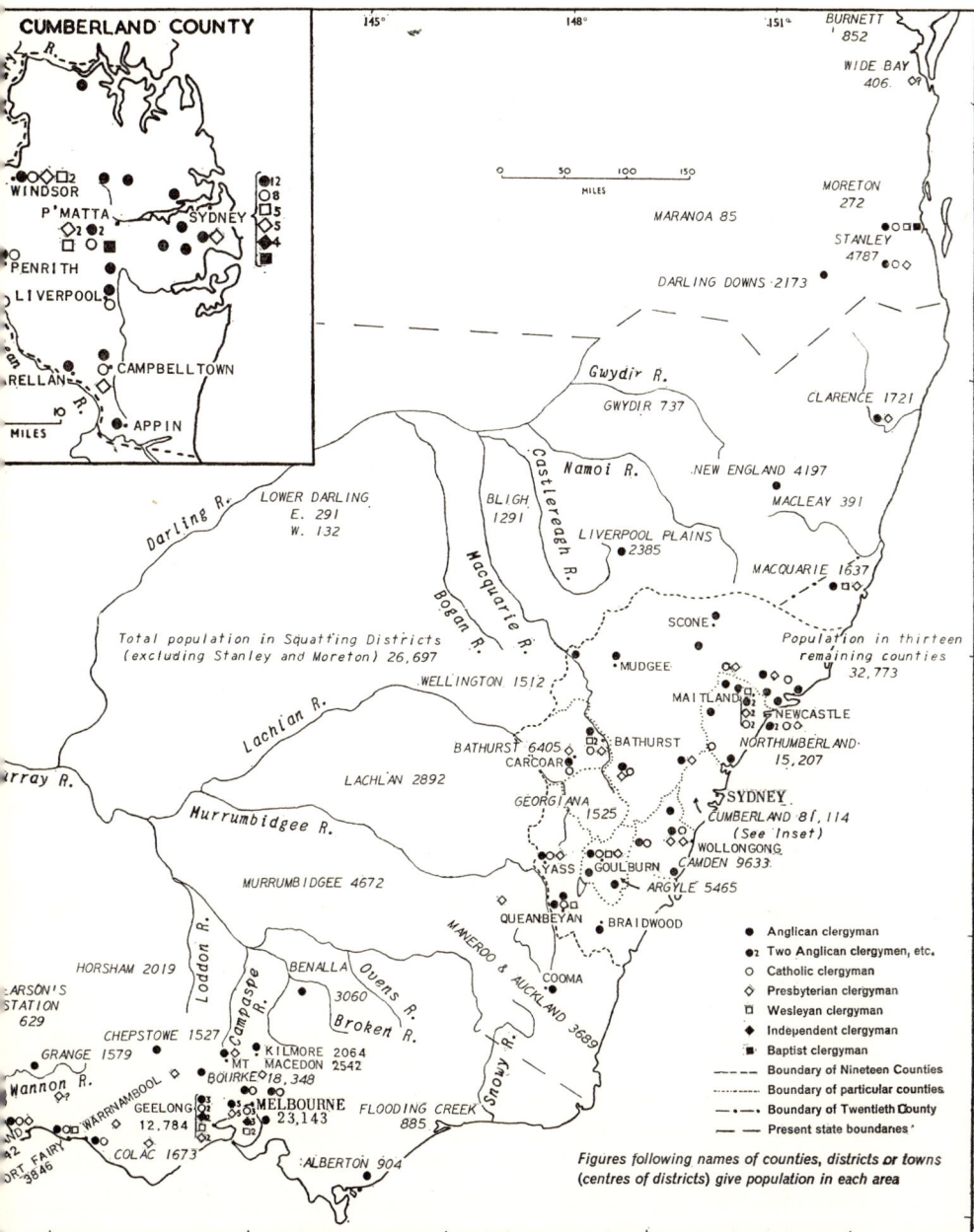

Fig. 3   New South Wales including Port Phillip and Moreton Bay
Stationing of Clergymen, 1850

1,055.[12] Although eighteen of the clergymen in 1850 lived in Melbourne, so also did twenty-three thousand people. (See Figure 3.) If the Melbourne clergy had a big advantage in compact parishes, each of them had—by an overall average—just about as many people to look after as any other of the clergy, and some of them, indeed, made tours from Melbourne into the outer districts. The people on the stations following the rivers out to the Murray had, of course, only the occasional visits of itinerating clergymen, and sometimes they missed even these. The Reverend W. B. Clarke (on an expedition as a geologist rather than as a minister) held a Christmas service in 1851 on the banks of the Indi River, the upper limit of the Murray, and among the small group of pioneers who attended were two men who had not seen a clergyman for eleven and eighteen years respectively.[13] There can be no doubt that this sort of thing was true for a rather large number of colonists; but it is equally true that many more colonials—always the great majority—had a fairly regular sight, even when they avoided the sound, of the clergy.

The case of Van Diemen's Land heavily underlines this point. For its population of seventy thousand (prisoners and all) it had eighty-seven clergymen (convict-chaplains and all), or a minister for every eight hundred people in 1850.[14] The position is worse there today, when there are 1,074 persons to each minister,[15] and had been much worse in 1836, when the ratio was nearly two thousand to one. The simple average is probably a better guide in Van Diemen's Land than it is elsewhere, for in the two districts of Hobart and Launceston there lived almost half of the population (thirty-four thousand) and about half of the clergymen, and most of the remaining people were concentrated in districts where they could be served by a clergyman. (See Figure 4.) The Van Diemen's Land clergy were predominantly Anglican; of the grand total of eighty-seven, fifty belonged to the Church of England, while the twelve Catholic priests made up the second highest number. So well served, indeed, was the Church of England that one minister who arrived in 1850 soon went on to New South Wales, believing that he was not really needed among the 'numerous and well organized' Anglican clergy in the colony.[16] There were also eleven Presbyterian, six Independent, six Wesleyan and two Baptist ministers, so that the people were reasonably likely to find a pastor to

[12] Population, 1961 census, approximately 2,930,000. Preliminary estimate of clergymen, 2,776.
[13] W. B. Clarke, *Researches in the Southern Goldfields of New South Wales* (Sydney, 1860), p. 119n.
[14] *Wood's Royal Southern Kalendar*, 1850, pp. 85-9.
[15] Population, 1961 census, 350,340. Preliminary estimate of clergymen, 326.
[16] J. D. Mereweather, *Life on Board an Emigrant Ship* . . . (London, 1852), p. 75.

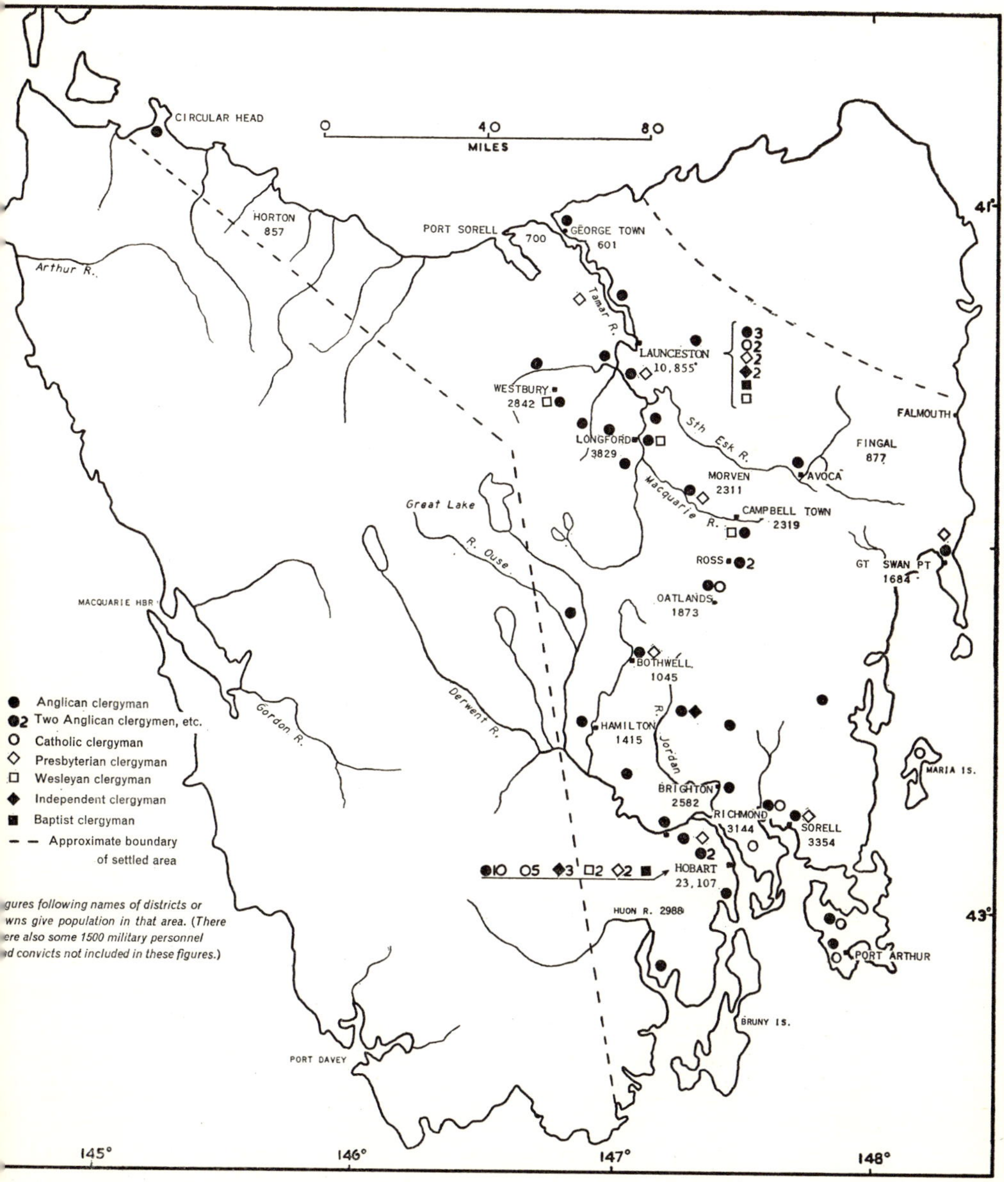

CIRCULAR HEAD

HORTON
857

Arthur R.

PORT SORELL

GEORGE TOWN
601

700

Tamar R.

LAUNCESTON
10,855

● 3
○ 2
◇ 2
◆ 2
■ 2
□

WESTBURY
2842

FALMOUTH

LONGFORD
3829

Sth Esk R.

FINGAL
877

Macquarie R.

MORVEN
2311

AVOCA

Great Lake

CAMPBELL TOWN
2319

R. Ouse

ROSS ● 2

GT SWAN PT
1684

OATLANDS
1873

MACQUARIE HBR

BOTHWELL
1045

● Anglican clergyman
●2 Two Anglican clergymen, etc.
○ Catholic clergyman
◇ Presbyterian clergyman
□ Wesleyan clergyman
◆ Independent clergyman
■ Baptist clergyman
‒ ‒ Approximate boundary
    of settled area

gures following names of districts or
wns give population in that area. (There
ere also some 1500 military personnel
d convicts not included in these figures.)

Gordon R.

Derwent R.

R. Jordan

HAMILTON
1415

MARIA IS.

BRIGHTON
2582

RICHMOND
3144

SORELL
3354

●10 ○5 ◆3 □2 ◇2 ■   HOBART
                          23,107

HUON R. 2988

PORT ARTHUR

BRUNY IS.

PORT DAVEY

145°   146°   147°   148°

41°

43°

MILES
0   40   80

Fig. 4   Van Diemen's Land
Stationing of Clergymen, 1850

suit them, though there was always the chance of, say, several Baptist families living in a district served only by an Anglican parson—and possibly a high churchman at that! Such ill-fortune apart, Van Diemen's Land colonists were well supplied with pastors.

The position in this colony highlights one other aspect of religious provision in Australia which may well have left a permanent mark on the nation's attitude to religion. Two-thirds of the Catholic priests and one-fifth of the Anglicans were attached to the 'Convict Department' and were, therefore, paid from Imperial funds and associated with the Government even more closely than were the other ministers. In one sense, these were imposed upon the colony: many of the prisoners, specially Protestant prisoners, had no desire to be supplied with clergymen; like the prisoners themselves, the clergy were there because authority willed it. In another sense, the convict chaplains were given to the colony: they were not present simply because the colonists sought them and supported them, but they ministered to both bond and free by the grace of the Government. A not dissimilar effect was produced by the Church Acts in both colonies. If colonists contributed half the cost of a church, the State supplied the remainder and often paid the whole of the clergyman's stipend, so that religious provision was almost as much the gift of the Governments as it was the achievement of the colonists. All this may have played a big part in determining Australian attitudes to religion. Belief that the Churches are on the side of privilege and authority rather than on the side of the workingman, and the idea of the Churches as feeble bodies, old and in need of crutches, instead of pulsing with vigorous life, are probably widespread in modern Australia. Some of this opinion would have its remote origins in old England, with its Church by law established and its chapels attended by the middle classes; but the idea could have sprung partly from the Churches' history in eastern Australia up to 1850. For in that period (and for longer) the Churches were not a part of the traditional scenery, but were very much a part of the official establishment. It was precisely because of this that they managed to become so well represented in the colonies.

What is more, the Churches represented were those already accepted in the homeland, and they continued to claim about the same proportional allegiance among the colonists as they did among the immigrants. They did this in spite of the truth in repeated claims that many colonists were indifferent to denominational labels and antipathetic to religious form and ceremony. It seems that this widespread indifference amounted to either complete failure to support the Churches or to an easy tolerance which allowed the traditional services to continue. Litur-

gical correctness and sectarian difference did not matter to many
colonists, but their habitual associations drew them to the chapels and
rituals of their fathers. Thus the numerical strength of the Church
of England in Australia, and the weakness of the Independents and
other groups with free forms of worship, were in marked contrast to
what happened on the American frontier, where Methodists and
Baptists in their most homely guise often swept the field. An even more
striking difference in the two frontiers is that the indigenous Disciples
of Christ arose with strength in America to express the common faith
of the frontier and to resist the entry of divisive denominations, while
the Australian Churches found no significant competition from any
new sect.[17] Part of the explanation of this must lie in the virtual
absence of fervent revivalism on any large scale in the Australian
colonies; but another part lies in the same sort of facts which are usually
appealed to when contrasting the two frontiers—their different natures
and extent, and the far greater dependence of Australian settlers upon
government. Here again the Church Acts apply. There was no State
aid to religion in America after the first settled colonies were left
behind, but Australians had both State aid and a form of it which
did not encourage local sects. The Acts supported the orthodox denominations named in their regulations, since grants were made only
where the required numbers of persons declared their adherence to one
of these Churches. When their Legislative Councils would help them
secure the denominations they were used to, and they themselves were
neither religious fanatics nor denominational cranks, the Australian
settlers were most unlikely to rally round strange banners. In any full
investigation into the reasons why the Churches of the British Isles
remained unrivalled as the Churches of Australia, and why the proportion of colonists belonging to each of them remained about the
same throughout the years, the Church Acts must be given due weight.

Whatever the reasons behind the shape of Church growth, the
churchmen themselves had reason to be pleased with at least the institutional development of their several denominations between 1835
and 1850. Yet an improved number of churches and clergymen did
not guarantee that Christian doctrine would be thoroughly disseminated
among the people. Conscious of a great religious ignorance among
many inhabitants, the Church leaders gave anxious thought to other
means of spreading the gospel. Their greatest hope lay in training the
young, for the children were impressionable even when the parents

[17] The Wroeites, who had several chapels, and these only in the larger centres of
population, and perhaps one thousand members by the end of the forties, were a very
minor exception. See M. Roe, 'Society and Thought in Eastern Australia, 1835-51'
(Ph.D. thesis, A.N.U., 1960), pp. 389-91.

were hardened in sin and indifference, and clerical eyes were jealously watching the schools. While most of the clergy were battling to keep State aid for their Churches, they were battling no less to keep out a State-directed, secularized system of education: for they feared this as much as any shortage of ministers and churches.

II

The Churches and Education

1835-1850

6

NEW SOUTH WALES:
THE CHURCH WALL OF RESISTANCE

1836: Protestants Prevent an Irish System

THE ANGLICAN CHURCH, traditional educator of the children of England and of English colonists, led the fight against the active entry of the British State into the field of popular education. The rival denominations, always resentful of Anglican power in the school systems and often equally anxious to combine religious with other teaching, were little less interested in the outcome. This was an issue, therefore, which absorbed the Churches' energies even more than the question of State aid. In both Britain and Australia the Church of England and the Nonconformist bodies resisted one government proposal after another, in their jealousy for their own position and doctrines, and their apprehension lest all Christian doctrine should be excluded from elementary education. The popular demand for secular knowledge being stronger than the desire for church schools and denominational instruction, the Churches finally lost the day; but they fought so hard and long that the education question is one of the most prominent issues in the Church history of the age.

From the foundation of the colony of New South Wales the public schools were essentially Anglican, though there were limitations to the Church of England's influence which were not unimportant. Thomas Bowden, headmaster of the main public school in Sydney, used the Lancastrian (or British and Foreign) system developed by Nonconformists in England, and he was himself a Methodist, as were other teachers sent out from the United Kingdom. Under Governor King, who retained control of the school and appointed the master, a Catholic school at the Rocks was granted State aid in 1793. This ceased when Captain Bligh came to the colony, but in 1822 Sir Thomas Brisbane agreed to pay one penny per week for every Catholic child attending Andrew Higgins's school in Sydney. This was 'the first direct subsidy for a denominational school' not controlled by the Government.[1] Yet

[1] V. W. E. Goodin, 'Public Education in New South Wales before 1848', *J.R.A.H.S.*, vol. 36, pts. 1-4, pp. 102, 191.

such phenomena were either accidental or incidental. The Imperial authorities had no intention of allowing the basic control of elementary education to pass from the hands of their established Church. In response to Macquarie's request for teachers 'untainted with Methodism or other sectarian opinion',[2] the Reverend Thomas Reddall, an Anglican, was appointed to take charge of the schools and to introduce the method and content of teaching favoured by the Church of England at home. Later Archdeacon Scott was appointed as 'Visitor of all Schools maintained throughout the Colony by His Majesty's Government'.[3]

Elementary education was still in the hands of the Church of England on 8 August 1836, a day on which Sir Richard Bourke signed two despatches, one of them marked 'separate and confidential', both of them written in a rage. The Governor had a plan for education which was being obstructed most prominently by the Right Reverend, and the right formidable, Dr W. G. Broughton, Lord Bishop of Australia. Bourke packed his despatches with criticism of the bishop, which revealed not just an impatience with temporary delay, but all the bitter fury of potential defeat.[4] For some years the Governor had been promoting the idea of copying the school system in operation since 1831 in Ireland. There the elementary schools were aided and directed by the State after the existing schools, mostly run by Christian denominations, had proved woefully inadequate. The new schools concentrated on providing a basic education for all, without distinction according to religious creed. No specifically denominational teaching was given except at stated times, when the clergy were entitled to come and teach the children of their own denomination. It was a system roughly of the kind familiar in Australia today, although the lesson books contained much more general religious teaching. It was adopted because Ireland was fundamentally divided over doctrine, the people being largely Catholic and the ruling caste (and many of the northerners) being Protestant. Governor Bourke, an Anglican who was both an Irishman and a liberal, saw freedom as the right and tolerance as the duty of all, and was impressed by the intrinsic value of literacy. The colony he governed urgently needed a better provision for education, and was peopled by a medley of denominations and a mass of the indifferent, so an adaptation of the Irish system seemed an ideal solution for New South Wales. Therefore, when Bourke proposed (in 1833) the policy which was to lead to the Church Act, he also proposed the Irish system for schools. He was confident of his case and of its acceptance. The

[2] Macquarie to Bathurst, 15 May 1818, *H.R.A.*, IX, p. 777.
[3] Bathurst to Brisbane, 21 December 1824, ibid., XI, pp. 419-20.
[4] Bourke to Glenelg, 8 August 1836, ibid., XVIII, pp. 466-78.

dissolution of the Church and School Corporation seemed to confirm the principles of religious equality and enlightened education, and to enable them to be implemented. Furthermore, the Secretary of State for the Colonies at that time was Lord Stanley, who, as Chief Secretary for Ireland in 1831, had first introduced the Irish system. Bourke pointed reproachfully at the unequal support given by the Government to the Anglican and Catholic schools in the colony, and tactlessly maintained that the schools would have to give way to something better, since they were quite insufficient for the 'sacred duty' of giving an education to the children in the colony. He was sure that Government schools 'regulated after the manner of the Irish schools' would be both suitable and acceptable to the colonists.[5]

Bourke's optimistic scheme, not the church schools, failed to win acceptance. In the first place it was over two years before the Governor received a definite instruction. Seventeen months after the date of his despatch, Lord Aberdeen (a new Secretary of State) wrote that he was not yet prepared to give any instructions, but was discussing the case with Dr Broughton, who was then in England.[6] The fact that the bishop was fully in the picture does much to explain the delay, for he was never one to surrender any Anglican advantage which could be retained. But there were other factors contributing to the lack of firm direction. There was 'the importance of the subject itself', and successive changes of government from Whig to Conservative and back to Whig, and also the complication that Lord Stanley thought of the Irish system as one to be confined to Ireland. Though the system was sometimes called Lord Stanley's, that noble lord 'should never have thought of recommending . . . [it] as in the least applicable to the very different state of England'.[7] Nor, for that matter, was it obvious to those at home that Australia was more like Ireland than England. Yet the scheme had an appeal to the Whigs, and Bourke had insisted that his colony was indeed unlike England. Finally, therefore, the new Whig cabinet decided to approve Sir Richard's suggestion.[8]

On 22 July 1836, the Governor laid on the table of the New South Wales Legislative Council two distinct documents.[9] One was the Bill

[5] Bourke to Stanley, 30 September 1833, ibid., xvii, p. 224 ff.
[6] Aberdeen to Bourke, 13 February 1835, ibid., xvii, pp. 656-7.
[7] Stanley to Hodgson, reprinted in *Colonist*, 19 January 1837, p. 23, from the *English Chronicle*, 13 August 1836.
[8] Glenelg to Bourke, 3 August 1835, and enclosure; Glenelg to Bourke, 30 November 1835 (No. 81); *H.R.A.*, xviii, pp. 58 ff, 201 ff.
[9] Recent writers have tended to think of the Church Act as being directly connected with education. This was not so: neither the Act nor the regulations under the Act mentioned schools. Only the 'principle of equality' accepted in the Act was appealed to in, e.g., Governor's Minute on Education, *V. & P.* (N.S.W.), 1839. Similarly, the 'half-and-half' subsidy of schools was a parallel to, not a provision of, the Church Act.

which became the Church Act; the other was a minute proposing a general system of education. The Council voted £3,000 for the establishment of 'National' (i.e., general system) schools, and all seemed well. In fact the vote was a gesture rather than an advance. The figure was placed on the Estimates, a contract was let for building a school at Wollongong, and a request was made for teachers to be sent out from England, but no more was done. Even the teachers, when they arrived, turned out to have been trained, not for the Irish, but for the British and Foreign system! By the time Sir George Gipps arrived as Governor, early in 1838, Bourke's plans 'were considered to be virtually abandoned'. Instead of the general system determined by the Council, Gipps found that an extended denominational schools system had 'tacitly grown up'. This was never formally approved by the Council, but Lord Glenelg, prompted by Bishop Broughton, had once told Bourke that schools might be subsidized according to amounts privately subscribed. After the passing of the Church Act, the bishop pressed the point and was successful in getting the Governor to treat schools in much the same way as the churches were to be dealt with. Anglican and Catholic schools established before 1837 continued to receive the fixed annual grant they had previously been given, and Bourke naturally allowed subsidies for the new schools of every denomination which applied for them; but Broughton had succeeded in strengthening the position of his own schools, old and new, and in reducing the chance of general-system schools being established. His Anglicans promptly claimed government aid towards a school built to rival the new government school being erected at Wollongong, using money donated by the English S.P.G. to qualify for aid! A Catholic school was also built at Wollongong, and plans were soon in hand for the erection of a Presbyterian school there; so the astonished Gipps chose to leave the general-system school empty, rather than add to the religious dissension.[10]

The Churches were finally responsible for the acceptance of Bourke's plan of State aid and for his plan of education lying on the table gathering dust. Sir Richard's two proposals had been made in the same despatch, approved in one answering despatch from the Secretary of State, brought before the Council on the one day, and both favourably regarded by that body. The two measures were considered to be com-

[10] Glenelg to Bourke, 12 May 1836, *H.R.A.*, xviii, p. 419; Broughton to Bourke, 26 November 1836, C.S.I.L. 36/10579 (Dixson Collection); Col. Sec. to Broughton, 19 December 1836, C.S.O.L. 4/3618/28 (ML); Gipps to Normanby, 9 December 1839, *H.R.A.*, xx, pp. 426-7; Gipps to Russell, 24 October 1840, ibid., xxi, pp. 58-9. A useful guide to sources is K. Grose, '1847: The Educational Compromise of the Lord Bishop of Australia', *Journal of Religious History*, vol. 1, no. 4, pp. 233-48.

plementary by the liberal Governor and the Whig cabinet at home, since both gave proper opportunity for all in the new, pluralistic society emerging in an age of enlightenment and reform. But the leaders of the Protestant Churches saw the measures as radically different, and they determined to resist the education proposals. The ground for Protestant opposition was prepared in 1834, when a group of Nonconformists decided to foster education along the principles of the British and Foreign schools in England. What particularly appealed to them was this system's use of the whole Bible, without note or comment, as a reading book. The Australian School Society was consequently formed to support the move, and in January 1835 a school was opened in Hart Street, Sydney. By the beginning of 1836 there were one hundred and twenty pupils in the boys' school, and twenty-seven in the girls' section.[11] In the same year, moreover, the society successfully petitioned the Legislative Council for State aid.[12] In this way publicity was given to a system of education, described as non-sectarian and suitable for adoption by the Government, before the Irish system was formally proposed to the Council, also as non-sectarian and suitable for adoption by the Government.

What was more important, the Irish system had aroused the strong opposition of Protestant churchmen since it was considered to favour Catholicism by using only restricted portions of the Bible. Supporters of the British and Foreign system maintained

> that the Holy Scriptures (the oracles of GOD) present us with the most perfect morality . . . and that as the education afforded by this [Australian School] Society is based upon the Scriptures, it is of a class sufficiently general to demand the co-operation of men of diverse sentiments.[13]

Numerous Protestants were content to have no more religious instruction than Bible reading in the schools, but they were content with nothing less. They were not made more amenable to the Irish system by the knowledge that Catholics had worked with Protestants on the school board in Ireland to produce a series of carefully selected and edited readings to be used in ordinary lessons, while the rest of the Bible could only be read at the specified time of religious instruction.[14]

[11] *First Report of the Australian School Society* . . . (Sydney, 1836), pp. 9-10; *Colonist*, 22 January 1835, p. 28.
[12] *V. & P.* (N.S.W.), 1836. Compare with Gipps's memo., 24 January 1839, on Mansfield and Allen to Col. Sec., 15 January 1839, C.S.I.L., 4/2434.1 (ML). The school did not get sufficient support from any quarter (*Herald*, 10 March 1836, p. 4), and was closed for want of funds perhaps as early as 1840 (Lowe Committee, Evidence, p. 5).
[13] *Report of the Australian School Society* . . . , p. iii.
[14] For the regulations, see *V. & P.* (N.S.W.), 1836.

Catholics looked with more favour upon the Irish system. Father John McEncroe attended one of the early meetings of the Australian School Society to say that Catholics could not combine in a system which placed the Bible—a difficult book in many parts—in the hands of children without explanation, but that the Irish system might be acceptable to them.[15] This preference only confirmed Protestant suspicions and made them more determined than ever to oppose the introduction of the Irish system. They argued: compromise between Catholicism and Protestantism was 'manifestly wrong in principle, if attainable in practice', and New South Wales was a British, not an Irish, colony.[16] And they lampooned:

> There were guests of every rank and station,
> Of every possible creed and nation;
> Mahometan, Christian, Turk and Jew;
> But the only dish was an Irish stew.
>
> An Irish Roman Catholic priest
> Got up in his place and blessed the feast,
> And then helped himself, as he well could do,
> To a trencher-full of the Irish stew.
>
> He dived right into it all in a minute,
> And showed there was never a Bible in it.
> 'For what,' said he, 'had the Bible to do
> Either inside or outside an Irish stew?'[17]

When Bourke gave notice of his intention to introduce the Irish system in his opening address to the Council on 4 June 1836, the Protestants began to organize their resistance. A meeting was called for 24 June, at which the chairman was Bishop Broughton, who had returned from England earlier in the month, and the secretary was the Wesleyan, Ralph Mansfield. The battle was taken up as the cause of Protestantism and the Authorized Version against Catholicism, and Bourke's plan was attacked as 'subversive of the fundamental principle of Protestantism' by its denial of free access to the whole Bible.[18] Bourke's intention to use the 'Scripture Lessons' was indeed a concession to Catholic opinion and a denial of a liberty in which Protestants gloried, and they grasped it as a stick for beating Bourke and keeping the Catholics in their place. A General Committee of Protestants was formed, which petitioned the Council against the Irish system, and was supported from Protestant pulpits and by three similar

[15] *Colonist*, 5 February 1835, p. 44.
[17] Ibid., 26 February 1835, p. 69.
[16] Ibid., 5 May 1836, p. 137.
[18] Resolutions, *H.R.A.*, xviii, p. 472.

petitions, including one from the bishop himself.[19] The four nominated members of the Council, representatives of the people in the sense that they were not members by virtue of holding colonial office, signed a protest against the Irish system. The *Colonist* continued its attack and an even more influential campaign was conducted by the *Herald*. Frequently its editorials damned Bourke's proposals. News from overseas papers of Irish crime and 'papist guile' was chosen for reprinting. Many letters of protest were printed in its columns, and letters from the other side were commented upon unfavourably in editorial notes. After 20 August, a third paper, the *Sydney Gazette,* passed into new hands and ceased to 'knock on the head every scarecrow argument that Bishop Broughton . . . and his small band of heterodox squire Thwackums' brought against the Irish system, devoting itself instead to attacking Bourke.[20] Other papers gave Bourke consistent support, among them the *Australian* and the *Monitor*. The latter spread itself over several columns to denounce Bishop Broughton and the Protestants who had come under his influence. It warned that half a century would not eradicate the religious antagonisms which were being aroused. It pleaded that the education of Protestants and Catholics together would lead to increased brotherliness in the next generation, and it condemned 'the unaffectionate assuming haughty spirit which refuses to consider the Roman Catholics as members of Christ's body'.[21] But this was not the popular view.

The opponents of the Irish system made the telling point that if Catholics were one-fifth of the population, Protestants made up the remaining four-fifths. This, they claimed, meant that the argument for the system in Ireland was an argument against the system in New South Wales; Catholics formed the large majority in the first country, Protestants the large majority in the second, and the wish of the majority ought to prevail—both by right and by Lord Glenelg's instructions. Bourke's plan meant that the Protestants would not get the degree of 'tolerance' that the Catholics would get. Much was made of the English inheritance of the Reformation, and of the peril to which the proposed system exposed it by acknowledging Catholic objections and playing down Protestant principles. It was claimed that many children needed to be taught religion and morality at school, since their parents were dissipated and too indifferent to care. And—the case against the system continued—since the Catholics were

[19] *V. & P.* (N.S.W.), 1836; Papers on Education, etc., 1804-68 (MS. ML); Bourke to Glenelg, 8 August, 7 October 1836, and enclosures, *H.R.A.*, xviii, pp. 467, 565-70.
[20] For the *Gazette*, see W. Foster, 'Education in New South Wales under Governor Sir Richard Bourke', *J.R.A.H.S.*, vol. 47, pt. 5, pp. 271-2.
[21] *Monitor*, 26 July 1836.

largely poor and of Irish convict origin, and most of the landowners were English and Scottish Protestants, the latter would have to pay for a system which would benefit mainly the children of Irish Catholic convicts. Highly inflammatory remarks were passed in this connection, but it was clearly effective to appeal to the pockets and pride, as well as to the faith, of the 'mentally and morally superior' English and Scots, and to play up the old issue of emancipist against free settler; for these were the arguments which led to the giving up of the attempt to establish a comprehensive system of elementary education in New South Wales in 1836.

The essence of the protest was 'No concession to Catholics at the expense of Protestants'; it was not an attempt to deny Catholics freedom of worship or the right to education. This important distinction is the key to the acquiescence which made the Church Act possible and truly effective, and to the Protestant clamour which caused the shelving of the Irish system. The Church Act was accepted by all because it meant aid for all, when all had need and none could be denied. The Irish system was defeated because, by deferring to Catholic attitudes to the Bible, it meant that the State would enter the field on the Catholic side; and because, by imposing State control instead of merely granting aid, it would reduce the power and independence of the Churches.

The victory was to the Protestants, and was achieved by the Protestants, not just the Anglicans. Every Protestant Church condemned the Irish system, and was represented at the meeting in June and on the sub-committees formed throughout the colony.[22] It had been the Nonconformists who established the Hart Street school on British and Foreign principles in 1835. It was a Presbyterian, the Reverend Dr J. D. Lang, who set out in 1844 'to atone' for his opposition to the Irish system in 1835, when—he claimed—the system was not understood; thenceforth he became an ardent supporter of the Irish system.[23] It was a Wesleyan, the Reverend John McKenny, who continued to believe it an honour to have opposed Bourke in 1836.[24] It was very largely the non-Anglican Protestants who (encouraged by Broughton) drew up a recommendation that the British and Foreign system be developed along with strictly denominational schools in 1836.[25] At the crowded meeting of Protestants, Broughton maintained that he had not thus stirred up the colony within ten days of his return from England, that the Reverend Samuel Marsden came out to the ship

[22] See *H.R.A.*, XVIII, pp. 472-4; *Colonist*, 12, 19 January 1837.
[23] J. D. Lang, *An Historical and Statistical Account of New South Wales ...* (Sydney, 3rd ed., 1852), II, p. 514. [24] *Herald*, 11 September 1844, p. 2.
[25] Lowe Committee, Evidence, pp. 10-11, 17.

before he landed and told him that Bourke's plan was 'generally considered' to be the first step towards 'schools without the Bible', and that it was only after some Dissenting ministers took the initiative in approaching him that he gave his support to the protesting movement.[26]

How truly the Protestants were united, however, and how well Broughton succeeded in using the Nonconformists for his own purposes, are other questions. The bishop was *subtil* to the point of lying in this campaign. In his anxiety to foster the feeling that this was not an episcopal manœuvre but a spontaneous Protestant response, he asserted that, prior to his return to the colony, he had 'never written a line nor spoken a word' even to his own clergy 'to induce them to second or support' his own dislike of a general system of education.[27] In fact he had written to Marsden, and to others of his clergy, giving them a strong lead in opposing the embryonic system.

> In my last letter I think you had my opinion upon the tendency of this [Irish school] scheme; but let me repeat . . . I am persuaded that the more these invasions of the Protestant faith are countenanced and sanctioned by others, the more it becomes *us* to stand aloof from them and resist them.[28]

Broughton was also ambiguous in what he said to the Nonconformists in the colony, so that many of those on the General Committee thought that the bishop was their champion, and went on expecting Broughton to support the introduction of the British and Foreign system. True, Broughton told the Committee that he wanted the Church of England catechism taught in his schools. He thought the Government could be induced to grant him this because the 'good man who had the first church here, had also the first school; wherein the catechism of the Church of England was taught', and he added that it would 'be useless to attempt combining in a general scheme of religious education' until they were agreed to such terms. But this was not all that Broughton said. The Government should support his schools 'so far at least as not to undo' those which had long been in existence—he said this also. The schools should include the Anglican catechism 'or some equivalent summary'. 'We might possibly agree,' the bishop went on, 'in a scheme which should employ the terms and

[26] W. G. Broughton, *A Speech Delivered at the General Committee of Protestants August 3, 1836* (Sydney, 1836), p. 4; *The Speech of the Lord Bishop of Australia in the Legislative Council, upon the Resolutions for Establishing a System of General Education, 27 August, 1839* (Sydney, 1839), p. 3; *Herald*, 4 September 1844, p. 3.
[27] *Speech . . . at the General Committee . . .* , pp. 4-5.
[28] Broughton to Marsden, 25 September 1835, Marsden Papers, I, pp. 584-5 (ML). See also, Broughton to Cowper and Hill, 26 June 1835, *Speech . . . in the Legislative Council . . . 1839*, Appendix B. By 1839 Broughton must have forgotten that he had denied such correspondence in 1836.

phrases of Scripture without attempting to give them an interpretation.'
It was an ambiguous speech indeed. Even if Broughton finished on a
firmer note, it was still one which did not jar on all Nonconformist
ears.

> At the same time, as I know that there are some who cannot take
> part in the system to which I have declared my adherence, I shall be
> glad to see them provided for upon ground of their own. If I might be
> permitted to offer a suggestion, it would be that a Sub-Committee be
> formed to consider upon what common ground those who cannot unite
> with me, can agree among themselves. . . . I shall most cordially and
> sincerely wish God-speed to all who are engaged in so good a work;
> and will most cheerfully contribute my influence and recommendation
> towards obtaining for you a share of the public support.[29]

Some non-Anglicans saw through the bishop's speech at once. Bourke
reported that after it was printed Nonconformists began to realize
'that, with a Churchman of the Bishop of Australia's principles, no
Dissenter . . . [could] long remain united'.[30] Years afterwards, the
Baptist minister, John Saunders, confirmed this. He said that it had
been generally expected in 1836 that all Protestants could combine
in any system which included the whole Authorized Version of the
Bible, but 'when it was found that the Bishop, who had lately arrived,
had influenced the minds of his clergy contrary to our views, there
was great disappointment felt, even by many of his own denomination'.[31] Others continued to believe that the bishop was in favour of
British and Foreign schools being introduced, as well as maintaining
denominational schools. Ralph Mansfield, an intelligent Wesleyan, and
the secretary of the General Committee, remained under that illusion
until 1839. The bishop, said Mansfield, never resigned from the committee, but simply ceased to attend—much to his surprise. The recommendation that the committee should work for the establishment of
British and Foreign schools as well as church schools was indeed put
on one side at the request of the bishop; but this was not because
Broughton expressed disapproval, as far as Mansfield remembered, but
because the bishop wrote suggesting that the matter be dropped until
it was known what the Government intended to do.[32]

Perhaps this was a classic case of everyone believing only what they
wanted to believe. Broughton gave, and obviously intended to give,
every opportunity for various interpretations of his position. He mani-
pulated the Protestant movement with great skill, and less honesty, so

[29] *Speech . . . at the General Committee . . .* , pp. 19, 20, 22-3.
[30] Bourke to Glenelg, 8 August 1836 (no. 86), *H.R.A.*, xviii, p. 469.
[31] Lowe Committee, Evidence, pp. 96-7.   [32] Ibid., pp. 11-12.

Catholic Church, Hyde Park, New South Wales, 1836

J. G. Austin, *Sydney and its Environs* (1836)

St James' Church and Supreme Court House, Sydney

J. G. Austin, *Sydney and its Environs* (1836)

that his prime aim of a denominational school system was not endangered. But he did not instigate the movement. There was an unfavourable reaction on the part of all the Protestant churchmen, so that the fate of the New South Wales schools in 1836 was decided, not by the liberal policies of the Government, but by the principles and pressures of the Churches of the Reformation.

1839: Anglicans Reject a British and Foreign System

The events of 1839 revealed the full extent of Protestant differences, and the dominance of Broughton and the Church of England. Sir George Gipps set out, in his turn, to establish a general system of education. Like Bourke, he favoured the Irish system, but realizing the futility of proposing it after the 1836 débâcle, he chose the arrangement next best in his eyes—the British and Foreign system. This he intended to develop while allowing the Churches the option of continuing their own schools with Government support in amounts equal to private contributions. In August 1839 he laid on the table resolutions to the effect that all classes were entitled to equal assistance from public revenue in the establishment of schools, that the extreme dispersion of the population demanded a comprehensive system, that such a system might embrace at least all Protestants, and that, if the public schools were Protestant, corresponding advantages should be offered to Roman Catholics. The Governor informed the Council that the resolutions formed a unity: all were to be voted for, or none.[33]

Gipps might have expected opposition. Although the British and Foreign schools in England had secured royal patronage (in the persons of George III and William IV), their founder was Joseph Lancaster, a Quaker, and they were supported by the Whigs, the Utilitarians and the Dissenters. The British and Foreign School Society was bitterly rivalled by the 'National Society for Promoting the Education of the Poor in the Principles of the Established Church', in which the key figure was the Reverend Andrew Bell, whose method of monitorial teaching was like Lancaster's, but who insisted upon the catechism being taught in his schools. In England after 1833 both societies received annual grants from the State, but the antagonism did not diminish between them. As the Whig Governor of a religiously-divided colony, rather than as an Anglican, Gipps was prepared to recommend the British and Foreign system; but it was a risky venture. In his opinion, however, the likelihood of opposition was very much reduced by a number of factors. He believed that the Protestants had been truly united in 1836 and would be in similar agreement in 1839. The

[33] *V. & P.* (N.S.W.), 1839.

British and Foreign system had been proposed by the Protestant sub-committee, approved by Glenelg in despatches, and favourably mentioned by James Macarthur in evidence before a select committee of the House of Commons in 1837.[34] With Macarthur's evidence again as a guide, Gipps thought to overcome the anti-catholicism of 1836 by placing Catholics outside the comprehensive system.[35] In the event, his expectations misfired. Truly, as a writer to the *Sydney Herald* remarked, the advocates of the comprehensive system mistook the materials with which they had to work.

Like many Nonconformists themselves, Gipps misunderstood Broughton's position and charged the bishop with inconsistency when the latter came out against his plan. But it was not inconsistency in 1839, but duplicity in 1836, of which Broughton was guilty. Too late Gipps realized that the bishop was only prepared to work with Nonconformists in opposing the Irish system, and not in introducing the British and Foreign or any other general system. It was not among the Anglicans, but among the non-Anglicans, that a change of ground had been made by 1839. Gipps might well have thought that they would be sure to back his scheme to the hilt. They were less exclusive in their doctrines and practice with regard to the Church, the Ministry and the Sacraments. They stressed their Bible rather than their catechisms; the British and Foreign system forbade catechisms and allowed the whole of the Bible to be read; it was actively supported by Dissent in England; and the school in Hart Street was still in existence. What more could the Nonconformists want?

They wanted their own schools. With a few exceptions, such as Presbyterians from Goulburn, who had been incensed by the demand that children attending the local Anglican school must also attend Anglican worship on Sundays, the 'Presbyterians and Dissenters' gave Gipps no support. They did not actively join the opposition, but they did not rally to his side. When the Governor realized that their attitude had changed since 1836, he put this down to 'the prospect opened to them of obtaining separate schools for themselves'.[36] Sir George was correct in this judgment, though the Nonconformists' attitude was not due only to changed colonial circumstances. Lord John Russell, then Secretary of State for the Colonies, agreed with Gipps that the British and Foreign system ought to be acceptable to all Protestants, but he

[34] Macarthur, however, had clearly stated that his preference was for a denominational school system—Minutes of Evidence, p. 180, Report of Select Committee on Transportation, *P.P.* (H.C.), 1837, vol. XIX, p. 1.
[35] Gipps to Normanby, 9 December 1839, *H.R.A.*, XX, pp. 427-8.
[36] Ibid. For Presbyterian petitions, see *V. & P.* (N.S.W.), 1839.

suggested that the Governor ought to know that in fact it was not acceptable.[37] Russell certainly knew, for he was at this very time in the thick of attempting to establish a comprehensive system in England, and was having an unhappy time with it. The Wesleyans in Great Britain provide a good example of what Russell was up against. Having been staunch opponents of the introduction of the new system in Ireland in 1831, the Wesleyans went on, in 1837, to declare themselves in favour of their own schools for England, wherein they could give their children 'a purely scriptural and Wesleyan system of education'. Their powerful leader, the Reverend Jabez Bunting, said at the next Conference that Lord Russell 'was acting under a coalition of O'Connell and Home Papists, etc., not to say infidels' in attempting to establish State schools. Even one Wesleyan's support of the Government's plan, because it would save the schools from complete secularization and from Anglican domination, merely underlined the tension which existed between rival denominations.[38] Thus the English situation influenced the course of events in New South Wales. The colonial Wesleyans, believing that they should have their own day schools, welcomed the English pronouncements and appointed a committee to foster their aim.[39] Some years later, the Reverend John McKenny explained the Wesleyans' position at some length. They had not intended to offer opposition to the British and Foreign system, but they had not been satisfied with it, either. Experience in England had shown that there was insufficient guarantee that the morals and evangelical beliefs of the teachers were what they should be; they did not like the exclusion of prayer and catechism; and they were very conscious of their English brethren's development of their own school system. A modification of the British and Foreign system, such as operated in Van Diemen's Land in 1844, would have been acceptable; but they preferred their own schools where practicable.[40] McKenny's review of 1839 thus illuminates the failure of the Nonconformists to rally to Gipps's aid.

Gipps came to grief, too, in his attempt to escape Protestant antagonism by making separate provision for Catholics. The Anglicans did not long leave him with such a hope. They had long-established and numerous schools, from which Gipps meant gradually to withdraw

[37] Russell to Gipps, 25 June 1840, *H.R.A.*, xx, p. 686.
[38] B. Gregory, *Sidelights on the Conflicts of Methodism, 1827-52* (London, 1898), pp. 116, 275, 268-9; Annual Address, *Minutes of the Methodist Conference, held at Leeds, 26 July 1837*, pp. 232-3.
[39] N.S.W. Wes. Dist. Min., 9 January 1839, Q. 27; 25 September 1839 (Special Meeting).
[40] Lowe Committee, Evidence, pp. 113-15.

aid. They faced the prospect of a complete exclusion of their clergy from the 'Protestant' schools, intended to replace theirs in the long run, yet the Catholics were to be aided to build schools—perhaps next door to the State schools—into which their priests would be free to come and go. Bishop Broughton sharply drew attention to the effect this could have on the alert minds of children. The Governor had been misled by a cry in 1836 that the British Government ought to provide separate schools for the offspring of Irish convicts; but this was a case of passing the buck from colonist to the Imperial authorities; it could not rightly be interpreted as a desire to see the colonial Treasury granting aid to one denomination which it denied to all others. The Anglicans also made this clear, as well as many other arguments, in the nineteen petitions against the British and Foreign system which they presented to the Council in 1839. The signatures on most of these were headed by clergymen, but not the least effective was one from some laymen of Kurrajong, which prayed for the continued support of the Anglican school system, on the grounds

> That your petitioners reside in a remote District . . . and that during many years they were, in consequence, as sheep having no shepherd. That during such time no attempt was made by any sect or denomination whatever, for their religious instruction and improvement, except by the Church of England, whose ministers came among them, and obtained for them the erection of a substantial School-house, wherein not only are their children carefully and religiously instructed, but Divine worship is regularly solemnized.[41]

It was a petition which lent weight to Broughton's claim that there was great attachment among the people—'*the people* in the strict and proper sense'—to the Church of England.[42]

On 27 August 1839, the Governor's resolutions were debated in the Council for six and a half hours. It was Broughton's day. After the bishop had delivered a long and powerful speech his Excellency withdrew all the proposals. Gipps remarked that if they were carried after all the opposition that had been shown, he did not think that he would be able to put the system into effect.[43] So another Governor was defeated in an attempt to establish a general system of elementary education in New South Wales. Although Gipps objected to the denominational system, 'tacitly' supported by the Treasury on the 'half-and-half' principle, this still had to be continued. The only alteration was that the

[41] *V. & P.* (N.S.W.), 1839.
[42] *Speech . . . in the Legislative Council . . . 1839*, p. 27.
[43] *Herald*, 28 August 1839, p. 2.

method of subsidy was changed to a penny-a-day per pupil from January 1842.[44]

Again the victors were the Churches. Sir George genuinely wanted a comprehensive system of schools, and the gradual abolition of church schools, both to give children a better chance of education and also to save government money. The denominational system, he thought, was so expensive that it could only be described as a 'mischief', and what had happened at Wollongong was a perfect example of it. The Anglican school was especially mischievous, since only £50 had been contributed locally and the English S.P.G. had contributed the £150 necessary to qualify for £200 from the Government. As Gipps pointed out, when grudgingly granting this pound for pound aid, such a method of raising money was no test of local feeling at all, and the Government could not keep up with sums donated by large public bodies or incorporated societies. He warned that no more gifts from the S.P.G., or similar groups, could be applied in this manner; the contributions must come from private and local citizens.[45] This was a great disappointment to the Church of England, but they, and the other Churches, had little to complain about. Anglican demands had basically prevailed, and the other denominations were not sorry. 1839 was a year of Anglican victory; the failure of Dissent to support Gipps was not without its effect, but the main cause of his defeat was that the strength of the Church of England was directed against him.

1835-1839: Catholics and the Proposed General Systems

The Catholics were comparatively quiet amid the storms which raged about them in 1836 and 1839. There was a good deal of uncertainty in their own minds at this period, due both to the *fait accompli* in Ireland and also to their difficult position in the colony. One thing they never doubted was that they must oppose the British and Foreign system—and this they made clear during the formation of the Australian School Society, when both Ullathorne and McEncroe stated their objections.[46] At this time, the Catholics showed at least a preference for the Irish system.

Bishop Polding once wrote to the press, under the pseudonym of 'Catholicus Ipse', arguing that the Irish system had smoothed down animosities in Ireland, and could do the same in New South Wales. He

[44] Public Education Regulations . . . 24 September 1841, enclosure, Gipps to Stanley, 17 December 1842, *H.R.A.*, xxii, pp. 427-8.
[45] Gipps to Russell, 24 October 1840, ibid., xxi, pp. 58-9.
[46] W. B. Ullathorne, *Observations on the Use and Abuse of the Sacred Scriptures* . . . (Sydney, 1834), p. 3.

went on in terms which suggested very little fear of contact in the schools between Catholics and Protestants.

> Open schools to us unhampered and unfettered, on the principles of equality. We ask no more—and the form of religion that perishes under the test ought to perish, for it has within it the germ of mortality.[47]

Well after 1836, responsible Catholics could support the Irish system, and claim that their priests did also. In 1844 the layman, Roger Therry, could ask his fellow Catholic, William Duncan, 'Are you not aware that the Roman Catholic clergy sanctioned the Irish system when proposed by Sir Richard Bourke in this colony?', and receive the answer, 'I have always understood that they gave it a sort of tacit approbation'.[48] Therefore it is not surprising that, in 1836, Protestants jumped to the conclusion that the Catholics had a great ambition to secure the Irish system, or that a newspaper should issue a warning that non-Catholics must be on the alert 'if they would not behold Roman Catholic and Irish Convict ascendency in New South Wales'.[49] Full credence continued to be given to this interpretation of 1835-6, for Gipps, as late as 1845, spoke of 'a remarkable change having taken place' in the sentiments of the Catholic clergy since the earlier years; and the *Colonial Observer* sought to explain this by declaring that in 1835 the Catholic Church 'to all intents and purposes' had Sir Richard Bourke as its 'head', but Polding had since taken up that position, wanted his share of 'denominational spoils' to continue, and had forced Father McEncroe to retract.[50]

The idea, and not only the *Observer's* style of writing, was exaggerated. Despite the bland assurances of 'Catholicus Ipse', the Catholics had never been certain that they would ask for no more than the Irish system, or that they had nothing to fear from it. It was not a liking for that system so much as a dislike of the condition of their schools which caused them to speak favourably of the proposed system in the mid-thirties. As McEncroe explained later, the Catholics had 'only two or three very indifferent' schools in 1836, and therefore they 'were not opposed to any experiment in education that promised to improve the then very defective education of Catholic children'.[51] So poor, in fact, were the Catholic schools, that Polding had been sickened by

[47] *Australian*, 23 August 1836, quoted in W. Foster, op. cit., pp. 272-3.
[48] Lowe Committee, Evidence, p. 23.
[49] *Herald*, 1 August 1836, pp. 2-3
[50] Gipps to Stanley, 1 February 1845, *H.R.A.*, xxiv, pp. 232-3; *Colonial Observer*, 15 August 1844, p. 1.
[51] P. F. Moran, *History of the Catholic Church in Australasia* (Sydney, n.d.), p. 864. See also *Herald*, 8 September 1844, p. 3.

their 'disgusting unruliness' when he came to the colony in 1835; and it was to prevent any school in the colony being so run-down, as well as to avoid the extravagance of separate denominational schools, that the influential layman, Therry, came out—and continued unwaveringly—in support of the Irish system.[52] But McEncroe maintained that, even at the time when Ullathorne and he were supposed to be championing the scheme, they had already decided against it. They had both agreed that there were too few priests in New South Wales for real opportunity to be taken of the time allowed for religious instruction. With insufficient clergy, the system would have been 'very dangerous to the Catholic children'. Polding was equally explicit by 1844: the Irish system was suited to Ireland, he said, but he would not choose it voluntarily for New South Wales. Ireland had the priests and pious parents to teach the children; but in the colony the priests were few and the bulk of the parents had to learn their religion from their children, rather than the other way round. The Catholic clergy had never been enamoured of the Irish system; they, as much or more than other denominations, wanted church schools. The Catholic attitude had not developed to the point reached after the publication of Pope Pius IX's *Syllabus of Errors* (1864), but the die was being cast even in New South Wales as far back as 1836.

The Catholic Church took no part in the public controversy of 1836. The only Catholic petition for educational rights came from the congregation of St Mary's, and merely prayed (with success) for a grant of money towards establishing an orphanage of their own, to save Catholic children from being instructed as Anglicans in the established orphanages. A letter from Polding was laid before the Council, pointing out the desperate shortage of priests in the colony and asking for aid in securing more. There was nothing presented in favour of the Irish system, or against it.

The Catholics were naturally more outspoken when Gipps made his proposal in 1839. J. H. Plunkett, a Catholic, was one of the four members of the Council who declared their support of the resolutions, but the official Catholic verdict was unfavourable. At first sight, the idea of giving a special grant in aid of Catholic schools appeared to be something the Catholics would welcome. A more careful consideration suggested that to be put in a special category was really to be put out on a limb which could be chopped off after a strong system of non-Catholic schools had been developed all over the colony. Catholic

---

[52] Lowe Committee, Evidence, pp. 44-5; R. Therry, *Explanation of the Plan of the Irish National Schools . . .* (Sydney, 1836); R. Therry, *Reminiscences of Thirty Years' Residence in New South Wales and Victoria* (London, 1863), p. 155 ff.

schools could not hope to keep up with State schools in reaching out
into the country, and the granting of special assistance would result in
even more animosity against Catholics. The pretty scheme did not show
much sign of lasting beauty. Bishop Polding and Dr Ullathorne discussed the proposals with Gipps, telling him that the conditions were
such that no Catholic could accept them. Gipps curtly ended the inter-
view with the words, 'In short I must adhere to the strongest party,
and I don't think you are the strongest'.[53] The Catholics had no cause
for worry. If they did not command the strongest party, neither did
Gipps. What they wanted was won for them, quite unintentionally, by
the Church of England. The Catholics simply waited, sending in no
petitions and making no other formal protest.[54] They were to become
loudly vocal only in 1844.

[53] W. Ullathorne, *Autobiography* . . . (London, n.d.), p. 167.
[54] Ullathorne wrote, 'After that we determined to make a public demonstration for
we knew that, if not the strongest by numbers, we were by our union'. A large pro-
cession was held, and judged a great success, but not until 25 August 1840, when
Gipps's proposals had long been laid to rest. A. G. Austin, *Australian Education,
1788-1900* (Melbourne, 1961), p. 42, is misleading in not making this time-lag clear.

7

THE WRITING ON THE WALL

1844: Clergymen versus a Select Committee

THE YEAR 1844 saw the third big move in the field of education. In spite of continued encouragement for Gipps from the Colonial Office, it was not the Governor but the Legislative Council itself which took the initiative. Members met unofficially on 19 June, agreed to form an investigating committee, and even named the members of it.[1] A general system of education was strongly favoured by the Council as a whole which, since the new constitution, had a majority of elected members—and no Bishop Broughton. On 21 June the Council officially appointed a select committee, under the chairmanship of Robert Lowe, 'to devise the means of placing the education of youth upon a basis suited to the wants and wishes of the community'. The Committee's report, presented in August, recommended the Irish system, which it tactfully described as Lord Stanley's. The Council supported its Committee. Early in September, John Robinson gave notice of motion to the effect that the Council accept generally the recommendations in the report; a month later, the Council voted, by thirteen to twelve, in favour of an amendment moved by W. C. Wentworth, which provided for the introduction of the Irish system, with the curious modification that, instead of the clergy going into the schools, the children should go out of them on one day for religious instruction.[2]

The almost even division of the Council on the issue showed the support still commanded by denominational schools (as well, perhaps, as doubt about the form of Wentworth's amendment), and so did a decision to continue aid to church schools which were then in existence. This aid was to depend upon the schools having an average attendance of fifty, and their buildings being properly conveyed in trust; this was rather stringent, especially in the matter of numbers, but the government aid was still to continue. The Council also had to defy many hostile petitions, with which it was bombarded almost from the first.

[1] *Observer*, 27 June 1844, p. 1.
[2] *V. & P.* (N.S.W.), 1844, vol. 1; *Herald*, 11 October 1844, p. 3.

Robinson presented a petition in favour of a system 'adapted to all denominations' from the mayor, aldermen and councillors of Melbourne, and this was backed by another from Dr Lang's break-away congregation of Presbyterians, both petitions being presented the sitting-day after Robinson's notice of motion. But the opposition was as quickly off the mark, and sent in more petitions. On the same day, three petitions were presented against the Committee's recommendations, and this was the pattern of the days which followed. Eighty-one petitions were presented; twenty-eight favoured the general system, fifty-two were against it, and one Presbyterian petition cut across both by perversely praying for what amounted to the British and Foreign system. The number of signatures opposed to the Committee's recommendations was also far greater than that in favour. The Governor reported that there were 15,118 signatures in protest and only 2,120 in support, and, although these figures are not completely accurate, they do not distort the truth.[3] The colonists who could be organized against the Irish system still exceeded those who could be organized in support.

Twenty-eight petitions were explicitly Anglican, and these, without exception, were against the Select Committee's recommendations. The Catholics, in contrast to their silence on previous occasions, sent four petitions against the proposals; the Wesleyans sent three; and seventeen others came vaguely from 'certain inhabitants' of various places (some of which, when examined, prove to have been Anglican petitions). Thus the fifty-two petitions against the recommendations were chiefly Anglican, Catholic and Wesleyan expressions of opinion. The sheer number of them eclipsed even the 1839 opposition (nineteen petitions) and caused Gipps to write, 'The Clergy throughout the Colony are at present even less disposed to co-operate in the establishment of a general system, than they were on the [previous] occasions'.[4]

This was not, of course, the whole story: there were the other petitions, supporting the Lowe Committee. Sixteen came from Melbourne and from the wards of the city of Sydney—from precisely those heavily populated areas where, it was usually claimed, the denominational schools could best operate. From Sydney also came a number of petitions drawn up by denominations which would not enter the Anglican-Catholic-Wesleyan camp, from Lang's Presbyterians,

---

[3] Gipps to Stanley, 1 February 1845, *H.R.A.*, xxiv, p. 232. Gipps only reported 50 petitions against, and 24 in favour; but a similar proportion of signatories (eight to one) emerges from the petitions which were printed in *V. & P.* (N.S.W.), 1844, vol. ii; *Herald*, 14 October 1844, p. 2, gave the numbers as 25,000 for, and 4,000 against.
[4] Governor's Message, 27 November, *V. & P.* (N.S.W.), 1844, vol. i.

from two congregations of Independents and Baptists, from the 'Australian Methodists'[5]—and one from 'Members of the Faith of Israel'. There was a significant increase in the number of these petitions in favour of the general system, from two in 1839, which favoured the system only for lack of something better, to the twenty-eight much more whole-hearted petitions of 1844. The demand for a State system of non-sectarian schools had at least become more vocal, and had probably gained an actually wider support.

Gipps, having been soundly thrashed five years before, strongly discouraged the legislature from persisting. He urged that the time was still not ripe, and thought that there was not a real majority in favour of the Irish system even in the Council itself.[6] But the Council asked for £2,000 sterling to be placed on the estimates for 1845 towards the establishment of schools on the principles of a 'General System of Education' under the superintendence of a board favourable to Lord Stanley's system. This was passed by the overwhelming vote of twenty-two to five. Next day, the Council negatived Cowper's motion for a further £2,000 to be included for the erection of schools 'for the humbler classes of society . . . according to the existing regulations'—that is, for church schools. Though the Council was steadfastly determined to foster a State system of education, Gipps dealt the death blow to its hopes on 19 December, when he declared that he did not think that alterations to the estimates could be made to any advantage.[7] One of his reasons was financial. There was already an estimated deficit due to supplementary votes, and the colony could not afford additional expense. In August he had complained about the Council, which was always at logger-heads with him; referring to the matter of the schedules, the police and the gaols (education was not his only problem!), he had written peevishly, 'The object of the Legislative Council is evidently to weaken the Government: and at the same time to run it if possible into debt'.[8] However, it was a second reason which was the decisive one for Gipps; denominational organization and influence were still too strong. The Governor genuinely wanted to see the Irish system established, but he considered that the opposition had really 'in no way diminished', and concluded:

[5] These were a small group of seceders from the Wesleyans. See *Herald*, 26 June 1844, p. 2.
[6] Gipps to Stanley, 1 February 1845, *H.R.A.*, xxiv, p. 232. For a contrary view, see *Observer*, 17 October 1844, pp. 2-3.
[7] *V. & P.* (N.S.W.), 1844, vol. I.
[8] Gipps to La Trobe, 17 August 1844, quoted in S. C. McCulloch, 'Unguarded Comments on the Administration of New South Wales, 1839-46 . . .', *Historical Studies*, vol. 9, no. 33, p. 31.

Without the co-operation of the Ministers of Religion, it seems to me scarcely possible to establish any system of Education, with a prospect of its being extensively useful.[9]

It was certainly true that most ministers of religion had shown their hostility to the Select Committee's recommendations. Since the Catholics were fighting openly on the same side as the Anglicans and Wesleyans, the anti-Catholicism of 1836 and 1839 was played down. The clergy concentrated on setting up and repudiating the doctrine that 'an impassable and indelible line should be drawn between secular and religious education'.[10] The Reverend Robert Allwood said, 'We hold that the principle upon which all education should be based is religion'. 'In our schools,' added Archbishop Polding, 'every hour when the clock strikes, the children cease from their work, and raise up their minds to Almighty God.'[11] The Select Committee was ready to admit that denominational schools might be a good thing in theory, but found its 'first objection' to them in their expensiveness.[12] Then, too, the original argument of Bourke, that the Churches' adherents were mixed and mingled in almost every scattered community, was still readily applicable; church schools simply could not be provided for every place, and probably half the children were receiving no education. Many who agreed with the Select Committee upheld the principle of the separation of Church and State. For some, this was a strongly religious protest; the Reverend Dr Robert Ross, an Independent, spoke of the Dissenters' objection to aid from the State in any form, and the Reverend Dr James Fullerton said that the Presbyterians were divided over the issue.[13] Other colonists, not necessarily religious, were far more convinced of the State's duty to educate in a general sense, and of the State's neutral position between sects, than they were of its duty to bow to the demands of Churches.[14] But, in this case, the demands of the Churches carried most weight with Sir George Gipps, who simply used his veto against his Council.

The *Herald* pronounced that the Select Committee had fulfilled one of the terms of its commission in making the enquiry, but that it had failed to fulfil the other: it had not recommended a system which accorded with the wishes of the community.[15] But the people for whose

[9] Governor's Message, 27 November, *V. & P.* (N.S.W.), 1844, vol. I. Gipps added a third and highly theoretical difficulty: the fact that the District Councils, which were required by the Constitution Act of 1842 to carry any such change into effect, had not yet been developed.
[10] Petition of the Bishop and Clergy of the Diocese of Australia, ibid., vol. II.
[11] Lowe Committee, Evidence, pp. 34, 47, 49.
[12] Lowe Committee, p. i.   [13] Lowe Committee, Evidence, pp. 101, 29.
[14] Ibid., p. 24; Petition of Citizens of Bourke Ward, Sydney, *V. & P.* (N.S.W.), 1844, vol. II; *Herald*, 7 October 1844, p. 2.   [15] *Herald*, 7 September 1844, p. 2.

children these elementary schools were intended simply wondered what all the fuss was about. Despite the formal victory of the petitions, the people as a whole did not know or care about the respective merits of church schools and Irish system schools. One of the defences of the denominational system was that the failure attributed to it was really attributable to the people's indifference to religion and education. The more truth there was in this, the less truth there was in the claim that the people wanted church schools. Anglican zealots could only say that the 'deeply rooted hereditary attachment' of the masses to their Church was 'latent'. Alderman George Allen, a Wesleyan, when asked if many people were unconnected with any Church, replied, 'I think many of the parents of the lower orders are careless about it; they neither care for their own souls nor for the souls of their children'. Dr Fullerton, the Presbyterian, agreed that the children of the 'humbler classes' would remain in spiritual ignorance unless taught at school, and added that many of their parents were unwilling to send them to a school of any kind.[16] The emancipated Solomon Wiseman, by then a landowner, said that education was 'a point on which he was not particular'.

> I have four sons; and I say to Richard, 'There's a herd of cattle for you', and to Tom, 'There's a flock of sheep—look after them': so in five years time they become rich . . . *Now that's what I call education.*[17]

Parents were sometimes known to seek education for their children so that they could rise above the 'disgrace' of labouring, and become 'clerks', but it is certain that many of the working classes did not care a straw for education, let alone for church schools. The clergy might have been justified in using this as an argument for the importance of their schools, which had so much to teach these people; but it was not true that a majority of the population actually wanted them.

On top of this, many of the leading citizens were indiscriminate in their support of two or more denominations. Low Church Anglicans like the Macarthurs were very ready to lay the foundation stone of a Wesleyan chapel and to give land for the erection of another, while, on the other side, such a prominent Wesleyan as George Allen could not even recollect what had led him to join the Wesleyans sixteen years earlier. One squatting family in the Western District, the Learmonths, secured for their neighbourhood the services of a minister of the Free Presbyterian Church, mainly because he was most readily

[16] *Report of the Church of England Lay Association for New South Wales* . . . *1844-5* (Sydney, 1846), p. 1; Lowe Committee, Evidence, pp. 5, 28-9.
[17] R. Therry, *Reminiscences of Thirty Years' Residence in New South Wales* . . . (London, 1863), pp. 121-2.

available; later they contributed towards the support of an Anglican clergyman as well.[18] People of this sort—and they were numerous—were most unlikely to prefer separate denominational schools to one combined school. Laymen tended to be like that—whatever their clergy might urge on them. Nine witnesses before the Select Committee decidedly favoured a general system; two were dissenting ministers and seven were laymen. Eight witnesses were equally decided in favour of church schools; four were clergymen (Anglican, Catholic and Wesleyan), and, of the four laymen, one was the master of St Philip's school, one was a Catholic schoolmaster, and a third was a member of the Society of Christian Brothers. Four other witnesses were either uncertain, or expressed a hope for some sort of combination of church schools and general schools. Of these, two were laymen, one was a former Wesleyan minister and the fourth was a Presbyterian minister. Clearly the laity, even of those denominations which petitioned for church schools, were to a great extent ready to accept a general system —unless, perhaps, they were teachers in church schools. These lay witnesses, in fact, said frankly that the opposition came almost entirely from the clergymen. Alderman Henry MacDermott believed that the laity were prepared to accept scripture 'selections' even though their Anglican bishop was not. Peter Steel and William Macarthur told the committee that the opposition was to be found 'chiefly among the clergy'. William Duncan, a Catholic, explained the matter by saying that the clergy did 'not like to give up power'. If only the clergy trusted the lay teachers more, complained W. T. Cape, the teaching of religion in the colony would be quite satisfactory.[19]

Many lay signatories of the petitions against State schools did not fully understand the issue. In one place, the parish clerk, sent around by the clergyman to collect signatures, and asked what was wrong with the proposals, admitted that he did not know. There was said to have been much misrepresentation, with people being told that they were signing a petition to have their children educated, a petition against Catholic government, and so on.[20] Numerous names therefore appeared on the petitions circulated by the clergy which should not have been there; it was easy to sign a paper, and risky to flout 'authority', so the names were added.

It was not widely thought, however, that the people would follow the

[18] N.S.W. Wes. Dist. Min., 1839, Q. 9; ibid., 1842, Q. 32; D. Allen, *Early Georgian, Extracts from the Journal of George Allen, 1800-1877* (Sydney, 1958), p. 59; *The Church in the Colonies . . . A Letter from the Lord Bishop of Melbourne* (London, 1850), pp. 37-8; A. G. Austin, *Australian Education, 1788-1900* (Melbourne, 1961), p. 61.
[19] Lowe Committee, Evidence, pp. 19, 23, 55, 60.
[20] *Herald*, 22 November 1844, p. 4; *Observer*, 21 November 1844, pp. 2-3, 19 September 1844, pp. 1-2.

clergy's lead in this matter for very long. Some of the witnesses told the Select Committee that the ministers would be able to keep the people with them, but others did not think so. The best answer was probably William Macarthur's. He did not believe that the community at large was really behind the clergy; by great exertion, the ministers could temporarily influence them, but they could not sustain their efforts.[21] That the obedience of many Anglicans and Catholics to their leaders had been willing enough, was admitted by one newspaper; but it went on to question whether the loyalty would long continue. The 'Church party' did not like the terms of the Governor's message, for this spoke of the attitude of the clergy rather than of the people; yet the Governor was honest: it was the clergy, and not the people, who were opposed to the general system. And, at the same time, the Governor was wrong: the dark ages had not returned, and the clergy were not to be feared.[22] If the clergy so far had sufficient strength to resist a general system, they did not truly have general support but were faced with a strengthening resistance among the people. The Churches had been winning battles, but were steadily losing the war.

1847-1848: The Establishment of a National Schools' Board

After the Churches had won their 'famous victory' in 1844, the matter was never left to rest by their opponents, especially Robert Lowe—that 'unruly member', as the *Herald* called him in disgust. The very next year, when the vote for education was proposed in the Estimates, Lowe moved that it be used for schools based on Lord Stanley's system. He withdrew his amendment when it appeared that nothing could be done just then, but Lowe's party continued to think that only 'the parsimony and over scrupulousness of Governor Gipps' had defeated them.[23] In October 1846, with Gipps gone, the Council renewed the attack. It requested the new Governor, Sir Charles FitzRoy, to include £2,000 in the Estimates for 1847 for Irish system schools, and to appoint a board to carry the project through. Lowe again moved the resolution, which was carried by twelve votes to ten. FitzRoy hedged. He replied that, even if the colony's financial position permitted such an addition, he was not prepared to act until he had opportunity to study the education question. His hesitation soon passed; he agreed to the inclusion of the sum in June 1847, and appointed a board to develop a 'National System' of schools. Progress was slow, but progress was made. The board applied for a master and mistress to be sent out from England, and set up a model school in the old military hospital in Fort Street

---

[21] Lowe Committee, Evidence, pp. 125-6. See also pp. 3, 29, 67, 78.
[22] *Observer*, 19 September 1844, p. 1; 12 December 1844, pp. 4-5.
[23] *Herald*, 10 October 1846, p. 2; *Atlas*, 1 January 1848, p. 2.

(which eventually became the famous Fort Street High School). The sum of £3,000 for the development of schools beyond the settled districts, originally intended for both denominational and national schools, was finally voted for the latter alone.[24] In 1849 the board reported that four schools had been established, and applications had been received from ten other places.[25] At last a general system was fairly launched and under way—and it was the Irish system proposed by Bourke in 1836!

The denominational schools were allowed to continue in receipt of State aid and in competition with the State schools. In January 1848, a Denominational Schools' Board was set up for New South Wales, and another for Victoria; but these were to control 'fiscal and temporal' arrangements only, leaving the matter of religious instruction to the clergyman who had the oversight of the school in his locality.[26] These schools continued to teach the great majority of pupils in New South Wales—Anglicans listing 5,375 pupils, Presbyterians 3,720, Catholics 3,445, Wesleyans 1,590 and Independents 323 towards the end of 1848. The total of nearly 13,500 was not only far greater than the National Board schools could claim, but was also twice as many as the colleges and private schools catered for.[27] The church schools hung on tenaciously and, from the point of view of secular education alone, were invaluable while the State was developing its own schools.[28]

The Churches accepted the coming of the State schools comparatively quietly after the peak of opposition in 1844. The government schools were far from impressive in their earlier years, and the church schools, numerous and long-established, did not compare at all badly with them—though even the most sanguine churchmen complained that unfair amounts were spent on the State schools. There were other things which seemed more dangerous than the new schools; in 1846, particularly, the prospect of the revival of transportation to New South Wales gave rise to greater horror, and protest against this kept the letter and leader writers busy in the press. To some degree, also, the Churches had despaired of their cause. Bishop Davis, of the Catholic Church, considered the Legislative Councillors to be 'a fearful set of infidels', who would soon succeed in destroying religion by their

[24] *Herald*, 6 June 1848, pp. 2-3.
[25] *V. & P.* (N.S.W.), 1849, vol. II. For the National Board's story see A. G. Austin, op. cit., p. 45 ff, and the same author's *George William Rusden and National Education in Australia, 1849-62* (Melbourne, 1958).
[26] Col. Sec. to McGarvie, 12 January 1848, C.S.O.L. 4/3622 (ML).
[27] N.S.W. Blue Book, 1848, p. 568.
[28] Aid to church schools was finally abolished by the Education Act in Victoria 1872, the State Education Act in Queensland 1875, and by the Public Instruction Act in New South Wales 1880.

St Stephen's Anglican Church, Penrith, New South Wales

Only minor alterations—the clock, a cement rendering and some stained glass in the windows—have been made to this building of the Church Act era, consecrated by Bishop Broughton on 16 July 1839

From an ink sketch by Dr John Dykes, 1963

St Andrew's Presbyterian Church, Evandale, Tasmania
The Executive Council granted aid for this church in 1838
under the Van Diemen's Land Church Act

system of education and their intention of withdrawing all support from the Churches.[29] The attitude of Bishop Broughton has been described as a new readiness to compromise, forced upon him by tremendous financial difficulties and the need to continue receiving State aid. It was quite impossible to persuade the popularly elected legislature to support only church schools; all that remained was to conciliate that body by not opposing the setting up of State schools to operate along with church schools.[30] Even in a pamphlet produced anonymously at this time to argue for the denominational system, it was admitted that in some places the Irish system would have to be adopted 'on account of its neutrality and greater comprehension'.[31]

Yet it is not to be thought that opposition from the Churches suddenly collapsed. When Broughton wrote the Governor about the schools in 1847, his letter could almost as well be described as a dogged rearguard action as an implicit compromise, for he insisted upon the maintenance of Church of England schools.[32] Charles Kemp was confiding to his diary bitter thoughts about Robert Lowe and the nominal Anglicans who would reduce their Church to the level of a sect, but he was cherishing a faint hope that the tide was about to turn in that Church's favour.[33] In 1848, a group of Sydney Anglicans were still proclaiming that none of their clergymen should be without a school, and were developing new Church of England schools throughout the colony, while their Melbourne counterparts were no less intent on increasing the number of their schools.[34] One of the agents for the National Schools' Board was G. W. Rusden, the son of the Reverend G. K. Rusden and a practising Anglican, but when he visited the Hunter Valley in 1850, the Bishop of Newcastle refused to see him, and he received similar—or worse—treatment at the hands of the Anglican clergy in many places. In the Legislative Council, the tireless Charles Cowper came into the lists periodically on behalf of the church schools. Catholics, in an attempt to get a larger amount of aid for their schools, presented sixteen petitions to the Council in 1849, and the Wesleyans annually reappointed their education committees to watch the situation. Denominational opposition died hard.

However, the *Atlas* was not far wrong when it claimed that men like Cowper were shaken by the strength of the opposition, and had lost

[29] H. N. Birt, *Benedictine Pioneers in Australia* (London, 1911), II, p. 166.
[30] K. Grose, '1847: the Educational Compromise of the Lord Bishop of Australia', *Journal of Religious History*. vol. 1, no. 4, pp. 239-45.
[31] 'Catholicus', *An Original Essay on Popular Education* . . . (Sydney, 1848), p. 10.
[32] Broughton to FitzRoy, 3 May 1847, 47/4785, C.S.I.L. 2/1717 (ML).
[33] C. Kemp, Diary 1847-8, 19, 22, 30 July 1847, 7 February 1848 (MS. ML).
[34] *S.P.G. Report* (Sydney, 1849), pp. 11-13, 16-17; *First Report of the Melbourne Diocesan Society* . . . (Melbourne, 1849), pp. 5, 12, 15.

their confident, contemptuous tone (something the *Atlas* had not done).[35] As a tactical move in a debate on schools beyond the boundaries, Cowper claimed that 'the spirit of the age' called for aid to every kind of school (including, in other words, the Anglican schools!); but, tactics or not, this was very different talk from the kind the Council had heard from Cowper in 1844. The need to live with the National system was becoming obvious to its opponents in the Churches, and they had to resign themselves as well as they could to its existence. Nor were they helped when Lowe was able to declare in triumph that the Bishop of Melbourne favoured a general system.[36] The hard core of neither party really changed, but the situation changed, and the Irish system won more support. Lowe and W. C. Wentworth made some remarkably anti-clerical speeches in the Legislative Council in 1848, probably made far less guarded by their sense of growing support.[37] The State schools had come to stay, and grow and be appreciated by the colonials. The church schools remained, receiving State aid for another quarter of a century; but many people must have agreed with Wentworth that they were a nuisance, to be tolerated only temporarily.

[35] *Atlas*, 20 May 1848, p. 246.
[36] Ibid., 13 May 1848, p. 241.
[37] *Herald*, 10 October 1846, p. 2; 6 June 1848, p. 3.

8

THE SCHOOL QUESTION IN
VAN DIEMEN'S LAND

1835-1838: Anglicans Resist Change

IN 1820 P. A. MULGRAVE was sent out by the British Government to introduce the Bell, or Anglican 'National Society', system of schools to Van Diemen's Land. He superintended schools between Ross and Launceston, and the Reverend William Bedford had the oversight of those between Hobart and Ross. Thus education in Van Diemen's Land was also given into the hands of the Anglican Church. By 1835 the schools, though financially assisted by the State, were under the control of Archdeacon William Hutchins. They were not, of course, confined to Anglicans, and the Church's oversight was not always strict. A majority of the pupils at the better of the two boys' schools in Hobart were sons of Dissenters, and the school was conducted on British and Foreign system principles, except that the *Book of Common Prayer,* and a short catechism, were used, and the Rural Dean called once a week. The standard of religious knowledge in the school was judged to be very low.[1] But the hand of the Church of England was itching to tighten its grip on the schools. In 1834, for instance, after the S.P.G. had made a gift of money towards the foundation of a school, the trustees applied for additional aid from the Government while, at the same time, intending to insist that the pupils should worship on Sunday in St David's Church.

About this time, however, the effectiveness of the colony's schools was questioned, and Lieutenant-Governor George Arthur asked the Colonial Treasurer and the Chief Police Magistrate to investigate. The former, John Gregory, recommended exclusively Anglican schools 'at the risk of offending Roman Catholic and other Dissenting parents'; the latter, Matthew Forster, favoured the British and Foreign system.[2]

---

[1] This was Mr Jones's school in Campbell Street—Report of Board of Inquiry upon the State of the Government Schools in Hobart Town, 31 December 1835, C.S.O. 1/843/17847 (TA).
[2] Arthur to Bourke, 2 February 1836, Papers of Sir George Arthur (MS. A1962 ML).

Arthur finally recommended the British and Foreign system for Protestants and separate aid for Catholic schools. He was convinced that the Anglicans could not have it all their own way, and warned the Council (before the Church Act) that legislation would have to be passed 'as regards both churches and schools'. Despite earlier rumblings from W. G. Broughton, the Lieutenant-Governor thought that the British and Foreign system—with 'such catechisms as may be approved' —would be acceptable in the colony, and he asked for teachers trained in the system to be sent out.[3] He was recalled before anything came of his proposals, but he had prepared the way for a challenge to Anglican direction of the elementary schools.

Sir John Franklin, Arthur's successor, thought he had found the answer to the school question, but the solution he propounded turned out to be no solution. In 1838, appealing to the Church Act passed the previous year, Franklin declared that the same principle of equality had to be adopted for the schools, but that there also had to be a compromise between a denominational system and a system in which the Churches had no direct control over schools. The system he envisaged might be labelled semi-denominational. Each school was to come under the control of the denomination which happened to have a majority among the pupils at its commencement, though each was to provide a separate class or classes in which the minority could be taught their catechisms. All thirty-two public schools in the colony were to come under the control of a huge board made up of numerous persons holding office under the Crown and all the clergy of every denomination.[4] That Franklin's scheme really pleased no party, is shown by its peculiar reception in the Legislative Council. On 12 July the plan was voted out by six votes to five, and ('will our readers believe us?', as the *Tasmanian* asked) was re-introduced and passed by nine votes to one on the next day.[5] Clearly the Council was in utter confusion over the scheme. The reasons were not merely the clumsy constitution of the proposed board, or an 'ignorance of the intention . . . and the probable effects' of the plan. There was a collision between rival opinions and between theory and practice. The Attorney-General said that, since the content of religious instruction could not be agreed upon, it should be left in the hands of parents and ministers and out of the schools altogether. The Chief Justice wanted precisely the opposite: money should be allotted to each denomination to allow each to develop its own schools.

[3] Broughton to Arthur, 24 January 1834 (A2172 ML); *Courier*, 12 August 1836, p. 4; Arthur to Glenelg, 4 May 1836, G.O. 33/22; Arthur to Stephen, 3 September 1836, C.S.O. 16/28/687 (TA).
[4] Opening Address, 30 June, *V. & P.* (V.D.L.), 1838.
[5] *Tasmanian*, 13 July 1838, p. 228.

The Colonial Secretary, who would not vote a farthing toward a school which taught no religion, argued that a denominational system was too expensive. And such was the Council's dilemma that Matthew Forster could persuade it to vote in what it had voted out the day before.[6] There was a long interval between the vote in the Council and any move to implement it. After three months the *Tasmanian* asked what had become of the 'ponderous scheme' and suggested that the Government ought at least to try it, but two more months passed before the board was constituted and the regulations drawn up.[7] These were to take effect from 1 January 1839, but were never made operative. Franklin's first plan for the schools simply faded out.

Its cumbersome machinery was a bad, but not the worst, feature. The board, it is true, was to consist of two judges, the Executive and Legislative Councillors, the clerk of the Council, all the police magistrates, all the assistant police magistrates and all the clergy of every Church (except the Baptist). But five were to be a quorum, and the board need not have been hamstrung by the difficulty of assembling its members. The main trouble was that the measure solved nothing as far as the Churches were concerned. There was a good reason for objection by non-Anglicans. As the *Tasmanian* expressed it, the scheme was 'vitally at war' with the very principle of equality it was designed to serve. Anglican children would usually be in a majority and the Church of England could claim most of the existing schools for itself. More often than not, the children of other denominations would have to attend schools which were essentially Anglican.[8] Yet there was also some ground for non-Anglican support. The Anglican monopoly was at least being challenged, and there were new possibilities of State aid for non-Anglican schools. A decision on a Catholic application for grants of £50 per annum to each of its two schools had been deferred until the arrangements for schools generally had been made, and these schools could have benefited by the new proposal. Similarly the Wesleyans commenced a school in Hobart at the beginning of 1839, hoping to get government aid for it. The Presbyterians, while apparently not very much wanting the new arrangement, were willing to co-operate in it.[9] In spite of their doubts, and in spite of the claims made by recent historians, it was not the Dissenters who caused the abandonment of Franklin's plan.[10]

[6] *Courier*, 20 July 1838, pp. 2, 4.
[7] *Proclamations, Government Orders and Notices* (V.D.L.), 1838, p. 270.
[8] *Tasmanian*, 21 December 1838, p. 404.
[9] Min. Exec. Coun., 30 May 1838, 8 January 1839, E.C. 2/6, pp. 147, 412 (TA); Waterhouse to Forster, 1 May 1839, C.S.O. 5/190/4602 (TA); V.D.L. Wes. Dist. Min., 3 October 1839, Appendix.
[10] That the Anglicans supported, and the Dissenters rejected, the plan is wrongly

The new arrangement was wrecked by the Anglicans. The Church of England had quite as much reason as any other for rejecting the scheme. Not only was the archdeacon losing personal control of the schools, but the Anglicans demanded a fully denominational system on principle. Although the immediate effect of the measure might have been to leave the schools very nearly as they were, the trend was away from Church of England direction and towards government control of education. This the Anglicans determined to nip in the bud. At the very first suggestion of Franklin's scheme, Archdeacon Hutchins opposed any change; if some alteration had to be made, he wanted each denomination to be given aid in proportion to its numbers. When the government notice was issued on 13 December 1838, the archdeacon immediately wrote his clergy. By 24 December all but one had informed him that they would withdraw altogether from schools managed according to the Lieutenant-Governor's plan; they would co-operate only if they received aid for schools which were truly their own.[11] It was this Anglican obstruction which forced the Executive Council to advise Franklin against bringing the new regulations into force until the matter could again be referred to the Legislative Council.[12] As the *True Colonist* very properly expressed it:

> When the Government attempted to establish a co-operation and union, as regarded secular education, by entrusting the management to a conjunct board, composed of all denominations, the Church of England ministers alone refused to act.[13]

1839-1842: Anglicans Boycott a British and Foreign System

In 1839 the Lieutenant-Governor tried again. By May he had come back to the system which Arthur had recommended—the British and Foreign system. In August more detailed information was given. There was to be a small lay committee in place of the board, and the clergy and the police magistrates would be invited merely to visit the schools and suggest improvements. The Bible in its entirety was to be read, and, as a further aid to religious training, Sir John proposed some monetary help for Sunday schools.[14] In September the new board's position was consolidated by a minute to the Council from Franklin, and by the issue of further detailed regulations. The Lieutenant-Governor quoted

suggested in C. Reeves, *A History of Tasmanian Education . . .* (Melbourne, 1935), p. 25; A. G. Austin, *Australian Education, 1788-1900* (Melbourne, 1961), p. 71; and R. Fogarty, *Catholic Education in Australia, 1806-1950* (Melbourne, 1959), I, p. 35 n.84.
[11] Min. Exec. Coun., 23 June 1838, 8 January 1839, E.C. 2/6, pp. 191, 411 (TA).
[12] Ibid., p. 466.
[13] *True Colonist*, 29 November 1839, p. 4.
[14] *Hobart Town Gazette*, 10 May 1839, p. 471; 9 August 1839, p. 923.

Sir John Herschel, of the Cape Colony, on the principles of a new arrangement for schools there; he had said:

> I would only remark in general that so long as Christian principles are broadly laid down as the basis of all proceedings, every thing calculated to perpetuate religious or civil distinctions between members of the same community, or to foster a spirit of domination on the part of any religious sect, ought to be most studiously and pointedly avoided.[15]

This declaration, taken from documents forwarded by the Secretary of State, was a great encouragement to Franklin, and he stressed that there had been 'a remarkable coincidence of opinion' at the Cape, in New South Wales (where Gipps was advocating the British and Foreign system) and in Van Diemen's Land. The chief remaining difficulty, according to Franklin, was a shortage of suitable teachers.[16]

This was not the chief remaining difficulty at all. Once more the main trouble lay in the intransigence of the Anglican clergy. The British and Foreign schools rejected all catechisms as categorically as the Anglicans insisted on the need for them. Also, while the whole Bible was read, the scripture lessons were reduced to mere reading lessons, the master simply questioning the children to see if they understood the literal sense of what was read. He was given the task, and the warning, of 'explaining Scripture by Scripture, and never seeking by any expression of his own opinions to draw away any child from the tenets of the particular Christian communion to which the child's parents may belong'.[17] In June 1839 Archdeacon Hutchins said plainly that his clergy could neither approve nor support the system. He would not deny useful secular knowledge to those who could not be instructed in religion, but he would not support a system based on 'loose and indefinite principles' for the sake of a small minority. He could not see 'either the wisdom or the propriety of risking the stability of nine out of ten for the mere chance of improving the tenth'. Eleven Anglican clergymen supported their archdeacon in a memorial to the Lieutenant-Governor, asking for denominational schools.[18]

Anglican clerical opposition did not, on this occasion, prevent the introduction of the British and Foreign system. The board appointed

---

[15] This system, outlined approvingly by the *Courier*, 30 August 1839, p. 3, provided for the daily reading of the Bible, for pupils to be taught by their own pastors at specific times, and for children to be exempted from religious instruction if their parents wished it.

[16] Lieutenant-Governor's Minute, 2 September, *V. & P.* (V.D.L.), 1839.

[17] Ibid., 1840.

[18] W. Hutchins, *A letter on the School Question, addressed to Sir John Lewes Pedder* . . . (Hobart, 1839); Addresses For and Against Government Schools, pp. 39-41, *V. & P.* (V.D.L.), 1840.

in August 1839 duly took charge of the schools and issued its own instructions. But two exceptions to British and Foreign principles were allowed by the board, in an effort to mollify the Anglicans. Early in March 1840 the masters were instructed to allow clergymen to teach religion to their children, and the board also departed from the 'no catechisms' rule.[19] The S.P.C.K. in England had published a small book for the use of young people, consisting of selected texts from the Bible followed by questions of a more searching kind than those normally asked in British and Foreign schools, and its use in the schools was approved by the Van Diemen's Land board of education.[20] It was an admirable compromise, but the Anglican clergy, with rare exceptions, remained adamant and unco-operative.

They were themselves under criticism at this time, and their pleas were suspect in many quarters. The resignation of T. H. Braim from the headmastership of the Hobart Town Grammar School, after being instructed to see that all pupils attended Anglican service on Sundays, had given some publicity to the pressures sometimes applied by the Church of England to scholars in its schools.[21] The *True Colonist* smelled out another instance. The Presbyterian, James Thomson, had written pamphlets attacking the ecclesiastical monopoly of the Church of England. When it reached the paper's ears that Thomas Wilkinson, schoolmaster of Bothwell, had refused to act as agent for the sale of Thomson's publication, it suggested that this was because Wilkinson was afraid that the archdeacon would put him out of his job if he handled the pamphlets. In many such ways this paper sniped at the Anglican clergymen and actively fostered public resentment against them.[22] On the other hand, the Anglicans had some strong press support. The *Courier*, nearly always sympathetic, sturdily followed the clergy's lead in arguing that 'the best plan would be to afford assistance as proposed by the Archdeacon, according to the number of children, whether of Protestant, Presbyterian [sic], or Catholic denomination, to follow their own course of education as each may see fit'.[23] But strong opposition to the Anglican stand was given in other ways—so much opposition that the clergy of the Church of England seemed to be very much in the minority.

Their petition provoked an immediate retort from Nonconformists and others. The Independent ministers, Price and West, and the Baptist

[19] Report of the Board of Education, ibid., 1840.
[20] *The Faith and Duty of A Christian, Digested under Proper Heads, and Expressed in the Words of Scripture*. The edition seen was printed in Hobart in 1851 'for the Van Diemen's Land Schools'.
[21] *Tasmanian*, 20 July 1838, p. 227.
[22] *True Colonist*, 12 July, 2, 9, 16 August 1839.
[23] *Courier*, 27 September 1839, p. 2.

pastor, Dowling, wrote from Launceston to support the Lieutenant-Governor's proposal, adding, 'We have herein expressed the views of our respective congregations'. The Reverend John Lillie wrote to say that the Presbytery of Van Diemen's Land had unanimously decided in favour of the system, and the Reverend Frederick Miller informed the Colonial Secretary of the support of the Congregational Union. Thomas Anstey, in presenting a favourable address from residents of Oatlands, pointed out that it was signed 'by members of the Churches of England, Scotland and Rome; by Methodists (both Calvinistic and Armenian [sic]), Independents, and Baptists'. Within the first six months of 1840, eight other addresses came in supporting the British and Foreign system. Altogether over nine hundred male persons signed them, among whom (as well as Independent and Presbyterian ministers) there was at least one Wesleyan minister, and one Israelite. The addresses were stereotyped—drawn up by the board of education, the Anglicans were later to claim, and the board to deny—and expressed the view that a community composed of all denominations, few in numbers and dispersed over a wide extent of country, could not support church schools. The new system did away with 'the exclusive system', and laid a sure foundation for the daily reading of the Bible.

> Thus provision is made for securing to the rising generation an habitual acquaintance with that 'form of sound words' contained in the Word of God, who will thus be furnished with a perfect rule of conduct, and an effectual safeguard against error.[24]

In contrast, only two petitions, bearing eighty-eight names, came in on the Anglican side up to the middle of 1840. In spite of the Anglican majority in the population, the Church of England clergy were not spontaneously supported by their people.[25]

It is not to be supposed that the proposed British and Foreign system was condemned only by the Anglicans, and that the other denominations considered it to be ideal. The *True Colonist* was critical of the scheme from the point of view of costs, courses and teachers' qualifications, and believed that the Presbyterian Church (with which its sympathies lay) was accepting it only for want of something better.[26]

[24] Addresses For and Against . . . , pp. 1-35, *V. & P.* (V.D.L.), 1840.
[25] J. D. Loch, *An Account of the Introduction and Effects of the System of General Religious Education established in Van Diemen's Land in 1839* (Hobart, 1843), section II, pp. 17-18, offers the explanation that no attempt was made to organize petitions, for the clergy—the proper representatives of the people on religious subjects—spoke for them. If so, Mr Loch was rather overstepping the mark in producing a pamphlet of two hundred pages. The policy of letting the clergy speak for the people was not adopted in New South Wales in 1839, and Loch's explanation may be viewed with some suspicion.   [26] *True Colonist*, 16 August, 4 October, 29 November 1839.

It was perfectly true that many non-Anglican Protestants were not enamoured of a general system. The archdeacon was soon to make effective use of strong statements made about this time by both the Presbyterians and the Wesleyans in Great Britain against government schools. As far back as 1837 the Wesleyans in Van Diemen's Land itself had declared that the institution of day schools at their principal stations would 'tend materially to advance the cause of Methodism'. They had commenced a school in Hobart in 1839, and their continuing ideal was to be shown in the establishment of a similar school in 1850 at Launceston.[27] It was not a difference in ideals, but in dominance and strength, which made the Church of England so unready to enter a general system and the Wesleyan and Presbyterian Churches so much more ready.

In 1840 the Catholic attitude was made finally and abundantly clear. Towards the end of 1839 the Vicar-General, the Reverend J. J. Therry, taking a calculated risk in the hope of getting guaranteed State aid, applied for the Catholic schools at Hobart, Richmond and the Springs to be classed as government schools. This was refused on the pretext that there were already government schools at two of these places and that a decision had been made, prior to Therry's application, to establish one at the Springs.[28] Therry, like all the Australian priests, was forced into some acquiescence in State schools by having a minority and a generally poor people. He had recommended Catholic parents to send their children to the British and Foreign schools, believing that Catholic scruples would be respected. When it was pointed out to him that Catholic children in Hobart Town schools were joining with others in prayers and Bible reading, he threatened to have them withdrawn. This he was not anxious to do, and he only asked that the regulations be strictly observed. In the same letter, indeed, he asked that either a Catholic assistant to the Hobart schoolmaster be appointed, or a branch-school be opened under a Catholic teacher.[29] If he could have introduced Catholic teachers and influence into the system, he would have gone along with it. But this was something of a manipulation of the system, and it was repeatedly refused. When Therry found that nothing could be done to make the government system more acceptable to Catholics, he began in earnest to organize his own schools. Similar steps were taken by the priest at Richmond. He provided the Catholic children in the government school with books to read instead of the

[27] V.D.L. Wes. Dist. Min., 1837 (Q. 31); 1845 (Appendix); 1850 (Appendix). The Hobart school was closed in 1840 for want of funds.
[28] W. Nairn to Therry, 10 December 1839, quoted in P. F. Moran, *History of the Catholic Church in Australasia* (Sydney, n.d.), pp. 251-2.
[29] Therry to Sec. of Board, 21 October 1840, ibid., pp. 254-5.

Bible. When the board heard of this, it ordered the books to be with-drawn. They were; and so were the Catholic children.[30] There was never any question in Catholic minds about the ideal principles of education, and they were not the principles of the new general system. As Therry told the Colonial Secretary:

> To persons believing that all religions are equally good in the sight of heaven, this system must appear unobjectionable, but to those who believe, as all sincere Catholics do, that there is but one true faith, a system of education calculated to alienate or even diminish their attach-ment to it must appear dangerous.[31]

In August 1840 the board directing the government schools was one year old. It was a month to be remembered, for the board presented its first report, Anglican petitions were presented against the continuation of the system and the Lieutenant-Governor spoke out. Two of the petitions were from private citizens praying for Anglican schools. They were signed by thirty and one hundred and twenty-three persons re-spectively, and were some indication of a wider public support for the Anglican clergy. Yet the one hundred and twenty-three included wives (no other petition had resorted to this), and the total signatories of the Anglican memorials between August 1839 and August 1840 amounted to only about two hundred and fifty—wives, archdeacons and all. Compared with the nine hundred signatures attached to the petitions in favour of the British and Foreign system, the Anglican effort was far from impressive. W. E. Nairn, a secretary of the board of education, was right when he said that the system of education 'was received . . . without disfavour by many of the laity of the Church of England', and that the lower classes did not take much interest—they talked about it, but neither clearly understood what was involved nor thought it important.[32]

A third petition was from the archdeacon himself. As might be expected of a mathematician and former Fellow of Pembroke College, Cambridge, Hutchins made out a good case. He made four significant claims. Anglican children were being denied their rights by the rele-gation of their ministers to the category of mere visitors; British and Foreign principles had been departed from by permitting ministers to give instruction, and by the introduction of *The Faith and Duty of a Christian,* so the granting of aid to Anglican schools would be no less consistent; there had been no expansion under the board, but only the re-opening of some schools which had closed through government

[30] *Courier,* 14 August 1840, p. 3.
[31] Therry to Forster, 17 October 1840, quoted in P. F. Moran, op. cit., p. 253.
[32] Report of V.D.L. Education Commissioners, 1845, G.O. 33/51, p. 988 (TA).

(not Anglican) ineptitude; and, fourthly, the archdeacon appealed to contemporary statements in support of fully denominational schools made by Nonconformists in Britain and also to a comment made by the early Nonconformist divine, Richard Baxter:

> He is not worthy of the name of Christian Schoolmaster who maketh it not his chief work to teach his scholars the knowledge of Christ and life everlasting.[33]

The report of the board of education hardly amounted to a satisfactory reply. It claimed that the number of scholars in the twenty-seven schools had increased from 785 to 1,145; that three of these schools were new; and that the erection of another three had been recommended. Since there had been thirty-two schools, with an average attendance of 843 children in 1838, Archdeacon Hutchins was close to the truth. The board attacked the Anglicans for the state of the schools when it had taken them over, for they had been quite inadequate in curriculum, equipment and methods of teaching; but it had to admit that it continued to labour under most of these disadvantages, including a lack of suitable teachers. What strengthened the board's case, and weakened the archdeacon's petition, was the stubborn refusal of the Anglican clergy to have anything to do with the schools. Although the board had allowed two large modifications of the system to meet the objections of the ministers of the Church of England, only five of their number would co-operate in any way. In contrast, the board claimed 'the cordial support' of the other ministers of religion.[34] The difference could not fail to be observed, and the community did not fail to remember it.

Sir John Franklin felt it necessary to make a statement about the situation. He defended the schools, both as the kind desired by the people and as giving an adequate amount of religious instruction; he confessed that he could 'by no means overlook or depreciate' the fact that the Anglican clergy were objecting, but he stressed that he had to be guided by what the community at large wanted. Sir John, however, was becoming increasingly uneasy, and he announced that he would leave it to the Legislative Council freely to decide whether or not to retain the British and Foreign system. The Council, not so easily intimidated, voted for its retention.[35]

---

[33] *V. & P.* (V.D.L.), 1840.

[34] Report of Board of Education, ibid. The five Anglicans were men such as the Rev. H. Bishton, whose small school had an Anglican mistress and only Anglican pupils. These clergymen were not really divided from their brethren.

[35] Addresses For and Against . . . , p. 43; Minute, 15 August; Resolution, 4 September; *V. & P.* (V.D.L.), 1840.

By 1842 the board of education could even report 'very important improvements'. Six couples trained in the British and Foreign system (including the now celebrated James Bonwick and his wife) had arrived from England and were settled in schools. The standard and scope of teaching had been raised strikingly, and 'even in the *least effective*' schools an acquaintance with the Holy Scriptures, as well as knowledge of writing and arithmetic, was being gained. There was an average total attendance of 1,460 children, compared with 785 when the board had taken over in 1839. But the position had not improved beyond recognition. The number of schools (as distinct from scholars) was not increasing, and it was to continue to fall a little in the next few years.[36] There was still a shortage of properly trained teachers. Above all, there was still the religious problem. Most schoolteachers were Anglicans, but most ministers of the Church of England still refused to give religious instruction in the schools.[37]

On the contrary, they launched another attack on the system. Twenty-one of these clergymen associated themselves in a petition for denominational schools. Only two in the colony did not sign—the Reverend H. Bishton, who had not signed the first, and a newcomer, the Reverend T. Spurr. Since their numbers had increased since 1838, and the second petition was prepared in the absence of both archdeacon and bishop (for Hutchins had died in 1841, and their first bishop and a new archdeacon had not yet arrived), it was clearer than ever that the Anglican ministers were opposed to the government system. It was clear, too, that the clergy were more anxious for an alteration in the system than were their people: for the petitions to which the people attached their names in 1842 were not concerned with schools, but prayed for a 'Usury Law' to give them protection as they tried to weather the storm of economic depression.

1843-1847: Bishop Nixon against Sir John Eardley-Wilmot

When the Right Reverend Francis Russell Nixon arrived in July 1843, he gave strong support to his clergy. He waited, perforce, until a new Lieutenant-Governor, Sir John Eardley-Wilmot, had settled in, summoned a Legislative Council and declared to it his profound belief in religious freedom. Then Nixon struck. On 24 October 1843, the bishop and his clergy petitioned that the money about to be voted for education be distributed among the denominations in proportion

---

[36] The 22 schools at the commencement of the board's life (as stated in the report) should have been 27 (see Table A in Appendix to Report). In 1842, 1843, 1844, there were 24, 24 and 23 government schools respectively, with 1,493 scholars in the latter year—*Statistics of Van Diemen's Land for 1842-4* (Hobart, 1845), p. 16.
[37] Report of Board of Education, *V. & P.* (V.D.L.), 1842.

to their numbers, for use in the development of church schools. Next day Nixon petitioned to be heard before the Council, and, the Council granting his request by eight votes to five, he was heard at length on 31 October. The Council room was crowded by 'the most respectable of the Community', and several ladies were in a room behind the chamber. The bishop began by saying that he was old-fashioned enough to believe that a country's prosperity depended on it having God's bless-ing. The statesman's duty was not confined to the temporal welfare of the people, but extended to the provision of an educational system which produced 'not moralists, but God's worshippers'. It was an evil to forbid catechisms and comment on the Bible in the schools, and the existing system acknowledged the objections of Romanist, Jew and Dissenter, but not the principles of the Church of England. 'The principle of liberty of conscience is for them, but the coercion of conscience for us', said the bishop. But, he asked, was conscience just Romish or Jewish? And had the Church of England fallen so far that it was a mere sect? Nixon began to condemn the schools on their practical working—and was interrupted by Eardley-Wilmot, who held up a copy of the board's report, saying that this flatly refuted these charges. The bishop went on to suggest that the Church of England was established—and was interrupted by the Attorney-General and the Colonial Secretary. Eventually Nixon was allowed to reach his grand conclusion: that posterity could never say 'that the first Lord Bishop of Tasmania was afraid to speak his mind, that he was recreant to his trust, or that he did not raise his voice, solemnly and sincerely, in behalf of the church, before God, and before his country'.[38] Obviously the bishop had impressed himself.

Unlike Bishop Broughton on a similar occasion, Nixon had not sufficiently impressed the Lieutenant-Governor, the Council or the people. The first result was the arrival of five petitions (with Independent and Baptist influences prominent) against any change. Two Wesleyan petitions were presented, asking that no change be made until sufficient time had been given 'to all parties to explain their views on this im-portant subject'. Only one petition in support of Nixon accompanied them. A good example of the case put for the general schools was a petition from inhabitants of Hobart. This said that the system had been recently introduced after much discussion and deliberation, it had been well received by the people, and to alter it would disturb the children and violate the contract with teachers brought out for the schools. Furthermore, to surrender to the demands of the clergy of one Church, especially after the introduction of *The Faith and Duty*

[38] *Courier*, 3 November 1843, p. 2.

of a Christian, written by an Anglican dignitary and published by the S.P.C.K., would be quite unreasonable. Compared with other Protestants' efforts, Anglican activity in the colony did not emerge very favourably; eighty children attended Anglican Sunday schools in Hobart and eight hundred and fifty went to non-Anglican Sunday schools, and the Nonconformist provision for 8,916 persons in their churches was not far behind the Anglican accommodation for 9,870. Yet the Church of England ministers had the presumption to claim that Dissenters should attend Anglican schools, but Anglicans should not have to attend other Protestant schools![39] It was a case well put, and its arguments had much support in the colony.

A week after the first petitions arrived, the Reverend John Lillie prayed to be heard on behalf of the general system and, in the next day or two, four petitions were presented against any change. In support of Nixon, eight petitions were received, one of them signed by 1,200 inhabitants of the colony. But up to the end of 1843 the petitioners supporting the general system remained well ahead, and, as the session continued into 1844, they increased their lead. Four more petitions, one bearing the signatures of 1,626 inhabitants of Hobart, favoured the existing system: while two, bearing the name of only one layman (J. D. Loch), asked for the school system to be reconsidered. Since the Anglicans laid claim to well over half the total population of the island, the support received by their clergy was very limited indeed. It was the minor denominations which really rallied, and which were joined—or not opposed—by many members of the Church of England.

The newly-arrived Sir John Eardley-Wilmot declared that he was not going to decide the matter. He certainly showed far more sympathy for the board than for the claims of the Anglican Church, but he concluded the matter with the words,

> shall I, finding a system carried on for four or five years, of which no complaint has been substantiated ... authorized by the home Government, and sanctioned by the Queen, consent that it be suddenly changed without notice, and without due consideration, and without consulting that authority at home, by which the system was originally established? To this my answer is, I cannot do so.

The documents for and against were to go to England; in the meantime the British and Foreign system was to go on.[40]

No one defended the physical conditions of the schools in general or denied that, in practice, many of them left much to be desired. That would have been too much to try to get away with. The school

[39] Ibid., 17 November 1843, p. 3.
[40] *Colonial Times,* 28 November 1843, p. 3.

at Cambridge, for instance, consisted of two rooms, a 'skilling' and a
sitting room, which housed the master and his family as well as the
pupils, and which was flooded in wet weather.[41] Towards the end of
1843 the resignation of James Bonwick from the key school in Hobart
gave added emphasis to the problem of finding good teachers and of
paying them adequately. When the Anglican lay champion, J. D. Loch,
published his long and scathing attack on the board schools,[42] even the
newspapers which supported these schools had to admit that some
of his criticisms were quite just. The *Colonial Times* reprinted long
extracts in successive issues with the comment that, while Loch had
been misled by some of his informants, other of his criticisms were
unanswerable.[43] Even the *Launceston Examiner,* an unlikely source
of any approval for Loch, treated his *Account* with initial respect before
beginning to find out and fire into the loopholes.[44]

The gravest weakness on the Anglican side was the attitude of the
clergy; the position they had taken up as a strong one, turned out to be
something of a trap for them. There was a lively correspondence in the
press at this time, and the Anglican clergy had to be defended by the
explanation that they could only hope to get the system changed by
completely dissociating themselves from the schools, since 'a single
visit . . . was always turned into an argument that they approved of
the system'.[45] Their more numerous detractors, however, continued
to try to turn the Anglican boast into shame.[46] Nor did the Church
of England ministers get much editorial support. There was 'something very unchristianlike' about complaining of the want of religious
education in schools they would not visit, and even the friends of
Bishop Nixon, it was said, thought that his speech was 'greatly calculated to mar his usefulness'.[47] The *Launceston Examiner* drew a
moral from the defeat of Sir James Graham's Factories Education Bill
in England: the colony could not be expected to change its system
when the objections of Dissent to granting the Church of England
control of education had caused the English Bill to be withdrawn. A
trump card, Tractarianism and its effects, was produced: Sir John
Eardley-Wilmot was wished 'the joy of the task' of deciding which of
'the various opinions which stand between Geneva and Rome' formed
the doctrine of a Church ranging from Evangelical to Puseyite. The
Anglican clergy were ironically acquitted of all base motives, since

[41] Ibid., 1 August 1843, p. 2.   [42] J. D. Loch, op. cit.
[43] *Colonial Times,* 5, 9, 15 August 1843.
[44] *Examiner,* 2 August 1843, p. 483.   [45] *Courier,* 18 August 1843, p. 3.
[46] Ibid., 11 August 1843, p. 3. See also ibid., 15 September 1843, p. 3; *Examiner*
12 August 1843, p. 510.
[47] *Colonial Times,* 8 August 1843, p. 2; 14 November 1843, p. 2.

they had been taught by the doctors of Oxford to cherish notions unsuited to their colonial circumstances. But who could be expected 'to expose their children to the instruction of a church whose creed no one knows, and no man pretends to know'? Eardley-Wilmot was warned: if ministers were to be insulted, ministers who had laboured at Port Arthur when no Anglican could be found to fill the station, the first free Legislative Council would 'lay the axe to the root of ecclesiastical establishments, and resolve the dignity of a bishop into its primitive nothingness'. And the Churches themselves were warned against dividing into hostile factions, contending for powers none could permanently possess.[48] The *Courier's* restrained and infrequent reference to the education question was no less revealing. For this paper, the question was whether the colony was to train up 'a race of men either dead to all principles, excepting, perhaps, those of cold worldly morality, or a God-loving and God-fearing people'. Yet, apart from publicizing Loch's *Account,* it said virtually nothing until 1843 was drawing to a close, and then contented itself with expressing a doubt about the suitability of the Anglican proposal, even if the existing system was a 'negative' one. When the Lieutenant-Governor announced his intention to refer the whole matter to the Secretary of State, the *Courier* was content to let the matter rest.[49] The tide of public opinion was not flowing in the direction the Church of England—and the *Courier* of 1839—had hoped it would.

Therefore, the Anglicans determined to by-pass the colonial authorities. Privately they produced a pamphlet, lacking both title and author's name, which contested the board's claims and pressed their own. It may be true that the Legislative Council had been asked to print the document and had refused; it may be true that, after the clergy paid for the printing themselves, a copy was sent to the board of education, which did not reply.[50] But this does not explain the division of the printing between the *Advertiser* and the *Colonial Times,*[51] or the pamphlet's existence being kept secret for six months until the *Launceston Examiner* accidentally got hold of one—and promptly printed a long extract.[52] It seems that the pamphlet was produced for secret despatch to influential quarters in England, there to be supported by Archdeacon Marriott, who was in fact being sent home partly to press

[48] *Examiner,* 8 November 1843, p. 696; 25 November 1843, p. 737. The Wesleyans, who had been in spiritual charge of Port Arthur from its commencement, were peremptorily replaced by an Anglican in 1843.
[49] *Courier,* 7 July 1843, p. 4; 3 November 1843, p. 2; 1 December 1843, p. 3.
[50] Claimed by the Rev. R. R. Davies, *Examiner,* 3 July 1844, p. 419.
[51] Asserted by *True Colonist,* 14 June 1844, p. 2. The editor had been unable to procure a copy.
[52] *Examiner,* 5 June 1844, pp. 355, 358-60; 12 June 1844, p. 371.

the case for Anglican schools, though the *True Colonist* was told that the archdeacon's visit had nothing to do with schools.[53]

The news broken by the *Launceston Examiner* was not well received in the colony, but, one way and another, the Anglicans had managed to confuse the situation so much that the Secretary of State's reply to Eardley-Wilmot's request for instructions was equally confused. Lord Stanley considered that there was sufficient weight in the charges brought against the schools to justify a commission of enquiry, not into the system, but into the working of the system. At the same time, while hasty changes were deprecated, Eardley-Wilmot might well decide that the system needed changing; if so, the denominational system in operation in New South Wales might be considered.[54] Bishop Nixon found this despatch 'more satisfactory than he anticipated',[55] but pity the Lieutenant-Governor, who had hoped to avoid making a decision, only to find that the Secretary of State claimed this relief for himself. Eardley-Wilmot dutifully shouldered his burden, and appointed a commission of enquiry in 1845. The commissioners—W. D. Bernard, Dr John Meyer and George Courtnay, comparative newcomers to the colony—were suspected of bias because they were Anglicans, a suspicion which was heightened by their enquiries being held behind closed doors and by the Lieutenant-Governor's decision not to publish the report, or even place it before the Council, but to send it home. This was unfortunate, for Eardley-Wilmot simply recommended that the system continue, except for the replacement of the voluntary board by a superintendent and an official department,[56] and the commissioners, far from having an Anglican bias, produced a favourable report. The schools did 'not merit the full measure of censure . . . cast upon them'. If children and parents, in any cases, had come to disregard the Anglican clergy, it was a natural result of Anglican withdrawal from the schools; but it was commonly recognized that the parents were 'almost entirely' concerned about secular instruction, and were 'frequently indifferent' to the religious instruction offered. Many improvements, the commission found, had been prevented by lack of money, not by any fault in the system as such.[57]

While word from England was once more awaited, the board suffered

[53] *True Colonist*, 14 June 1844, p. 2, A. Nixon to Woodcock, 3 April 1844, N. Nixon (ed.), *The Pioneer Bishop in Van Diemen's Land, 1843-63* (Hobart, 1953), p. 24. According to Mrs Nixon, there were three matters entrusted to the 'faithful and good' archdeacon: endowing the Church; the education question; and superintendence of the Convict Chaplains.
[54] Stanley to Eardley-Wilmot, 24 August 1844, *V. & P.* (V.D.L.), 1847-8.
[55] A. Nixon to Woodcock, 30 December 1844, N. Nixon, op. cit., p. 41.
[56] Eardley-Wilmot to Stanley, 13 June 1845, G.O. 25/11 (TA).
[57] Report of Education Commissioners, 23 May 1845, G.O. 33/51, pp. 591-5 (TA).

from the Lieutenant-Governor's extreme caution, by being forbidden to increase the number of schools.[58] In the Estimates the amount proposed for government schools was actually reduced by £1,000, although this was not really an educational matter, being rather one aspect of the position taken up by the 'Patriotic Six', the members who put the whole fiscal arrangement under fire before resigning amid the plaudits of the population. Hence economic difficulty as much as educational policy denied the board a fair chance of proving itself. Yet the dogged Anglicans managed to get sufficient money privately subscribed to engage in a school building campaign. In the south they did more building of schools than of chapels.[59] In the Deanery of Longford, to the north, two brick and eight weatherboard Anglican schools were erected before their funds were exhausted; then, since six more schools were contemplated in areas where there were no State schools, the clergy asked the Government for financial assistance.[60] Support for the Longford clergy's petition was given by the *Courier*, which argued that it was an economy of public funds, and that the board was never intended to prevent such voluntary efforts.[61] Dissenting ministers from the area petitioned against it; the *Launceston Examiner* opposed it as an attempt to get public money in defiance of government policy;[62] and the Government ignored the request.

The year 1846 opened with the government schools in stagnant existence, and the Anglican schools increasing in number. In April, shortly before leaving for a trip to England, Bishop Nixon delivered his first charge to the clergy. He spoke 'in the language of regret rather than of complaint' about the deficiency of schools in an island which, year after year, had a mass of evil cast upon its shores. It was difficult to establish Anglican day schools, especially in country districts, but the Church of England must no longer be outdone in zeal by Dissenters in establishing Sunday schools.[63] There was little menace in these words, and Sir John Eardley-Wilmot may have been pleased with the bishop's moderate tone. But Nixon was soon to have some of his difficulties removed, and the Lieutenant-Governor to suffer a grievous shock. The despatch dealing with schools came, not from Stanley, but from W. E. Gladstone in liverish mood. Unable to master his dislike of Eardley-Wilmot, the new Secretary of State had mastered the docu-

---

[58] Report of Board of Education, 13 August, *V. & P.* (V.D.L.), 1845.
[59] *Herald of Tasmania*, 18 July 1845, p. 2; *S.P.G. Report* (Hobart), 1844-5, pp. 9-11.
[60] Petition of the Clergy . . . , 4 August, *V. & P.* (V.D.L.), 1845.
[61] *Courier*, 9 August 1845, p. 2.
[62] Petition of . . . Ministers . . . , 21 August, *V. & P.* (V.D.L.), 1845; *Examiner*, 6 August 1845, p. 499.
[63] F. R. Nixon, *A Charge Delivered to the Clergy . . . at the Primary Visitation . . . April xxiii, MDCCCXLVI.* (London, 2nd ed., 1848), pp. 31-2.

ments sufficiently to turn them against the Lieutenant-Governor and the board schools.

Gladstone savaged Eardley-Wilmot for substituting laconic comments for the full report he had been asked for, and agreed with a Catholic complaint that the British and Foreign system gave 'an exclusive support to Independency'. He condemned the schools for their inefficiency and the whole system for its inadequacy. In short, he was less than fair; especially since he was not prepared to direct that a denominational school system be introduced. For all his denial of Eardley-Wilmot's claim of a popular support which included that of many Anglicans, it was obvious that Gladstone was not quite sure that the Lieutenant-Governor was wrong. But there were two things about which Gladstone was sure: a strict interpretation of the British and Foreign system's rules was to be insisted upon; and aid from the Treasury, at the rate of one penny or a penny halfpenny a day per child, was to be granted to church schools.[64]

In this way, and not through any majority opinion in the colony, the educational system came at last to be modified. Gone was all hope of simply adjusting the British and Foreign schools to allow more scope for religious instruction. The government schools had to be operated on the narrowest basis, while rival denominational schools were to be assisted from Government funds. The only safeguard for the State schools was that they were regarded as catering adequately for Dissenters, and aid was given only to Anglican and Catholic schools.[65]

Although a Catholic objection had been taken into account by the Secretary of State, this sabotage of the board schools was essentially an Anglican achievement. But some of the means used to secure the Anglican goal were despicable. Part of the reason for Gladstone's unexpected attack on Eardley-Wilmot was that he gave shocked credence to rumours that the Lieutenant-Governor was a notorious lecher, and the despatch on schools was soon followed by despatches removing him from his post. Ostensibly, and to some extent truly, this was due to his mis-management of the convict system and other inefficiency; but looming large among the reasons was this charge of irregularities in his private life.[66] The sexual morals of the Lieutenant-Governor may not have been impeccable, but they were not blatantly improper. The staunch Anglican, Chief Justice Pedder, did not like Eardley-Wilmot, in either public or private life, but he claimed that the 'infamous

[64] Gladstone to Eardley-Wilmot, 3 March 1846, *V. & P.* (V.D.L.), 1847-8.
[65] Bradbury to MacCaig, 22 August 1848, Board of Education Letterbook of Outward Letters, 1847-51 (TA).
[66] The relevant despatches are printed in *P.P.* (H.C.), 1847, vol. xxxviii, p. 513 ff.

stories' charging the man with 'the grossest immorality' were 'utterly
without foundation'.[67] That injustice was done to Eardley-Wilmot (who
died in 1847 before leaving the colony) was widely maintained in Van
Diemen's Land at the time, even by such narrow persons as the
members of the Hobart Wesleyan Leaders' Meeting,[68] and was admitted
by Gladstone himself a little later.[69] Eardley-Wilmot suspected that the
rumours had been spread by free settlers who opposed the new probation system, and blamed them for it.[70] Such persons doubtless contributed to the scandal-mongering, but one guilty person emerges more
clearly than any other—the Lord Bishop of Tasmania. Nixon, in a
letter quoted in the House of Commons when this matter was debated,
declared that the rumours were 'utterly groundless'.[71] But he was here
beating a retreat, and Gladstone wrote him in indignant reproof:

> I consider that it *was* upon your Lordship's authority in no small degree,
> though perhaps not in a degree greater than upon any other authority,
> that I wrote.[72]

The best that can be said for Nixon is that Gladstone was shown
letters written by the bishop to the Reverend Edward Coleridge, but
Coleridge was known to have Gladstone's ear, and Australian bishops
deliberately worked through him.[73] It was known, or suspected, in the
colony that the Anglican clergy had a hand in reporting, and exag-
gerating, Eardley-Wilmot's misdemeanours,[74] but, by fair means and
foul, they got their way as far as schools went.

1848: A Triumphant Interval for Anglican Schools

Wilmot's successor, Sir William Denison, knew what he had to do.
He did not follow his own preferences. He did not try to gauge the
public will. He simply announced a new scheme close to the ideals of
Gladstone. The position at this time, early in 1848, was that the board
controlled twenty-two schools, the Catholics four and Anglicans twenty-
four—such had been their vigorous expansion. Only about half the

[67] Pedder to Arthur, 18 February 1846 (A2170 ML).
[68] They referred to Eardley-Wilmot's 'injured character' and resolved to record the important service he had rendered religion in the colony—Minutes, 15 February 1847, Hobart Wesleyan Leaders' Meeting Minute Book, 1830-52 (Wesley Church, Hobart).
[69] See Kathleen Fitzpatrick, 'Mr. Gladstone and the Governor: the Recall of Sir John Eardley-Wilmot from Van Diemen's Land, 1846', *Historical Studies*, vol. 1, no. 1, pp. 31-45.
[70] Wilmot to Gladstone, 26 September 1846, P.P. (H.C.), 1847, vol. xxxviii, p. 529.
[71] *Hansard*, 7 June 1847, vol. xciii, c. 201.
[72] Gladstone to Nixon, 24 June 1847, British Museum MSS., Catalogue MS. 44,365, folios 307-9.
[73] Broughton to Coleridge, 15 August 1850, B.P.
[74] *Courier*, 20 October 1847, p. 2.

2,759 children enrolled at the colony's elementary schools were attending the government schools. Denison found that there were as many
children again of school-going age, but claimed that his Government
could not afford the £11,000 it would have taken annually to provide
schools for them all, and urged that a rigid uniformity in all schools
was undesirable. He therefore proposed that a committee of ratepayers,
elected each year for every district, should decide the type of education
to be given in the local school, and that a capitation tax of five shillings
per annum be levied for education.[75] The proposal was given only
dubious support, editorially and by letters, in the *Courier*, where most
support was to be expected; and the non-official members of the Legislative Council flatly rejected it, arguing that the poll-tax would be
ruinous, and that the scheme would increase religious dissension.[76]

At this point the existing penny-a-day system for Anglican and
Catholic schools was called into question from both sides. Dissenters
raised the objection that the system 'had the effect of punishing those
Churches who concurred with . . . [the] Council in the General System
for the sake of peace and the common good, and of rewarding the
disaffection of its opponents'. From the other side, the Reverend R. R.
Davies pointed to the success of Anglican schools even with that small
assistance, and asked that it be increased to not less than twopence a
day. Other petitions came in also—two against the penny-a-day allowance, and three from Catholics seeking its continuation.[77] On top of
this the non-official councillors drew up a scheme of their own, which
came to nothing, but added to the uncertainty as to what the colony's
school system was to be.[78]

Both the board schools and the Anglican and Catholic schools, on
their penny-a-day, continued through 1848. By October there were
twenty-five board schools with about 1,200 pupils, four Catholic schools
with 350 pupils, and no less than thirty-three Church of England
schools with over 1,300 pupils. The Anglican clergy were as determined
to develop their own schools as they were to break the State schools,
and they were succeeding. It was a strenuous attempt to do good, but
both its ethics and its value were questioned. That nine of their schools
were held in buildings used for worship could be considered cheating.
They were also paying a heavy price from the point of view of teaching
standards. Only two masters and one mistress had been trained for
teaching; five masters and three mistresses held tickets-of-leave; and

[75] Minute on Education, 9 March; Minute on Finance, 17 March; Report of the Public Day Schools; *V. & P.* (V.D.L.), 1847-8.
[76] *Courier*, 11, 18, 22 March 1848; Denison to Grey, 7 August 1848, G.O. 33/64 (TA).
[77] *V. & P.* (V.D.L.), 1847-8.
[78] *Courier*, 5 September 1849, pp. 2-3.

five other masters had originally been transported. In contrast, all the teachers at the board schools were free persons, and eight masters were trained teachers.[79] That part of the Anglican argument for church schools which rested upon the depravity of the parents was to some extent given away by the use of ex-convict teachers.

In September 1848, the Lieutenant-Governor announced yet another scheme—the last before 1854. The cost of the schools to the Government was to be reduced, and the demands of the Anglicans and Catholics met. Masters would have no fixed salaries but would be paid a penny-halfpenny per day for each child up to the number of sixteen and a lower sum for children above that number. The Government would establish a normal school to train teachers. The Lieutenant-Governor, through an Inspector of Schools, was to appoint the teachers, but the recommendations of ministers of religion would be taken into account. The Inspector would have general charge of the schools, but supervision by ministers would also be asked for. The schools were to be open to all denominations, and the British and Foreign system could be followed or a school could be connected with one denomination, whichever was chosen by the parents of the majority of children attending. As far as possible the Inspector was to carry out the wishes of the clergyman in any school placed in the charge of a Church. Books were to be supplied by the Government, but not the buildings. As well as the government grant, teachers could receive fees from the parents. It was all to come into effect from the beginning of 1849.[80]

The board of education, feeling quite superseded, resigned in September 1848, and the British and Foreign system teachers, originally brought out from England, followed suit.[81] Three petitions were presented against the new scheme in October, but the system was duly put into effect. In August 1849, one of the councillors, Thomas Gregson, tried vainly to undo it. He successfully moved that no convict or emancipist should be allowed to teach in a public school, but he lost his motion (three votes to ten) that fixed salaries be paid to teachers and that education 'merely of a secular character' should be given in the public schools.[82] The Council did not want to start another rumpus any more than it wanted to spend additional money.

At the beginning of 1850 there were seventy-one schools assisted by the Government under this arrangement. Only eight were still run on

[79] Report of Board of Education, 23 October 1848, *V. & P.* (V.D.L.), 1848.
[80] Address, 12 September; Finance Minute, 21 September; ibid. Circular to Masters, Board of Education Letter Book, January-December 1848, pp. 161-2 (TA). *Hobart Town Gazette*, 7 November 1848, pp. 1109-10.
[81] Report by the Inspector of Schools, Thomas Arnold . . . for 1850, pp. 1-2, *V. & P.* (V.D.L.), 1850.　　　[82] Ibid., 1849.

British and Foreign principles, the others being four Catholic and fifty-nine Church of England schools. Between 1836 and 1850 the public schools in Van Diemen's Land had moved from being almost exclusively Anglican, through eight years (1839-46) of being non-Anglican, and two years (1847-8) of being half Anglican, to being principally Anglican once more. It must have seemed that the Church of England's persistence had finally been rewarded. Yet the Anglican victory was neither complete nor secure. Catholic schools, while few, were soundly established and State-aided. It was possible for a majority of parents to decide to take the local school out of the hands of the Church of England, and there were still the schools which continued to use the British and Foreign method. General systems of education, indeed, were better understood and widely approved by the colonists, while the implacable opposition of the clergy had hardened the feeling that, if the State had a duty to educate, it would have to be along comprehensive, not denominational, lines. This was true, despite the number of schools which went over to Anglican control in 1849 and the number of schools previously built by them; this was a forced growth and an unreliable verdict, due to the vigour of the clergy and the confusion of the people. The Church of England was enjoying only a brief interval of triumph before public opinion finally turned against it. In 1854 a modified form of the Irish system was introduced by the Government, and the Anglican and Catholic bishops were glad enough that the system was no worse than that.[83]

The end result was that the Churches were left farther outside the schools than they might have been if the Anglicans (in particular) had not worked so hard to stay at the centre. Clergymen, zealots in their own eyes, were popularly judged to be bigots. Instead of concentrating on teaching at least those basic religious truths which were common to all denominations, the clergy turned religious instruction into a bone of hopeless contention. Thus they helped to foster the modern secular system of education, the very thing they meant to resist.

[83] See A. G. Austin, op. cit., pp. 134-9.

9

DAY SCHOOLS AND SUNDAY SCHOOLS

Religious Instruction in the Day Schools

IN EVERY SCHOOL run on the principles of the Irish system there hung a chart bearing a legend which began, 'Christians should endeavour, as the Apostle Paul commands them, to live peaceably with all men. *Rom. ch. xii,* 18'. As well as allowing one day a week for religious instruction superintended by the pastors of the various Churches, schoolmasters in the Irish system schools were instructed to see that the lesson on the chart was 'strictly inculcated'.[1] Furthermore, the books used in these schools were heavily weighted with Christian sentiments and doctrine. There was a volume of sacred poetry from which the children might read:

> Jesus Christ my Lord and Saviour,
> Once became a child like me;
> Oh that in my whole behaviour
> He my pattern still might be!

One of the standard reading books contained a lesson on 'Milk, Butter and Cheese' which concluded thus: 'A sacred writer compares the word of God to milk, because as it belongs to milk to nourish the bodies of babes, so it belongs to the word of God to nourish the souls of those who have turned to God, and become as little children. . . '.[2] This was quite normal. Lessons on 'The Dog' and on 'Silver' pointed out that 'the dog seems to be used as a name for Satan, Psalm xxiii, 20', and moved from the use of silver in Solomon's temple to its use as a figure for 'the word of God (Psalm xii, 6)'. A lesson on 'Money' was even more frankly homiletic when, after dealing with the convenience of money in making exchanges, it continued:

> We are cautioned in Scripture against the love of money. It is a foolish
> and wicked thing for men to set their hearts on money, or on eating and

[1] *Regulations . . . for Aid towards the Building of School Houses . . .* (Sydney, 1849).
[2] See W. A. Duncan, *Lecture on National Education . . .* (Brisbane, 1850), p. 9; *Colonial Observer,* 29 August 1844, p. 2.

drinking, or on fine clothes, or on anything in this present world: for all these are apt to draw off their thoughts from God. Our Lord Jesus Christ, therefore, tells us to 'lay up for ourselves treasures in heaven'.

In addition to seventy-five general lessons of such a nature, this particular book contained twenty-four 'Religious and Moral Lessons', consisting of 'The Birth of Isaac and Expulsion of Ishmael', 'Trial of Abraham's Faith', and other paraphrased biblical extracts. Verse lessons included hymns by Dodderidge ('O God of Bethel! by whose hand thy people still are fed') and Heber ('From Greenland's icy mountains') as well as the more likely item, "Tis the voice of the sluggard'.[3] On top of all this, the Irish system provided another book of scripture lessons, which were edited selections from the Bible, with obscurities and archaisms explained in footnotes. At the end of each passage there were numerous questions, intended to elicit the general sense of the reading. The appearance at Christ's transfiguration of 'Moses the lawgiver, and Elijah the chief of the prophets, both attending on Christ, showed the agreement of the law and the prophets concerning him, and their fulfilment in him'. The saying, 'No man having put his hand to the plough, and looking back, is fit for the kingdom of God', was explained thus: 'It was a proverbial expression, that if a man who is ploughing looks back, he will not make a straight furrow. No person who purposes to follow the Saviour, and who looks wishfully back on worldly things, as loth to part with them, will be received by him as a disciple'.[4] Such passages, explanatory notes and general questions, taken together with the scripture references, hymns and moral injunctions in the ordinary lesson books, and the provision for denominational teaching on one day a week, enabled a great deal of religious instruction to be given. The supporters of the Irish system had a good case for denying that their schools were irreligious, and for maintaining that they laid a broad basis upon which further doctrine could be developed in church and at Sunday school.

The rules for the British and Foreign schools more quickly show reasons why there was such strong opposition to general systems. Here there was no provision of one day each week for the ministers to give instruction, and, although it was boasted that the entire Bible was taught in the schools, the biblical teaching was very limited. This was how the masters were instructed to teach scripture:

suppose the sentence to be read is, 'Seek ye the Lord while he may be found; call upon him while he is near', the Master should ask such

[3] *Third Book of Lessons for the Use of Schools*, reprinted for the V.D.L. Public Day Schools (Hobart, 1845).
[4] *Scripture Lessons for the Use of Schools, New Testament, No. 1* (Sydney, 1849).

questions as these—Who are to seek? *Answer,* All men. Whom are we to seek? *Answer,* the Lord. When are we to seek the Lord? *Answer,* While he may be found.[5]

To have been so confined must have been hardly satisfactory for any religious instructor. To the Reverend William Dry it was downright 'cruel to fill a child's mind with Scriptural phrases without teaching him the Christian faith'.[6] Bishop Broughton wanted to know what was the use of enabling boys to 'acquire a kind of fluency in the use of Scriptural terms, without the remotest conception of what the sense is'. All that would be asked by a British and Foreign schoolteacher when 'Son of God' was read would be, 'Who is called Son?', and 'By whom?'.[7] The objectors were right when they declared this to be an inadequate system of religious education.

At the same time, these theoretical confines in British and Foreign schools were not necessarily observed in practice. Sometimes, 'through fear of *giving too much* instruction', teachers gave '*too little explanation*', but the reverse could also happen. James Bonwick, educated and trained as a teacher in schools run on these principles in England, maintained that the masters were 'very unconfined' in reality and that religious instruction had been much extended 'in recent years' (this was in 1845), although debatable subjects were usually avoided. He himself 'would teach . . . the doctrine of the Trinity, the Atonement and Justification, but . . . would not explain . . . the Sacraments, or put any question concerning them'.[8] Faced with the curiosity of the child, and anxious to spread the gospel, a British and Foreign master would often go beyond the standard questions when he thought it desirable and safe to do so. In the modified form of the system operating in Van Diemen's Land after 1839 there was no need for a teacher to go beyond the law, since special instruction by ministers was permitted, and *The Faith and Duty of a Christian* was provided for general use. The latter contained very leading questions and was practically a catechism. Selected texts were arranged under headings such as Religion, God, Church, Christ, Baptism, Redemption, Duty, Reward and Punishments, and the questions included, 'Doth baptism engage to newness of life?', 'What constitutes the unity of the Church?', 'Hath Christ promised to be present in his Church?' and 'Did Christ command the wine also to be received?'.[9] These were questions of a very

[5] Report of the Board of Education, Appendix E, *V. & P.* (V.D.L.) 1840.
[6] W. Dry, *Sermons* (Launceston, 1850), p. 82.
[7] *The Speech of the Lord Bishop of Australia in the Legislative Council . . . August, 1839* (Sydney, n.d.), p. 22.
[8] Report of V.D.L. Education Commissioners, 23 May 1845, G.O. 33/51, pp. 600, 1060, 1065-6 (TA).
[9] *The Faith and Duty of a Christian . . .* (Hobart, 1851), pp. 34-7. The verses pre-

different order from 'Who are to seek? Whom are we to seek? When are we to seek?'. Since this book was the original product of the Anglican Bishop Gastrel and the S.P.C.K., the staunchest Anglican critics of the system actually operating in Van Diemen's Land were not justified in condemning it as roundly as they did.

There were deeper reasons why all general systems were opposed by so many of the clergy. They held their fundamental beliefs to be tremendous certainties from which it was perilous, indeed sinful, to waver; and they were therefore more inclined to break than to bend before the inevitable restriction of doctrinal teaching in general systems. The fight for the faith, the whole faith, and nothing but the faith, seemed particularly desperate at that time. They feared the influence of the Enlightenment, which encouraged the repudiation of Christian dogma, the glorification of human reason and the toleration of whatever vaguer forms of religion survived as being reasonable. The Englishman, Tom Paine, had not only his scorn for revealed religion but also his disciples, and so had many another enemy of orthodox religion—or of the established Church of England, which came to the same thing in the eyes of many clergymen belonging to that Church. Liberalism, Utilitarianism, Radicalism, Dissent and the practical difficulties in the new industrial cities of England all seemed to be placing the Anglican Church in jeopardy; and some of them threatened the survival of Christianity itself. The Anglican clergymen were particularly apprehensive, in Australia no less than at home, for their privileged position made them all the more acutely aware of the shaking of the Church in France by the combined effects of the Enlightenment and the French Revolution, and the continued rumblings of revolution over Europe. The French Revolution was recalled as 'a convulsion in which all that was venerable, and virtuous, and holy, seemed about to be swept away before the torrent of anarchy and infidelity', and the persistent troubles on the Continent were regarded as 'powerful proofs of the fearful mischiefs arising from education without a due regard for Divine Revelation, and the inculcation of religious principles'. The Anglicans wanted to protect Australia from this very thing. An Evangelical, the Reverend W. B. Clarke, believed that experiments in education were 'experiments in morality', and that the ignorance and vice of the convict population made Australia 'the very last country' in which they should be allowed. His high church bishop agreed, and declared that the popular notion of 'no privileges' would not be directed against the Church of England alone, but, unless checked, would be pushed for-

ceding these four questions were Romans 6:4, Ephesians 4:4-6, Matthew 18:20, 1 Corinthians 11:25.

ward until there was no Church or religion in Australia.[10] Though the other denominations contributed to Anglican difficulties, they shared many of the wider fears, and some were inclined to agree that the exclusion of controversial doctrine from the schools could mean the exclusion of crucial doctrine. Many people, in most of the Churches, expected that vagueness, indifference and scepticism would follow the introduction of educational systems in which religious teaching was marginal. John McKenny, the Wesleyan, maintained that denominational schools were essential 'if religion were not to be thrown overboard'. 'Catholicus' warned that 'neutrality and scepticism go hand in hand', and a Catholic petition insisted that no system 'should be introduced which would, in any way, interfere with the sacred and inalienable rights of parents and pastors to impart religious instruction to their children'.[11]

Robert Lowe, as chairman of the Select Committee on Education in New South Wales, posed the key question from the other, more secular side. 'Why', he asked, 'is it necessary that religion should be coupled with the art of reading, when nobody considers it necessary that it should be coupled with the art of shoemaking?'[12] W. A. Duncan, a member of the board of education, put the same point of view positively.

> Religious truth is as much a part of education, undoubtedly, as grammar or geography. But it does not follow that they are both to be taught at the same hour, or by the same person . . . it does not follow that the art of *crochet* and the science of *crochets* are to be taught by the same individual, or at the same hour.[13]

Though these were examples of a point of view well put, the churchmen had a point which was quite as sharp. The foundations of the child's later life were laid at the elementary school stage: teach him there, not only to read, but to read the right books with the right approach, and he would be prepared for life, whether he became a shoemaker, a master of the science of crochets, or even the chairman of a select committee of the Legislative Council. In and by itself, the ability to read need only assist spiritual decline. As the Reverend John McGarvie, of the Presbyterian Church, saw it, men were already 'less energetic for Religion' than they had been in the previous century:

[10] H. T. Stiles, *A Sermon, Preached at St. Matthew's Church, Windsor . . . 18 June 1845 . . .* (Sydney, 1845), p. 9; *Report of St. Philip's Parochial Association . . .* (Sydney, 1850), p. 5; *S.P.G. Report* (N.S.W.), 1840, p. 13; W. G. Broughton, op. cit., pp. 12-13.
[11] *Herald*, 11 September 1844, p. 2; 'Catholicus', *An Original Essay on Popular Education . . .* (Sydney, 1848), p. 9; Petition of the Rev. J. T. Lynch . . . , *V. & P.* (N.S.W.), 1844, vol. 1. [12] Lowe Committee, Evidence, p. 35.
[13] W. A. Duncan, op. cit., pp. 10-11.

'Then the Church and pulpit were the vehicles of knowledge, now it is the daily Press. . . . They hear one Sermon, but read six newspapers weekly, the Bible never'.[14] Furthermore, a teacher was not satisfactory just because he could give a formally correct lesson in anything, even in doctrine; he ought also to be a man who would exert a good personal influence on the pupils.[15]

It was not that the clergy were opposed to education. Broughton, Clarke and McGarvie, no less than Lowe, were university graduates, and, like Lowe, McGarvie wrote newspaper editorials. It was a question of emphasis and of the overriding purpose. The Reverend Robert Allwood, also a graduate, was not opposed to educating the lower-class children when asked if he did not think it 'a fearful thing for the rising generation to grow up without education'; what he said was something different: 'If by this question is meant secular instruction, I would say that it is a far more dreadful thing for them to grow up without religion.'[16] Bishop Broughton would have been ashamed to think that the study of natural science was inconsistent with a man's being religious, but insisted that such studies, in themselves, could never be a substitute for revealed religion or lead men to the most important truth of all.[17] On a more prosaic level, Clarke said, 'Instruction, without a proper religious balance, . . . can never fit a man for such a conduct and bearing in life, as shall make him . . . even an honest tradesman in the moment of commercial temptation'.[18] It was, therefore, something other than obscurantism which caused the clergy and their lay supporters to make difficulties over one educational scheme after another. They were fighting for their faiths, for the power to instruct the young in the way of salvation, and against the tendency of the community to place literacy before devotion. So, at any rate, it seemed to them.

Despite the churchmen's fears for the future of religion, no one who entered the debate on schools spoke avowedly as an unbeliever. 'Let it not be supposed,' wrote one Catholic lay champion of the Irish system, 'that by the separation of religious from secular and moral instruction, it was part of the plan that religious and moral instruction be neglected or excluded.'[19] Thomas Gregson, proposing that education 'merely of a secular character' be given in public schools in Van Diemen's Land, protested that it was only the fact

[14] J. McGarvie, Diary, 4 January 1843 (MS. ML).
[15] Lowe Committee, Evidence, pp. 44-5.　　　　[16] Ibid., p. 12.
[17] *Church of England Book Society Report* (Sydney, 1841), pp. 17-18.
[18] *S.P.G. Report* (N.S.W.), 1840, p. 12.
[19] R. Therry, *Reminiscences of Thirty Years' Residence in New South Wales . . . .* (London, 1863), p. 157.

that the colony was so divided by religion which forced him to suggest leaving religious teaching to parents and ministers.[20] 'I am not an indifferentist on this subject', declared W. A. Duncan, speaking as a Catholic, 'my creed is longer, I believe, than the creeds of most of you.'[21] Robert Lowe insisted that he did not want children 'to be brought up irreligiously'; he only wanted to keep religious creeds out of the teaching of reading, writing and arithmetic, so that the colony's schools could be as open to all as were the colony's roads.[22] The common point at issue was whether or not a reasonable religious education could be given without having a multiplicity of denominational schools.

The men who advocated one comprehensive system maintained that this was the only way to get education to the colonies' children, anyway. Separate denominational schools in every community would be absurd, impossible to staff and prohibitively expensive. Surely, they argued, it was better to unite in achieving what was practicable than to insist upon pursuing an ultimately unattainable objective. John Robinson, a Quaker member of the Select Committee on education in New South Wales, followed this practical line in the course of cross-examining Bishop Broughton.

Robinson: Do you think it is possible to expect practical religion from any man not in a position to read his Bible?
Broughton: Yes; I should say that some of the best men I have ever known, so far as practical religion went, were among the old peasantry of England, who could not read their Bible.
Robinson: Did they reside in the neighbourhood of a church?
Broughton: Yes, close to a church, and under constant charge of the clergyman.
Robinson: Supposing a man to be two hundred miles from a church?
Broughton: Then, thinking as I do, that the teaching of the Church is necessary, he must be in a very embarrassing situation, to say the least.
Robinson: Do you not think it would be an advantage to such a person to be able to read?
Broughton: Yes; still I do not think merely reading the Bible would teach him religion, in any sense of the word, if he had no other source of instruction.
Robinson: Do you not think a higher power would assist him?
Broughton: That power would assist him only as he used proper means.[23]

It might be pardonable to call Robinson the realist, even if he did

[20] *Speech of Thomas George Gregson in the Legislative Council, on the State of Public Education* . . . (Hobart, 1850), pp. vii-viii.
[21] W. A. Duncan, op. cit., p. 10.　　　　[22] *Herald*, 10 October 1846, p. 2.
[23] Lowe Committee, Evidence, p. 87.

have the advantage, over Broughton, of his uncomplicated Quaker creed and practice. The ideal might have been for all the colonists to be Protestants, or Anglicans, or Quakers; but they were not. The ideal might have been for the State to pay for four denominational schools and four teachers where one would do from the point of view of teaching the Three R's and some broad religious knowledge; but this was an impossibility. The ideal might have been for no colonist to move farther out than the Churches could reach him and instruct his children; but squatters and shepherds did not act in this way. In the difficulties of the actual situation, the State was ready to offer a system of education which could embrace as many children as possible by giving general instruction and as much religious teaching as the Churches could agree upon. This was a reasonable offer when there were a variety of denominations, so many nominal Christians, and such a problem of illiteracy among both old and young in the colonies. It was also reasonable for Robinson to argue that, if a man were deprived of much religious exercise and consolation, it was better for him to be able to read his Bible (and catechism and prayer book) than to be unable to read. None other than Archbishop Polding remarked that 'it would be a very erroneous argument to contend that only those who attended divine worship were imbued with the principles of religion'.[24] Broughton himself had pleaded with isolated settlers to maintain the practice of family prayers if nothing else were possible,[25] and the bishop was being perverse before the Select Committee in the hope of obstructing one system to secure another. He and his clergy were unduly stubborn and were thereby led into actions which rather belied their words. The Anglican clergy were very slow to admit that, as soon as Dissenters and Catholics had been granted equality as citizens, they themselves no longer had the right to control the State schools. They spoke of their vows to instruct the young in the creeds and articles of the Church of England, yet left themselves open to severe criticism, in Van Diemen's Land particularly, by refusing for years to attend the board schools to instruct the Anglican children in them. They felt that they were forced to offer this sacrifice to stave off even greater loss, but it is highly questionable if their desperate decision was either necessary or realistic. After all their splashing attempts to swim against the tide of popular opinion, they eventually turned to swim with the current, wearier and farther behind than they might have been.

[24] *Herald*, 10 September 1844, p. 3.
[25] Broughton to a private friend in England, 17 February 1846, *H.R.A.*, xxiv, p. 783.

Even their cherished schools could scarcely be called successful. The denominational theory was immensely hard to practise, for church schools shared with State schools the shortage of teachers, the typical incompetence of teachers, the squalid condition of school buildings, the shortage of equipment and the irregular attendance of children. The denominational schools were not shining examples of what schools ought to be, but simply helped to perpetuate and extend the general muddle. School books provide a good example of the confusion. All over the colonies all sorts of books were used in all sorts of schools; parents chose the books which were the cheapest; all books were in short supply, and few schools had a complete set of any series. The result was 'that the variety of books brought to school by the pupils was so great that it often disorganized the work of the teacher and paralyzed completely any attempt at the simultaneous method'. This was something which would not have happened under one general system. The church schools could not even justify their part in this confusion by claiming that their books were better in any way. One series of books used in some Catholic schools was 'expensive, and in many ways unsuited for use in Australia'.[26] The books produced for Anglican schools were, in the opinion of Commissioner Wilkins, 'decidedly the worst series of School-books used in the colony'.[27] Comparison of an ancient history book written for Wesleyan schools with a geography book compiled by James Bonwick, the British and Foreign system man, reveals no more religious teaching in the former than in the latter; the Old Testament material in the one was not in the least evangelical, and the geography of the other included the early conversions to Catholicism in Japan, the refusal of government aid for religion in the United States of America, and the assertion that the 'Christian religion teaches us that it is only by the merits of Christ our Saviour, that we can hope for heaven'.[28] Indeed, it was to the books of the despised Irish system that the church schools often turned—either wholly or in part. In Victoria the Denominational School Board bought Irish system books from the National School Board for use in its own schools, and Catholic schools in New South Wales and British and Foreign schools in Van Diemen's Land also used them. Even a reader specially printed for Catholic schools in Sydney drew much of its material from the Irish system

[26] R. Fogarty, *Catholic Education in Australia, 1806-1950* (Melbourne, 1959), I, p. 104.
[27] A. G. Austin, *Australian Education, 1788-1900* (Melbourne, 1961) p. 57.
[28] W. B. Boyce, *A Brief Grammar of Ancient History, for the Use of Schools*, printed for the Wesleyan Committee of Education (Sydney, 1850); J. Bonwick, *Geography for the Use of Australian Youth* (Hobart, 1849).

books, including the 'Hymn to the B.V. Mary' written by the Protestant, though ardent Tractarian, John Keble.[29]

The plain fact of the matter was that denominational schools often taught very little, if any more religion than the State schools. It sounded well to report of Anglican schools in Van Diemen's Land that the Bible was read in every school, and that examinations were frequently held in the school room by the local clergyman, or occasionally after prayers in the neighbouring church, at which 'in some localities' the children attended one or two mornings in the week.[30] But this was vague, and the vagueness was emphasized by the phrase 'in some localities'. One of the arguments against the Irish system was that the insufficiency of clergymen prevented them from taking the opportunities to give religious instruction, and one of the objections to relying on Sunday schools to teach specifically denominational points of view was that the clergy were too busy to attend them; so it is very unlikely that the ministers were constant and effective visitors to many of their schools. The idyllic claims are suspect; and so are the teaching methods in Anglican schools, where children might be taught to memorize the order of the books of the New Testament by means of this jingle:

> Read the Gospels and the Acts,
> If you want to know the facts,
> Rom—Cor—Cor—Gal—Ephe—
> Phil—Col—Thess—Thessalee—
> Tim—Tim—Ti—Philemon—
> Hebrews—Jacobus—Pet—Pet—John—
> John—John—Ju—Revelation.[31]

Even the time allotted to religious instruction in the denominational schools was not significantly longer than in the general system schools. Government schools in New South Wales gave instruction for twenty-eight hours each week, of which five were devoted to religious instruction.[32] The St James' Model School (Anglican) allowed about four hours each week for Bible reading, collect learning and so on, and about two hours for prayers and singing.[33] In Catholic schools,

---

[29] *The Second Reading Book . . . .* published under the direction of His Grace the Archbishop of Sydney (Sydney, 1850); *Herald*, 9 September 1844 (Supplement).
[30] Report of Board of Education, *V. & P.* (V.D.L.), 1848.
[31] L. S. Bethell, 'The Development of Education in Northern Tasmania', *Papers and Proceedings, Tasmanian Historical Research Association*, vol. 3, May 1954, p. 30.
[32] Secretary of Board to Teachers, 1 March 1851, Appendix F, *Regulations for the Establishment and Conduct of National Schools in N.S.W.* (Sydney, 1853).
[33] *Rules for the Church of England Schools of the Middle District* (Sydney, 1853). The introductory note is dated 31 January 1850.

only about four or five hours a week were allocated to religious exercises and instruction.[34] Although particular tenets might have been taught, and frequent brief recollections encouraged, in the church schools, the general practice and actual achievement do not support the idea that the denominational schools were any more effective than schools run on the Irish—or some other—general system. The unfavourable verdict passed in 1835 on the Hobart school visited each week by the Anglican Rural Dean—that the standard of religious knowledge was not very high[35]—remained the typical verdict passed on the standard of Christian teaching in the schools generally in the middle of the century. Inspector Thomas Arnold could not find much knowledge of the Bible among school children anywhere in Van Diemen's Land in 1851 (though nearly all of them were in Anglican schools), and he reported that religious instruction usually consisted of memorizing catechism, prayers and hymns. In New South Wales, in 1856, William Wilkins reported a 'deplorable' ignorance of religion in the schools; both he and G. W. Rusden found that the catechisms were taught but not explained, and that consequently 'even the modicum learned was generally . . . not understood at all'. They were quite convinced that the State schools gave as much religious instruction as the denominational schools.[36]

The denominationalists had, therefore, a fine theory that they could not practise. It is more than likely that the Churches would have achieved greater success in promoting Christian teaching if they had pooled their resources with the Governments in the mid-thirties and had entered wholeheartedly into a general system which allowed considerable scope for religious instruction. As it was, met all along the line with the Churches' intractability, and witnessing the Churches' own failures to handle their schools well, the Governments naturally lost patience with the strict denominationalists and became less sympathetic towards including religion in the schools' curricula. Present difficulties with religious instruction in Australian State schools are largely the result of the failure to develop a co-operative and well integrated system then.

The Role of Sunday Schools

Sunday schools today are devoted entirely to religious teaching, but many of the nineteenth-century Sunday schools in England and Wales (though not usually in Scotland) taught reading as well. In 1835, for

[34] Regulations for Catholic Schools, 1848, R. Fogarty, op. cit., II, pp. 490-1.
[35] C.S.O. 1/843/17847 (TA).
[36] A. G. Austin, op. cit., pp. 56-7; R. Fogarty, op. cit., I, pp. 116-17.

instance, most of the eighty-six Sunday schools in Manchester were prepared to teach their scholars to read, while ten taught writing and three offered courses in arithmetic. In addition, thirty-nine of them had evening schools associated with them in which the Three R's were taught.[37] For many of the working classes, in fact, Sunday schools were 'the only instrument for the education of the Children . . . in universal use'.[38] This double aim of teaching reading as well as religion was sometimes continued in the colonies, and made the Sunday schools doubly relevant to the question of education in colonial Australia. The Reverend Richard Johnson spoke of teaching on Sundays as early as 1793 on the grounds that many in New South Wales knew 'not a letter in the Alphabet'. In 1813 the Independent missionary, W. P. Crook, used to ride out from Sydney ten miles every Sunday morning to teach eight or ten children to write. A correspondent in the *Sydney Gazette* in 1815 urged the need for Sunday schools in the colony so that people could be taught to read and thus enabled to study the Bible, and in that year the New South Wales Sunday School Institution was established, under the direction of Wesleyans and Independents, whose Sunday schools flourished and spread, at first with the assistance of the Anglican clergy, but soon in rivalry with Church of England Sunday schools.[39] As the Sunday schools developed they continued to pay some attention to teaching children to read.

In 1846 a Sydney Wesleyan Sunday school reported its need of twenty-five 'first spelling books',[40] and it was not alone in this, for Peter Steel, a private schoolmaster in Sydney, had said a couple of years earlier:

> The method of conducting Sunday Schools in this Colony is very inefficient, the time of the masters being completely frittered away in giving elementary knowledge to the scholars in place of religious instruction; in fact, teaching them to read a spelling book in preference to communicating a saving knowledge of the Book of life.[41]

Wesleyan records in Van Diemen's Land include references to 'the knowledge of letters', 'literary welfare' and bills for 'alphabet boards', and their Sunday schools were paid a fine tribute in this regard by Elliston's *Almanack*, which said that the good they had done was 'almost incalculable'.[42] The Independent Sunday school at Port Fenton

[37] *P.P.* (H.C.), 1835, vol. VII, p. 870.   [38] Ibid., 1843, vol. XIII, p. 477.
[39] V. W. E. Goodin, 'Public Education in New South Wales before 1848', *J.R.A.H.S.*, vol. 36, part iii, pp. 160-2.
[40] Minute Book of the York St Sunday School Teachers' Committee, 1846-50, Report for Quarter ended 31 December 1846 (ML).   [41] Lowe Committee, Evidence, p. 62.
[42] *Proceedings of . . . the Hobart Town Wesleyan Sunday School Union . . .* (Hobart, 1834), pp. 3, 15; ibid., 1846, p. 4; Elliston's *Hobart Town Almanack . . .* (1837), p. 87.

in 1845 was the only school of any description in the district, and in 1850 the establishment of a Presbyterian Sunday school near Evandale was commented upon thus:

> The children in such cases are too far from a township to attend week-day school, and the parents too poor to board them away from home. So that any knowledge they possess, not only with respect to religion, but even the elementary acquisition of reading and writing, will in all probability have been communicated to them at these Branch Schools, up to the time of their leaving the parental roof.[43]

Most of the Sunday schools, too, had libraries from which the scholars could borrow books, and must have done much to develop reading skills, and the powers of retention and of expression, by their insistence upon reading and memorizing hymns, scripture and catechism, for which—as in Tom Sawyer's Sunday school—they sometimes had a ticket system which led on to a prize.[44] Whatever may be said in criticism of the Churches for obstructing elementary education, in their Sunday schools they pushed it on a little.

Peter Steel, however, had exaggerated the position. Religious instruction rather than the teaching of reading was most prominent in colonial Sunday schools. In regulations for the Sunday schools of Sydney Presbyterians (1835), Hobart Independents (1845) and Hobart Wesleyans (1839), and in the Launceston Independents' *Address to Parents* (1837), there was no mention of any instruction other than in religion. The real emphasis was revealed, in a grand manner, by a Methodist intention 'gratuitously to communicate Christian instruction to children of all denominations'.[45] It was as a means for providing the denominational teaching excluded from the day schools, not for the sake of the Three R's, or even one of them, that the Governments valued the Sunday schools and voted them some financial assistance at various times.[46]

Here again the Anglicans were the main stumbling block. As well as stubbornly refusing to surrender gracefully the day schools, they were disinclined to develop vigorous Sunday schools in many places. Within their communion the Sunday school tradition was not uni-

---

[43] *Fourth Annual Report of V.D.L. Sunday School Union* (Hobart, 1846), p. 7; ibid. (1851), p. 9.
[44] Minutes of Sunday School Committee, 1830-42, 13 August 1830 (Wesley Church, Hobart).
[45] *General Rules of the Wesleyan Methodist Sunday Schools in the Hobart Town Circuit* (Hobart, 1839), p. 1.
[46] *Hobart Town Gazette*, 10 May 1839, p. 472; Report of Board of Education, *V. & P.* (V.D.L.), 1842; ibid., 1845; N.S.W. Col. Sec. to McKenny, 8 June, 14 July 1837, C.S.O.L. 4/3618 (ML).

versally strong,[47] and many Anglicans were therefore scornful of suggestions that Sunday schools could make up any ground lost in the day schools. As the board of education in Van Diemen's Land once put it, the Anglicans resented this suggestion because there were

> comparatively *few Sunday Schools in existence in connexion with their Church.* In *Hobart Town,* where the population is in great measure of the Church of England, there is but *one* Church of England Sunday School, at which about 60 children attend; while of other denominations there are several Schools, with an attendance of upwards of 1000 children. In the Interior the disproportion is even greater.[48]

Anglican excuses were not convincing. If there were more Dissenting ministers than Anglican clergymen in Hobart, and the latter had heavier parochial duties among more parishioners—which was one explanation offered from the Anglican side[49]—there should have been more teachers and scholars for the Anglicans; the laymen, not the ministers, conducted the Sunday schools and built them up, as is indicated by the minute, 'Unanimously agreed that each Teacher shall bring three new Scholars by next Sunday'.[50] But this was in a Methodist Sunday school; the Anglicans were all too indifferent about this means of helping the children of the colonies, a fact which Bishop Nixon admitted in urging his people in 1846 not to be any longer outdone by other denominations in establishing Sunday schools.[51] The common Anglican attitude to Sunday schools was unfortunate, and, since they managed to provide no permanent substitute, the religious and secular education of the children was thereby hindered, not advanced.

Over the years the influence of the colonies' Sunday schools on the manners and outlook of young people must have been considerable. It is tempting to add them to the list of suggested factors which produced the striking increase in sobriety and morality among the early generations of Australian-born compared with their parents.[52] Visitors to Sydney on behalf of the London Missionary Society attended the Reverend Samuel Marsden's annual examination of the Parramatta

---

[47] While the total number of Anglican Sunday schools and scholars was probably greater than the Dissenters' in England as a whole, in many places the Church of England was far behind. See *P.P.* (H.C.), 1835, vol. XLIII, p. 399; ibid., 1843, vol. XIV, pp. 140, 231, 221.

[48] *Examiner,* 25 November 1843, p. 741 (quoting the Report of the Board of Education).

[49] Report of V.D.L. Education Commissioners, 23 May 1845, G.O. 33/51, p. 1003 (TA).

[50] Minute Book of the York St Sunday School Teachers' Committee, 1846-50, 9 November 1846 (ML).

[51] F. R. Nixon, *A Charge delivered to the Clergy . . . April xxiii, MDCCCXLVI* (London, 2nd ed., 1848), p. 32.

[52] See K. Macnab and R. Ward, 'The Nature and Nurture of the First Generation of Native-born Australians', *Historical Studies,* vol. 10, no. 39, pp. 289-308.

Sunday school scholars in 1824. (As an Evangelical, Marsden took more naturally to the Sunday school movement than many Anglicans did.) The visitors were deeply impressed by the attitude and knowledge of the one hundred 'scions of wild stocks' who were present, reporting that many of them were ashamed of their parents, and wept over their ways, while only one '*young* man' in Parramatta was known to be a drunkard.[53] Sixteen years later, the Parramatta Wesleyans noted that those who were on trial for membership of their Church were principally young persons born in the colony, and that these bade fair to have exemplary characters.[54] However, a direct and definite connection between Church and Sunday school influence and the improved behaviour of the native-born cannot be made with any certainty. Puzzled temperance society members in Van Diemen's Land, for instance, decided that the native-born must be 'constitutionally temperate', due to 'some physical cause', for most of them had almost no religious and moral training.[55] Then, too, if something like thirty per cent of Van Diemen's Land children between the ages of two and thirteen were enrolled at Sunday schools in the late forties,[56] as much—and more—can be claimed for the youth of England. By 1833 the number of Sunday school scholars in England and Wales was over one and a half millions, having trebled since 1820, though the population had increased only by about sixteen per cent. There was, therefore, a surprisingly large— and an increasing—enrolment of children at the English and Welsh Sunday schools in the second quarter of the nineteenth century.[57] How much the great expansion of the Sunday schools was an effect, and how much it was a cause, of the growing religious seriousness in Britain in the second quarter of the nineteenth century is a matter for conjecture. Just what influence the Sunday schools in the colonies had on the children is equally unsure. Yet it is quite certain that very few in the first fleet would ever have been to a Sunday school; and it is at least worth pondering upon a section of a colonial Wesleyan Sunday school report, which read:

> By Sabbath School efforts many children are instructed who would be spending the Sabbath-day in idleness and mischief, in dirt and rags . . . [They] come clean and neat to school, and are saved from vicious com-

---

[53] J. Montgomery (ed.), *Journal of Voyages and Travels by the Rev. Daniel Tyerman and George Bennet, Esq.,* . . . (London, 1831), II, p. 167.
[54] N.S.W. Wes. Dist. Min., 1840, Appendix 1.
[55] *Report of the V.D.L. Temperance Society* (Hobart, 1837), pp. 17-18.
[56] Estimated roughly from the 1848 census and from the list of enrolments at Sunday schools (1845) in G.O. 33/51, pp. 547-8 (TA).
[57] *P.P.* (H.C.), 1820, vol. XII, p. 341; ibid., 1835, vol. XLIII, p. 399; ibid., 1843, vol. XIV, p. 755. The reports spoke specifically of 'children'; they did not use a term which could have included adults.

panions—many, whose parents care not for their souls, are taught to regard the Lord's day—to attend the house of prayer, to respect the Word of God, and to love the people of God. Many are learning our Catechisms, and . . . may be able to resist the pernicious errors which are springing up around us.[58]

What is least questionable is that the Churches and churchmen who were lukewarm about Sunday schools, and hotly opposed to general-system day schools, actually hindered the cause of religion. Their ideals did not grip the imaginations or inspire the loyalties of enough colonists, and their positive campaigns had finally negative results. The Sunday school men were at least building something permanent, for the people generally responded to their efforts, and Sunday schools long remained popular with families who were associated very little with any other aspect of Church life.

[58] *Proceedings of . . . Annual Meeting of the Wesleyan Sunday Schools, in the Hobart Town Circuit* (Hobart, 1851), p. 5.

SCHOOLS FOR THE HUMBLER CLASSES

COLONIAL JACK may not have tipped his hat to his master as carefully as he may have done in the homeland, but he certainly had, and knew that he had, his social superiors. The Australian colonies were not the egalitarian societies often developed in the American frontier areas, but were always communities in which the class distinctions were maintained. The Churches, especially the most powerful of them all, the Church of England, were naturally geared to the prevailing class structures; and this told against them in their attempts to evangelize the masses through the schools.

Nothing less than the conversion of the children of the poor was the Churches' aim in coming into the education fight. Nothing more could be their aim: for the public elementary schools in the colonies were intended, by and large, for the labouring classes. The wealthier were expected to use private tutors and private schools, not the developing State school system, for their children's education. 'It is to be remembered,' Sir Richard Bourke had said, 'that the National Schools are intended for the great mass of the people requiring gratuitous instruction'.[1] Years later, a Van Diemen's Land committee on convict expenditure still insisted that the chief object of the elementary schools was 'to provide instruction for the destitute children of Convicts, or the offspring of those who have been Convicts', and added, with a basis of truth beneath the exaggeration:

> The children of the free participate, but only to a limited extent. The depauperated condition of the emigrant labourer, occasioned by Convict competition, has caused an increase of expenditure under this head.[2]

All this applied as much to the denominational schools, fully supported or subsidized by the State, as to the State schools proper. In 1841 the New South Wales Government issued regulations for church schools in which it was laid down that the 'first duty' of inspectors was to find out which pupils did not need government assistance. The new regulations were issued precisely because the authorities thought of the schools as being provided for the lower classes and disapproved of them

[1] Minute on Estimates, *V. & P.* (N.S.W.), 1836.   [2] *V. & P.* (V.D.L.), 1848.

being used by parents who could afford to educate their children elsewhere, or at least without calling upon a subsidy towards tuition fees.[3] The point needs emphasis, for it can easily be overlooked: the fight over the schools was fundamentally a fight for the working classes.

Churches, Governments, upper-class citizens and newspapers were overwhelmingly of the opinion that the children of the working classes should be made literate. 'Let it not be supposed that I would withhold instruction in sound, secular knowledge, where I had not the power of accompanying it with religious instruction,' said Archdeacon Hutchins, in making the point that his Church did have that power and that the State should preserve it.[4] Sir William Denison supported one of his proposals with the argument that persons in the upper classes of colonial society would benefit by having better educated servants; his Colonial Secretary spoke of the exploded fallacy that education for all was dangerous to the State; and his Attorney-General brusquely agreed—the children must be educated.[5] A writer to a Sydney paper expressed such a common belief when he said that every child had a right to knowledge, that the New South Wales Select Committee on education found it unnecessary even to discuss secular education: there was no question about that.[6] The only protest came from the churchmen who warned that purely secular education, without adequate religious instruction, would lead to wickedness and anarchy; and this was not a rejection of popular education.

The undesirable element, the patronage which could stick in the gullets of the poor who resented their position, came out clearly in an editorial which argued both for popular and for religious teaching on the preciously pious grounds that a scriptural education

> inculcates patient endurance, and in the occupation of the more humble walks of life, affords such food for the mind as will beguile the tedious hours, and teach us [sic!] to seek refuge in higher contemplation, smiling at the vanities and empty glories of this world, as transitory, and not in any way connected with intrinsic happiness.[7]

In so far as such attitudes were common, were maintained in the face of nascent ideas of social equality and social reform, and were reflected in the lives of the Churches and their clergy, they militated against the Churches' educational efforts being appreciated by the people.

[3] Enclosure, Gipps to Stanley, 17 December 1842, *H.R.A.*, XXII, p. 428; Enclosure No. 2, Gipps to Stanley, 8 May 1847, ibid., XXIV, pp. 337-8.
[4] W. Hutchins, *A Letter on the School Question* . . . (Hobart, 1839), p. 8.
[5] Minute on Education, *V. & P.* (V.D.L.), 1848; *Courier*, 22 March 1848, p. 2.
[6] *Herald*, 16 June 1836, p. 2; Lowe Committee, p. 3.
[7] *Courier*, 6 April 1838, p. 2.

This was, in fact, the situation. The Churches, in fighting for schools in which an ideal religious education was given, were not fighting for schools in which an ideal social equality was practised. The boys at the two Hobart schools under Anglican oversight in 1835, for instance, were the sons 'principally of petty Shopkeepers, Mechanics, Laborers [*sic*] and Publicans—and some . . . Convicts holding Tickets of Leave'. Far from these mingling with scions of grander families, the marked character of the provincial dialect of Mr Jones and his son, the teachers at the better of these two schools, rendered them 'ineligible for the tuition of boys from a higher sphere'.[8] When government schools were attended by children of the wealthier classes, as happened on occasion, the children of the poor tended to be excluded. In Van Diemen's Land, at Richmond, Clarence Plains and Greenponds, the masters were accused of wanting their schools 'respectable', and the middle classes of preventing lower-class children from mixing with their own, so that the State schools were turned into 'classical academies' and even received boarders.[9] One way or another the children of disparate social groups were kept apart for their schooling. And the children of the clergy themselves did not usually go to the schools about which their fathers had so much to say.

The way the young colonial gentlemen were educated (unless, or until, they were sent home to England) may be illustrated by the schooling of James Hassall in the thirties. A grandson of Samuel Marsden, and son of the Reverend Thomas Hassall, young James went to the King's School, Parramatta, with boys bearing such proud colonial names as Blaxland, Nicholson, Oxley, Antill, Suttor and Macarthur. After several years there, he was taught at home by a governess and a tutor. Later still, he went as a boarder to a school opened at Mulgoa by the Reverend Thomas Makinson. Once more the scholars consisted of boys such as the sons of the land-owning Cox family and the grandsons of the former Governor King. After a time, another change was made, Hassall going as a resident pupil, together with two Nortons, two Oxleys and G. F. Macarthur, to the home of the Reverend Robert Forrest, newly appointed incumbent of Campbelltown and Narellan. Each pupil was charged £100 a year by Forrest, who managed by this means to feed himself, and them, as they might have been fed 'at any gentleman's table', being always provided with 'wine and other luxuries'.[10]

By the late forties the colonial upper and upper-middle classes were

---

[8] Report of Board of Inquiry . . . 1835, C.S.O. 1/843/17847 (TA).
[9] *Courier*, 5 September 1849, p. 3.
[10] J. S. Hassall, *In Old Australia* . . . (Brisbane, 1902), pp. 13-14, 25-6, 41.

very well served by schools established with their children in mind. No longer was it necessary for prosperous settlers living away from Hobart—the Brodribbs, Thrupps and Buxtons—to use the government orphanages as substitute boarding schools![11] There were the Hutchins' School in Hobart and the Launceston Church Grammar School (and, as finishing schools, the Hobart High School and Christ's College). In New South Wales there were the Sydney College and the Australian College, as well as the King's School at Parramatta, and the first of these—considered the best of the three—was teaching no less than two hundred and six students in 1845. On the opening day of the Hutchins' School, there were enrolled the sons of the Attorney-General, of the Senior Colonial Surgeon and of other surgeons, army officers and landowners, thus indicating for whom this school was intended.[12] The King's School was not ultra-exclusive (and the cost was only £28 per annum), so that James Macarthur could describe it as a place where 'the children of the middling classes as well as of the most respectable families' received an education, and in 'middling' he included 'tradespeople'. But there was still the distinction, the lower limit, which was made specially clear in Macarthur's further remark that respectable colonists did not like sending their children to school in Sydney because it was 'a sea-port town' and the inhabitants were 'to a great extent emancipated convicts of low character'.[13] The same class distinction was revealed in the comment of Port Phillip Anglicans that, 'with the exception of the Grammar School adjoining St Peter's Church, which was erected with money from England, and is intended for boys of a different class, there is as yet in all Melbourne only two school buildings belonging to the Church of England'.[14] Supplementing the bigger and most prominent schools were the private academies— Cape's in Sydney, Woolls' in Parramatta, the school for young ladies run by the Misses Deane in Sydney, and many other small educational ventures which sprang up in both colonies. Their importance is indicated by the enrolment figures. There were probably little under five thousand pupils in private schools in New South Wales, compared with considerably less than eight thousand in the denominational and State schools, in 1844.[15] In Van Diemen's Land in 1848 there were well over two thousand pupils in the hundred or more private schools, and only about three thousand scholars in the sixty-five government and

[11] Statements of Sums due for the Maintenance and Education of Boys and Girls not on the Foundation at the Orphan Establishments, 31 December 1830, C.S.O. 1/122/3073 (TA).
[12] The Hutchins' School Register of Admissions, August 1846-April 1892 (TA).
[13] Select Committee on Transportation, *P.P.* (H.C.), 1837, vol. XIX, p. 181.
[14] *First Report of Melbourne Diocesan Society*, 1849, p. 15.
[15] Lowe Committee, p. i.

church schools.[16] All the private schools were not highly respectable; in fact, they contributed their share to the 'Fagan system' schools, from which a child might return saying, 'We have got a holiday; my mistress is drunk, and my master is gone to the treadmill'.[17] Many of them, too, were short-lived and otherwise unsatisfactory. Yet, in many others, middle-class children gained a reasonable commercial education, and upper-middle-class children the foundations of a classical education, while the denominational and State schools were left to the poor.

One odd facet of the education debates was the silence of the clergy on religious instruction in private schools. It is arguable that middle-class children were more likely to be taught the faith by parents and ministers than were the youngsters from the poorer homes; it is much less realistic to assume that religious instruction was prominent in the typical private school. The College High School in Elizabeth Street, Sydney, offered young ladies 'a sound English Education, as well as the higher, fashionable, and finishing accomplishments', and promised boys an education 'without flogging or beating'; but its advertisement spoke not a word about religious training.[18] J. F. Castle's school accounts, relating to Calder House in Sydney during 1838-9, included small sums for the odd Bible, prayer book or a seat in the church, so spiritual things were not entirely neglected among the boarders, but there is no indication that they were stressed. When Castle opened a new school, Austenham House, in 1846 his prospectus offered both elementary and higher instruction in mathematics and languages, flaunted a Mons. H. Perrier as French and Italian master, held out hopes of fitting boys to enter the professions or a university, and promised to make them acquainted also with 'those studies which more immediately belong to the business of every-day life'; but no mention was made of religious instruction, though Castle was an evangelical Anglican.[19] Though nobody seemed to think of this as a retort to the Churches' emphatic criticisms of the godless general systems for elementary schools, it does suggest that the clergy were rather blind to the shortcomings of the private schools and unduly critical of the curricula offered in the schools for the humbler classes.

This, however, is incidental to the main point, which is that the clergy fought for control of the elementary schools but did not fight alongside the people whose children were sent to them. Of all the things which lessened the chance of the Churches' views being accepted

[16] Report of Board of Education, *V. & P.* (V.D.L.), 1848.
[17] *Courier*, 5 September 1849, p. 2; 8 September 1849, p. 3.
[18] *Herald*, 3 January 1843, p. 1.
[19] J. F. Castle's School Ledger (A.N.U. Archives 7/17/1) and Prospectus, *Austenham House School* (Sydney, n.d.) contained therein.

by the working classes generally, one of the gravest was that the clergy naturally took class distinctions for granted, and identified themselves with the higher classes, while the Australian workers were beginning to live by the code that one man was as good as the next. That the identification of the clergy with the upper classes was particularly true in the case of the Church of England, which had most to say and most influence to bring to bear against the general systems, could not be lost upon the workers. That the clergymen had not come from a working-class background, that their training and manner of living accentuated their different social position, and that it was the most natural thing in the world for this to happen, do not alter the situation and its consequences. Nor does the absence of any militant spirit of reform or revolution among the workers mean that, apathetically or subconsciously, they did not resist the clergymen's arguments for church schools. The parsons wanted them, but they were parsons, not the people.

It may be that the eventual success of the Catholics in establishing their own schools was partly due to their many Irish priests being close to the ordinary Irishman; and possibly this points up the significance of the social factor in the Anglican failure. But the facts do not stand out in bold relief; they blur and overlap. After all, none of the Churches neglected the poorer people and, in this sense, they stood with them. Captain Michael Fenton once paid the clergy a pretty compliment in the Van Diemen's Land Legislative Council, when he argued that the ministers of religion should be able to exercise real control of the schools since they alone had a real concern for the poor.[20] If the Anglican clergy appear as the villains of the piece in that colony during the years in which they refused to enter the government schools, they must at the same time be credited with the development of thirty-three schools of their own by 1848, while their counterparts in New South Wales were operating sixty-six schools for the poorer classes. The long years of Wesleyan hard work, including educational work, at Port Arthur and Point Puer alone are sufficient to refute any charge of indifference to the lower classes, and this denomination had sixteen schools in New South Wales in 1848. The contribution of the Presbyterians in New South Wales to the education of the working-class children was at that time forty-six schools. For their poor, the Catholics had several schools in Van Diemen's Land and thirty-seven in New South Wales.[21] The Baptists and Independents had been sturdy, if

---

[20] *Courier*, 5 September 1849, p. 3.
[21] Board of Education Report, p. 8, *V. & P.* (V.D.L.), 1849; *N.S.W. Almanack and Remembrancer for 1848*, pp. 49-53.

not entirely satisfied, supporters of the general systems in both colonies, and were thus in a different category. Ministers of religion were also prominent in one other avenue of working-class education—the Mechanics' Institutes, which aimed at giving instruction to working men by lectures, library facilities and classes for reading, writing and arithmetic. Perhaps the Reverend Henry Carmichael, foremost in the establishment of the Sydney Mechanics' Institute in 1833, can scarcely be included in this category, for he had 'all but renounced religion';[22] but in the southern colony another Presbyterian, the Reverend Dr John Lillie, was the backbone of the Hobart equivalent, and other Nonconformist ministers were closely associated with it.[23] The Reverend John West, an Independent, founded the Launceston Mechanics' Institute in 1842, and his brother minister, Charles Price, gave the first lecture.[24] It was to this body that Price spoke on education in words which might be expected to live in the memories of those who heard him. He praised the new schools in England, calling them 'refreshing fountains' of learning, and contrasted them with 'the mud holes . . . opened in this colony for the bespattering of the working classes'. 'If the working classes felt their true position,' he went on, 'they would not for a moment subject their children to the baneful influence of so degrading a system.' There was no 'aristocracy of mind', but the greatest ideas could be grasped by 'the sturdy mind of the operative'.[25] The part of Price's address which dealt with religion must have been delivered to an audience all the more sympathetic because of his outspokenness on their behalf.

Such wholehearted champions of the poorer classes did not speak up from the ranks of the Anglican clergy; they served, but stooped to serve the poor; they were often benign, but they were seldom brotherly. In Hobart in 1845, and again in 1846, an attempt was made to get a newspaper established with the professed aim of encouraging the working classes to associate themselves with the Church of England; but this was an individual layman's effort, which failed anyway.[26] An established newspaper was closer to the truth when it snarled that the colonists wanted a higher degree of education than that which England, 'under prelatic rule', had deemed sufficient for her working classes.[27] The workers had only to look at the parsons' children to know that they stood in different categories. Both James Hassall and G. F. Mac-

[22] G. Nadel, *Australia's Colonial Culture* (Melbourne, 1957), p. 113.
[23] *Report of V.D.L. Mechanics' Institution, 1849* (Hobart, 1850), p. 4.
[24] L. S. Bethell, 'The Development of Education in Northern Tasmania', *Papers and Proceedings, Tasmanian Historical Research Association*, vol. 3, May 1954, p. 32.
[25] C. Price, *The Intellectual Improvement of the Working Classes . . .* (Launceston, 1850), pp. 5-6.   [26] *Hobart Town Herald*, 18 July 1845.
[27] *True Colonist*, 4 October 1839, p. 4.

arthur, whose school careers were so close to each other and so devoid
of denominational school influences, became Anglican clergymen. The
Reverend William Cowper educated his children at home, and one of
them became a minister. The Reverend W. B. Clarke's wife took their
children to Ireland for schooling—where they, and she, remained for
fifteen years! The sons of the Reverend W. Garrard and of the Reverend
P. Palmer attended the Hutchins' School in Hobart, while Bishop
Nixon's children were taught at home. Even the chairman of the Van
Diemen's Land Wesleyan District, the Reverend Nathaniel Turner,
was spending £48 per annum, exclusive of clothing, on the schooling
of his twelve-year-old son in 1844, a fact which clearly indicates a
private school.[28] Not all Wesleyan ministers were involved in such
expense, for they reported to their controlling body in England, which
had just reduced their allowances, that as soon as a boy was capable
of being taught to read he had either to be instructed at home or sent
to a school at the cost of at least £8. 8s. a year, while a girl at a 'first
school' cost £12 a year.[29] The Reverend J. Jennings Smith, Anglican
parson at Paterson, New South Wales, had eleven children and one of
the lower incomes, so that, while he and his wife had hoped that one
of their sons might be educated for the ministry, they had been forced
to place them all in 'mercantile situations'. The clergy, therefore, were
not always financially comfortable and able to send their children to
the best schools. But this did not mean that many of their children
were sent to the nearest public elementary school; on the contrary, the
usual absence of the parsons' children from these schools meant that
the common people could not feel that the ministers of religion, as
a body, were truly standing with them, or that the struggle over the
schools was one in which they ought to identify themselves with the
clergy.

What is more, when the clergy personally conducted schools (as
distinct from the schools directed by their denomination) the boys in
them had to be of a class to help them financially and of a class wanting
to go beyond elementary education. Makinson's and Forrest's schools,
attended by James Hassall, were typical. Another example is the school
opened by the Reverend W. Sowerby in Goulburn in 1838, which was
attended by 'about sixteen of the sons of highly respectable families'.[30]
The number at Sowerby's school underlines the fact that he did not set
out to provide for all the children in the neighbourhood, (although he
did not mind Presbyterian boys attending his school, providing they

[28] Castle's school at Sydney, for instance, charged £50 per annum in 1846.
[29] V.D.L. Wes. Dist. Min., 4 October 1844, Q. XIX.
[30] *S.P.G. Report* (N.S.W.), 1840, p. 31.

never went to the Presbyterian minister for religious instruction even out of hours!). After the Presbyterians had hired a master for a school, they were able to claim that, of forty-five children at Goulburn between five and twelve years of age, only fourteen went to Sowerby's school, compared with twenty-seven attending theirs.[31] Similarly, a school run by an Anglican deacon at Hamilton, Van Diemen's Land, was closed due to the small attendance, but a ticket-of-leave man opened a school a little later which was 'generally attended by the children of the lower orders'.[32] Nor was this exclusive tendency confined to the Anglican clergymen. In Van Diemen's Land, for example, the Presbyterian minister, J. Mackersey, had a boarding school at Campbell Town (numbering among his pupils the future Sir Richard Dry), while even the Reverend Charles Price's school was attended mostly by boys who were to become 'ministers of religion, barristers, conductors of the press, merchants, officers in the army and in the civil service'.[33] While boys could grow into men who climbed in colonial rank, the suggestion once more is that these were schools attended almost exclusively by the sons of the more respectable inhabitants.

It may seem that the clergy as a group just piled mistake upon mistake; but it is more fair to see them often caught up in situations not of their direct making, and largely beyond their powers of mending. While many of them simply did not see that their class allegiances were damaging to their cause, they had not made the class distinctions and they would hardly have achieved any more success by spurning the leading citizens; they were themselves leading citizens in a class-conscious community, and there was little they could have done about it, even if it had occurred to them that they should. If, too, the Anglican clergymen refused to admit that what was expedient might also be right in the colonial education system, this was—as least at the beginning—only natural. They were convinced that the Church should educate and they were by no means as sure as later generations are that the people would not accept church schools. The Catholics, becoming increasingly insistent upon having their own schools, managed to secure the general obedience of their people, and it was only reasonable that the Anglicans should also try to hold their people at this point. The colonial clergy had not made the indifference of the English masses, they had not made the convict system, and they had not driven men out into the bush; this was a situation which was made by others,

[31] Petitions from Goulburn Kirk Session, and from Parents and Guardians, *V. & P.* (N.S.W.), 1839.
[32] Report of Education Commissioners, 1845, G.O. 33/51, pp. 720, 723 (TA).
[33] L. S. Bethell, op. cit., p. 77; J. Fenton, *The Life and Work of the Rev. Charles Price of Launceston* (Melbourne, 1886), pp. 76, 83.

and all they could do was to face it by doing what was most obvious
and natural to them.

Even so, they blundered badly in assessing the actual situation and
in not adapting themselves to it. They read the signs and panicked;
they feared the danger and resisted; they did not see the opportunity
and co-operate. They had not made the situation, but they need not
have made it worse. It was generally recognized that the poorer classes
sent their children to school 'almost entirely for the sake of the secular
instruction' and with 'too often little regard to the religious instruction',[34] yet the Anglican clergy kept their heads in the clouds of erst-
while glory and insisted that the bulk of the population was Anglican.
To be able to explain 'to some degree' the low attendance at Church
of England Sunday schools by pointing to the opening of sixteen new
Anglican day schools in Van Diemen's Land, where five hundred
children were taught in the way they preferred,[35] was both a plausible
argument and an impressive achievement. Yet it was not well conceived
policy. People who sent their children to school for 'learning' and not
for religion, were not going to prefer Anglican to general schools as
the State's own system began to gather strength. If it was an argument
for church schools that the ignorance and indifference of the parents
(many of them the nominal Anglicans who formed the bulk of the
population) made a great deal of religious teaching imperative in the
schools, the Anglican clergymen were badly losing ground in refusing
for years to go into the board schools to give it. When they were offered
a good deal of time and printed material for religious teaching, and
flatly rejected it, they were inviting a blow from the hand held out
to feed them.

The Anglicans' influence, prestige and determination, together with
their inability to rally effectively their so-called people, cause them to
be singled out. Other Churches shared the same educational ideal, but
Catholics, had they been more influential in public affairs, might have
won the day, for they better controlled their people; and the Wesleyans
—less sure of the ideal, less influential politically, and more ready to
be influenced by events—tended to be weak reeds and to lean with
the prevailing winds. Perhaps there was wisdom here, as well as weakness; for the Anglicans came to grief by being too stubborn for too
long. Dissenters were always sensitive to anything smacking of Anglican
privilege, and the people generally, believing far more in literacy than
the Thirty-nine Articles, were less deaf to their Governments' complaints about the expenses of a multiple school system than to the

---

[34] Report of Education Commissioners, 1845, G.O. 33/51, pp. 594-5 (TA).
[35] Ibid., p. 597.

Church of England's protests against reducing the amount of dogma taught at school. The Anglican clergy played for the highest stake—a predominantly Anglican religious education in the public schools, and, to be fair, a people taught to love God and the Church. By misjudging the situation, long and badly, they lost more than their ideal school system; the potential sympathy of the ordinary people, and the most likely method of successfully teaching their children, were lost to them also.

Nor was it only with the working classes that the Anglican clergy over-reached themselves: they did the same with the governing classes as far as the school systems went. They said too much, and their arguments became self-defeating. Bishop Broughton and his men claimed that it was morally wrong for the State to support truth and falsehood, and that it should support truth only. This, especially since it meant supporting Anglicanism rather than any other denomination, was too strong for a liberal State and liberal Christians, and could only have the long-term effect of convincing men that the State should not support any religious denomination. When this extreme position was met with the extreme voluntaryism of a churchman like the Reverend Dr J. D. Lang, government support of religion was all the more likely to be given up.[36] After non-Christians, like the Jews of New South Wales in 1845-6, attempted to get government aid, the policy of the State was thrown further into the melting pot, and the most extreme demands on the Governments were sure to be the first rejected. The humbler classes got their schools, but, precisely because of the uncompromising attitudes of the Churches generally and the Church of England in particular, religion was not very prominent in their curricula, and the civil and educational authorities were less than ever inclined to think that the religious content was worth the trouble it caused.

[36] Compare with J. S. Gregory, 'Church and State, and Education in Victoria to 1872', *Melbourne Studies in Education, 1958-1959* (Melbourne, 1960), pp. 22-8.

III

Religious Opinion and Practice

II

RELIGIOUS INDIFFERENCE
AND THE CHURCHES' MISSION

Practical Atheism

FOR ALL THE clergymen's political agitation and school-building, many children received little or no religious teaching; for all their preaching and church-building, many colonists neither heard the sermons, nor wanted to hear. The pastors' problem lay not merely in a scattered flock but with the many who were content to be lost. One Anglican group declared that white Australia was 'itself a Missionary field', and a body of Independents poured scorn on the sentimentality which concentrated attention upon missions to 'the perishing heathen' when their own kindred and countrymen were more exposed to the wrath of God than were those who sinned in ignorance of Christ.[1] The churchmen's heavy demands on the State for financial assistance and their vehement opposition to anything other than church schools were prompted and sustained by their awareness of a great need to evangelize the colonies.

Part of their problem was rational argument against orthodox Christian dogma or even against religion itself. The people who came to the colonies were not all immune to the movements in thought associated with D. F. Strauss's *Leben Jesu* (1835-6, translated into English in 1846), H. F. Milman's *History of the Jews* (1829), the Reverend R. D. Hampden's liberal views expressed in his 1832 Bampton Lectures and in his argument that graduates of Oxford and Cambridge should not have to subscribe to the Thirty-nine Articles, the rejection of Christianity by the likes of George Eliot, F. W. Newman and J. A. Froude in the thirties and forties,[2] and the anti-Christian writing of radical Tom Paine. The last, for instance, was sometimes read aloud by a group of wild young men coming out to Australia on an emigrant

[1] *S.P.G. Report* (Hobart), 1844-5, p. 7; *Report of V.D.L. Colonial Missionary . . . Society*, 1843, pp. 5-7.
[2] See H. R. Murphy, 'The Ethical Revolt against Christian Orthodoxy in Early Victorian England', *American Historical Review*, vol. LX, no. 4, pp. 800-17.

ship in 1850, a group which assailed the Bible with what believers called 'clumsy jests', though there was nothing clumsy in their challenge, 'Don't quote your Bible to prove your Bible: we must have other arguments'.[3] In the colonies already there were other, and more respectable, citizens who argued either for most unorthodox Christianity or for practically no religion whatever. E. S. Hall was moving towards the time of writing his turgid manuscript entitled the 'Credulity of Deism'.[4] The litigious G. M. C. Bowen had long since published his *Language of Theology* in which he had argued that the universe was God and that Christ was an attitude of mind.[5] Charles Harpur, the poet, hating the domination of any Church over education, politics or society, was also very much of a religious radical,[6] and Henry Melville, sometime editor of the *Colonial Times,* produced a privately-circulated rejection of Christianity in the forties, professing to have had his eyes opened by the science of geology.[7] There was sufficient questioning of the faith to make an Australian journal conclude that men no longer believed a religious doctrine just because they had been taught it, but investigated its truth for themselves.[8]

Yet the real problem for the churchmen did not lie in repudiation of religion on any acutely intellectual grounds. The Reverend William Dry rightly asserted that there were few colonials who would have denied that there was a God,[9] and even men like Bowen and Harpur remained deeply religious in their way. The greatest worry to Church leaders was what they described simply as practical atheism, a condition which had many causes and assumed many forms, but which was not truly philosophical. Some of it came from the old country, from such places as parts of Birmingham where many had 'always been quite heathen'.[10] Some of it developed from isolation and constant labour in the Australian bush, where thousands lived without any religious observance and even the devout could find that their 'general way of spending Sabbath morn^g—alas!' was in riding fifteen miles to tend cattle, not to attend service.[11] There was also, of course, sheer human cussedness in the religious neglect: as a convict of respectable parentage once admitted, he had become an 'infidel' not because he

---

[3] J. D. Mereweather, *Life on Board an Emigrant Ship* . . . (London, 1852), pp. 4, 34-5, 61-2.   [4] Dated 1855-6 (MS. 3221 ML).
[5] G. M. C. Bowen, *The Language of Theology Interpreted, in a Series of Short and Easy Lectures* (Sydney, 1836), pp. 311-12.
[6] J. Normington-Rawling, *Charles Harpur, an Australian* (Sydney, 1962), p. 152.
[7] H. Melville, *Exposition of Various Admitted Modern Theories, both Philosophical and Mythological* . . . (Van Diemen's Land, n.d.).
[8] *Melbourne Church of England Messenger,* June 1852, pp. 161-2.
[9] W. Dry, *Sermons* (Launceston, 1850), Sermon VIII.
[10] *P.P.* (H.C.), 1843, vol. XIII, pp. 160, 163.
[11] J. F. Castle, Private Journal, 1838-52, 16 February 1840 (A.N.U. Archives).

'had carefully examined the subject, and found any reasonable objection to the truths of Holy Scripture', but because he 'wished to be an infidel, and hoped there was no future state' for he would fare badly there if there was.[12] The carelessness comes out in comment after contemporary comment. Clergymen in both Sydney and Hobart said of working-class areas that there was little 'professed unbelief', but that '*practical* unbelief' led to a great deal of lying about on Sundays and to very little church attendance.[13] A Sydney minister denounced the 'prancing of horses and the rolling of chariots and the splashing of boat oars, and the revelry of parties, the disgusting ribaldry and profaneness of drunkenness' which threatened to 'drown in their united din the songs of holy praise and joy . . . within the walls of the Sanctuary', and the Superintendent of Police admitted that so many people went outside the city to amuse themselves that it was impossible to enforce the law on Sunday observance.[14] Sydney was sometimes considered the worst of the cities in this respect, but the Wesleyans in Hobart might not have agreed, for they spoke of the house of God being 'forsaken by many' while 'practical infidelity, like a flood' spread over the land.[15]

City, suburb and rural area were much the same. In the Castle Hill and Dural areas the greater number of people were described as having 'a contempt for religion, or, at the very best, a faint and imperfect sense of its value or importance',[16] and similar comments were passed at various times on Richmond, Goulburn, Yass and many another area. How completely many of the bushworkers were estranged from the Church was not always realized even by the itinerant chaplains themselves. The Reverend J. D. Mereweather, coming from Van Diemen's Land to the Riverina, described a service held in a wool-shed one Sunday for a number of 'very attentive' shearers and rouseabouts.[17] But a station-owner in the district also wrote a book in which he may have recalled the same service; he told, anyway, of a Mr M——r riding in one day and turning out to be an ordained man recently arrived from Tasmania. It was shearing time and the owner tried to arrange

[12] J. Backhouse, *Narrative of a Visit to the Australian Colonies* . . . (London, 1843), p. 161.

[13] F. H. Cox, *Public Worship. A Letter to . . . the Parish of St. John Baptist* . . . (Hobart, 1850), pp. 7-8; J. D. Lang, *Address, on behalf of the Australian Presbyterian Church Society* . . . (Sydney, 1850), pp. 2-3.

[14] W. Yate, *To the Parishioners of St. James' Church* . . . (Sydney, 1836), pp. 12-13; Report from Committee on the Shooting on Sunday Prevention Bill, *V. & P.* (N.S.W.), 1841.

[15] D. Mackenzie, *The Emigrant's Guide* . . . (London, 1845), pp. 30, 51; *Report of Wesleyan Methodist Sunday Schools* . . . (Hobart, 1843), p. 5.

[16] *S.P.G. Report* (N.S.W.), 1840, p. 37.

[17] J. D. Mereweather, *Diary of a Working Clergyman in Australia* . . . (London, 1859), p. 139.

the service requested by his visitor, but all thirty-odd men had an excuse for not attending until he promised a glass of rum to every man who came to the service and behaved during it. They all came, and were moderately pleased by the parson, but very much more pleased by the rum, for, 'wiping their mouths on their sleeves, they said they would not mind having a parson and Church service every day in the week, on the same terms'. Mr M——r continued in ignorance of the reason for the men's orderly attendance, and therefore—according to the squatter—completely misinterpreted it in a book he later wrote.[18] Nor was it only Protestants who ignored their Churches; even Catholics, with a much greater reputation for faithfulness to their religion, had to be rebuked by their bishop for carelessness.

> The world and its business usurp that place in our hearts which God alone should occupy; hence indifference to prayer, hence neglect of attendance at Mass, hence years follow each other in rapid succession, and the Sacraments are not received . . . the sacred name of God is blasphemed worse than among the Gentiles; the holiness of an oath is trampled under foot; the Sunday is no longer deemed a day consecrated to the Lord; children grow up in the habits of sin unchecked and unheeded.[19]

The reading of prayers to families and to hands, while by no means unknown, was not the general practice, and servants were not always willing to come when asked. J. F. Castle was one who read prayers to his men, but for the first twenty months he was with them on his land he had not done so. Presbyterian squatters in the Western District often had good intentions in this regard, but here—as in other places— it was only the coming of the station women and children in the later forties which produced much actual practice.[20] Even where the faith was theoretically acceptable, practical indifference often prevailed.

Leaving the British Isles, often for ever, to venture over wide oceans in tiny ships before landing on harshly alien shores, might be expected to leave migrants more ready to acknowledge dependence upon God. Yet this does not seem to have been usual. A few were converted on board ship (as a few are converted everywhere), but the long, idle months spent amid the boredom and temptations of the voyage left

---

[18] 'A Pioneer' [J. Phillips], *Reminiscences of Australian Early Life* (London, 1893), pp. 79-83.
[19] J. B. Polding, *The Pastoral Instruction for Lent, 1837* . . . (Sydney, 1837), p. 4.
[20] J. Backhouse, op. cit., p. 500; J. F. Castle, op. cit., 22 August 1841; M. Kiddle, *Men of Yesterday* (Melbourne, 1961), pp. 112-13; J. O. Balfour, *A Sketch of New South Wales* . . . (London, 1845), pp. 77-8; T. Sharpe, Journal Kept at Norfolk Island 1839-40, pp. 63-5 (ML); *Report of Melbourne Diocesan Society, 1851*, p. 9.

many migrants changed for the worse rather than for the better. J. D. Lang therefore denied, with strong emotion, the ancient maxim, '*Non mutant animos qui trans mare currunt*'.[21] J. D. Mereweather spoke to the same effect out of the same bitter experience. A Wesleyan spokesman for some of the passengers had accepted his offer to lead daily prayers, saying that while their creeds differed their danger was common; but, four months later, in such a gale that 'the sea rushed by, a mass of wild foam, as if it were too hurried to form into billows', the prevailing mood on board was very different.

> The people below did not seem frightened, or penetrated with a feeling that God was exerting, or allowing the Evil Spirit to exert, the power of his might. They were neither praying to their Saviour, or [*sic*] the Blessed Virgin, or the Holy Saints; but they were grumbling sadly that their dinners were not nicely cooked.[22]

In this frame of mind many migrants arrived in their new land. They nostalgically adopted the place names of the homeland, but they were not more inclined to retain the faith of their fathers or to embrace the faith their fathers had also spurned. In large numbers they planted themselves in the ground prepared for them in the colonies, in the soil of preoccupation with material things and neglect of the spiritual, and on Sundays they washed their shirts or joined the boating excursions around the harbour.

This was the background for the Churches' mission to white Australia. It was not, of course, the whole picture, for this included the welcome given by a big section of the people to the Church Acts, and many another indication that the faithful were in the land. Even the remote bush, an area particularly prone to religious neglect and often indeed suffering from it, was by no means devoid of the Churches' representatives and of those who sought and welcomed them.

The Bush Pastors

It was, and is, sometimes claimed that the only seriously persistent ministry to the sheep and cattle stations was that of the Catholic priests. These men certainly did excellent pastoral work in the bush and were, indeed, sometimes seen where no other clergyman had appeared. John Fidler, a Wesleyan local preacher, came out to Australia because he read of a convict who had been contacted only by a Catholic priest.[23] A bushman wrote in 1847, 'At present, except a stray Catholic priest,

[21] J. D. Lang, *An Historical and Statistical Account of New South Wales . . .* (London, 1834), II, pp. 241-2.   [22] J. D. Mereweather, *Life . . .*, pp. 5, 67.
[23] J. Fidler, Recollections, Methodist Church Papers, Uncat. MSS. 197/4 (ML).

no preacher or teacher ever penetrates the far interior'.[24] W. C. Wentworth claimed that he had never heard of a clergyman visiting the squatting districts 'except perhaps a stray itinerant Catholic'.[25] Another squatter mentioned only a Catholic priest and a Presbyterian minister as occasional visitors to his runs.[26] Catholics themselves encouraged this claim that they were the real bush pastors, and denigrated the Protestants' efforts. 'There is nothing that so strikes the Protestant population as the great distance the Catholics come to assist at Mass, whilst they themselves reckon four or five miles too far to travel that they may listen to their minister,' wrote J. B. Polding, adding in an unworthy moment, 'who, on his part, considers it a great hardship to leave his house in order to read the service.'[27] Such claims have been given new life in a recent history where it is uncritically written that 'itinerant Catholic priests were seen in the bush more often than were those of any other denomination'.[28]

There is, however, overwhelming evidence to the contrary. A comparison of tours by the bishops reveals no Catholic superiority. Polding's own travelling energies were enormous. Called to Wollongong to attend a dying man, he described the trip as 'just 85 miles from Sydney—a comfortable ride for one day and a half' and, since the man lived, was ready to return to the district in a few weeks to keep him on the path to which the accident had directed him. A little later, Polding made his 'first pastoral tour of extent', being away from Sydney four Sundays and going to Goulburn, Yass and on beyond the boundaries. A letter survives which the bishop wrote once from Moreton Bay before setting out on a visitation tour of nearly five hundred miles to Sydney. 'We must pack up and off,' he concluded. 'We carry a blanket each for the bush, a pair of pistols for show, Altar things, etc. etc.'.[29] Years later, he and Dr Gregory travelled more than eleven hundred miles by buggy in the southern districts of the diocese.[30] All these, and more, besides trips to Van Diemen's Land and even Western Australia, were undertaken by the head of the Catholic Church. But Bishop Broughton made voyages to these colonies, too, and he was no less active in touring the bush. Almost the first thing he did upon his return to Sydney in 1836 was to visit Bathurst. In 1840 he was out beyond the boundaries in the Tumut area, meandering back to Sydney via Yass, Limestone Plains, Braidwood and the other centres of settle-

[24] J. Sidney, *A Voice from the far Interior of Australia* (London, 1847), p. 23.
[25] *Herald*, 6 June 1848, p. 3.   [26] Ibid., 23 May 1848, p. 2.
[27] P. F. Moran, *History of the Catholic Church in Australasia* (Sydney, n.d.), p. 230.
[28] R. Ward, *The Australian Legend* (Melbourne, 1958), p. 88. Only one of the sources cited by Ward actually supports his claim.
[29] H. N. Birt, *Benedictine Pioneers in Australia* (London, 1911), I, pp. 317, 321, II, pp. 61-2.   [30] P. F. Moran, op. cit., pp. 446-7.

ment. In 1845, between June and August, he was away visiting New-castle, Maitland, Paterson, the River Allyn, Singleton, Muswellbrook, Scone, Mudgee, Bathurst and stations as well as towns along the way. Towards the end of that year he went to Geelong, Melbourne and Launceston, and these trips were typical—not the total—of his journey-ings.[31] Dr Polding therefore did not have any edge over his rival, especially if it is noted that Dr Broughton was six years his senior. Nor did the Catholic Bishop of Melbourne put to shame the Anglican Bishop of Melbourne. Dean Coffey explained his speaking for the Catholic Church in one public controversy by the fact that Bishop Goold had 'gone to search out the poor man in the Bush'; but Bishop Perry, the Anglican, was no less a travelling man but was 'distinguished as a *working* minister' who went into the interior.[32]

The persistent, arduous labour of ordinary Catholic priests must also be recognized. Priests were stationed in pairs, when possible, partly to enable one to itinerate while the other stayed at the main centre.[33] The two priests at Bathurst were reported to have twenty-six stations to visit once a quarter, the closest being twenty miles from Bathurst and the farthest (Dubbo) being one hundred and thirty miles away.[34] To this may be added the example of the Reverend Charles Lovat in the Yass-Goulburn area, as revealed in this random extract from his report in 1839:

> 2nd December, Gundaroe, 27 miles from Yass; 3rd, Goulburn, 45 miles from Gundaroe; 6th, Bungadore, 40 miles from Goulburn; 8th, Molonglo, 14 miles from Bungadore; 9th, Queanbeyan, 12 miles, at least; 11th, Goulburn, 40 miles (about); 12th, Gunning, 30 miles from Goulburn; 13th, Yass, 30 miles from Gunning . . .

In that year, also, the priest at Penrith travelled four and a half thousand miles, the man at Windsor covered between eight and nine thousand miles and the priests at East and West Maitland each travelled more than three thousand.[35] Within and without the boundaries, the Catholic clergy toured as assiduously as any.

But this did not mean that they were seen more often than the other clergymen. If the Catholics at Maitland each travelled about

[31] *S.P.G. Report* (N.S.W.), 1837, p. 40; ibid., 1840, p. 32; *The Church in Australia: Two Journals of Visitation to the Northern and Southern Portions of his Diocese, by the Lord Bishop of Australia, 1843* (London, 1845).
[32] 'N.J.C.', *Catholics, not Idolators* . . . (Melbourne, 1850), p. 5; J. B. Clutterbuck, *Port Phillip in 1849* (London, 1850), pp. 67-8.
[33] P. F. Moran, op. cit., p. 238. This practice, by no means universal, also reduced the area in which a priest might be seen; two men stationed one hundred miles apart could have travelled into more country.
[34] J. Kenny, *A History of the Commencement and Progress of Catholicity in Australia* . . . (Sydney, 1886), p. 197.
[35] H. N. Birt, op. cit., I, pp. 445-7.

three thousand miles a year, an Anglican minister (G. K. Rusden, who was neither young nor a bushman) had done the same in that district five years earlier, and had soon been joined by a second parson who took charge of a district one hundred miles in length.[36] In 1840 it was reported of another, the Reverend Robert Cartwright, who had been in the colony since 1810, that he 'had just returned from a distant excursion to the river Lachlan, whither he had gone at the express desire of Whitton, lately executed at Goulburn for bush-ranging and murder, in order to warn some of his associates against the danger of following his evil course'. Cartwright's home base was then at Burrows, several miles north-west of Yass and close to the boundaries of location, and he had to be a travelling parson, having once been 'minister of the district of Yass, the entire County of Murray, and the Western Division of the County of King'.[37] One of the ministers who helped reduce Cartwright's original parish was the Reverend Edward Smith, appointed to Queanbeyan in 1838 under instructions 'to visit at regular periods some stations 75-80 miles off'.[38] Since the Catholic priests at Bathurst have been mentioned, it should also be noted that Anglican, Presbyterian and Wesleyan ministers were all stationed there before them. Nor is it at all surprising to find that at least Anglican ministers were frequently in a district before Catholic priests. In New South Wales as a whole there were seventeen Anglican clergymen and only seven Catholic priests in 1836; by 1844 the respective numbers were about sixty to thirty; and in 1850 there were approximately seventy Anglicans to just under thirty Catholics.[39] The number of people to whom the Anglican clergymen had to minister increased over the years, but they were not at any disadvantage compared with the Catholic priests in this regard. In the early forties Anglican and Catholic clergymen each had much the same average number of 'parishioners', and by the end of the forties the Anglicans had to minister to roughly one thousand persons each compared with the Catholics' two thousand.[40] When numbers are considered, the claim that the Catholics gave better attention to their scattered flocks becomes at once improbable; and when the recorded tours of the Anglicans are examined, the claim becomes absurd.

Ministers of other Churches also played a part, sometimes an im-

[36] W. W. Burton, *The State of Religion and Education in New South Wales* (London, 1840), pp. 206-8.
[37] *S.P.G. Report* (N.S.W.), 1840, p. 33; Acts and Proceedings of the Bishop of Australia, I, p. 58 (Diocesan Registry, Sydney).
[38] Report of Committee on Immigration, p. 839, *V. & P.* (N.S.W.), 1838.
[39] See chs 1 and 5.
[40] Figures gained by dividing the number of clergymen into the numbers of adherents recorded in the censuses of 1841 and 1851.

portant part, in the bush mission. In 1836 the Wesleyan minister at Bathurst was regularly riding twenty-six miles between services on one Sunday, and forty miles to three appointments on the next, and by 1839 the Bathurst Wesleyan circuit was one hundred miles in length. In 1842 it was reported that Methodist ministers were riding once a quarter the seventy miles from Sydney to Wollongong, and during the forties they were being stationed at Goulburn, Queanbeyan, Scone and a few other places then a good way out. They were not great bush tourists, for they had too few ministers and more than enough work in the heavily populated areas, but they were not unknown.[41] An Independent, the Reverend Charles Price, was at Port Stephens for some years in the thirties, but he was an exception to the general rule that Independents and Baptists did very little bush work in New South Wales.[42] On the mainland these were not the men who challenged the Catholics as bush pastors, but in Van Diemen's Land the Independents did a great deal of pioneering in the interior. At the end of 1836 the Reverend Joseph Beazley arrived in the colony specifically for work in the bush, a task he faithfully carried out and in which he was joined, a few years later, by the Reverend John West, Alexander Morrison, William Waterfield and one or two other ministers—all of whom spent at least some time outback.[43] Here, too, the Wesleyans, while regretting their inability to go from farm to farm, or to make more than occasional visits to many places, itinerated widely through the island.[44] As for the Anglicans in Van Diemen's Land, by 1850 they had fifty clergymen (including six 'Missionary Chaplains' besides ten 'Convict Chaplains') compared with the Catholics' dozen. If the latter had been four times more active in their journeyings than the Church of England ministers, they would still have been no more in evidence. But, in fact, the Anglicans were so much in evidence that John Mereweather, arriving in 1850, soon transferred to New South Wales to get a neglected area to work in.[45]

Mereweather's wish was fulfilled in the Riverina, where he was energetically riding about while the nearest Catholic priest was a hundred miles away, in the Irish settlement at Kilmore, forty miles from Melbourne.[46] In a nearby area, entered by crossing the boundary

[41] J. Colwell, *The Illustrated History of Methodism* . . . (Sydney, 1904), p. 246; N.S.W. Wes. Dist. Min., 1839, Q. 28; ibid., 1842, Q. 32; ibid., 1845, Q. 27.
[42] Compare with M. Kiddle, op. cit., p. 447.
[43] *Report of Van Diemen's Land Home Missionary* . . . *Society*, 1837, 1838, 1839, 1843; *Colonial Times*, 28 May 1844, p. 3.
[44] V.D.L. Wes. Dist. Min., 1 November 1838, Q. xxviii, xxxii; ibid., 11 February 1836. See also J. Orton, Journal 1832-9, pp. 180-5 (MS. ML).
[45] J. D. Mereweather, *Life* . . . , pp. 75-6.
[46] J. D. Mereweather, *Diary* . . . , p. 115.

of the County of Murray from Michelago, and continuing beyond the
Snowy River ('a deep and rapid stream, very difficult to cross'), sterling
work was done by another Anglican, the Reverend E. G. Pryce. For
four years Pryce had no home but the squatters' huts; and, for the first
six months at least, he never stayed in one place for more than three
days, except for one week when he had a bad cold. Between 1843 and
1848, as well as itinerating in his own enormous district, he twice went
to Gippsland and Twofold Bay—a round trip of eight hundred miles
or more; and Pryce was only one of the five Church of England chaplains (supported mainly by the S.P.G.) appointed for duties like these
beyond the boundaries.[47] The young James Hassall, for all his select
schooling, worked hard in the saddle after ordination; stationed at
Bungonia in 1849, he rode nearly six thousand miles in his first year—
a fit inheritor of his father, the Reverend Thomas Hassall, who had
been called 'the galloping parson'. His fellow clergyman, G. E. Gregory,
was drowned while crossing the Molonglo River in 1850, one of five
Anglicans to die in this way within a few years.[48] At the end of the
forties, Melbourne Anglicans were keeping a clergyman itinerating
around the stations on the Campaspe, Loddon and Murray Rivers, on
the 'Adelaide Boundary line' near Portland and Mount Gambier, down
the Wimmera, and on the Goulburn, Ovens and Broken Rivers.[49] In
1849, the Reverend F. T. C. Russell took up duty at Coleraine and
itinerated between Casterton and Hamilton, down to Heywood and
across to the South Australian border, an area of some two thousand
square miles.[50] The list is monotonous but magnificent, providing poor
support for Polding's malicious remark that Protestant ministers did
not much like stirring from their houses.

Lest too much be said on the Anglicans' behalf, and too little on the
Catholics', it should be mentioned that Catholic priests—Geoghegan,
and Walsh, and Slattery—also had good reputations as itinerants in
these southern areas at various times. But there were also the Wesleyans—the first to hold service in Melbourne, the first to be established
at Geelong, the only ones to establish a mission to the aborigines, and
whose ministers were to be 'characteristic figures on the goldfields'.[51]
Dissenters, indeed, were acknowledged by Bishop Perry to have preceded Anglicans in many places in his diocese. His own Church, he
said wearily, was 'continually anticipated and shut out, through her

[47] *The Church in Australia, Part II. Two Journals of Missionary Tours in the Districts of Manéroo and Moreton Bay* . . . (London, 1845), *passim;* 'A Maneroo Squatter', *Herald,* 1 July 1848, p. 3; Broughton to S.P.G., 3 April 1845, *H.R.A.,* xxiv, p. 494.
[48] J. S. Hassall, *In Old Australia* . . . (Brisbane, 1902), pp. 73, 81.
[49] *Report of Melbourne Diocesan Society,* 1849, pp. 13-14; ibid., 1851, p. 9.
[50] M. Kiddle, op. cit., p. 445.   [51] Ibid., pp. 111, 446, 196-7.

own sloth and lukewarmness, from places which she has been invited
and even entreated to occupy, but has refused to do so until it was too
late'.[52] But this, while pointing up an area of Anglican weakness, is not
a claim for Catholic pre-eminence. Perry's lament was not over Catholic activity; it was that Wesleyans and Presbyterians were more often
seen in the bush than Anglicans. Presbyterian ministers were well
regarded as travellers in the interior, though they were handicapped
by their schisms, which sometimes meant two men being stationed
where one could have done the work. They were mentioned on occasion,
along with Catholics, as the only ones who had visited an area. A Presbyterian minister, the Reverend James Forbes, was the first minister of
religion to settle in Port Phillip (where not only had the first service
been conducted by a Wesleyan, but also an Anglican and an Independent had settled before the first Catholic arrived). The experiences of
some of the early Presbyterian ministers give a clue to part of the
origin of the claim that Catholics were more active than others; for
they did more than the squatter was always ready to admit. The
Reverend Andrew Love, an early Port Phillip Presbyterian, met a settler
in Geelong and asked if he would contribute to the church building
fund. The man refused, saying, 'You and Mr. Forbes are two very
indolent men. He stops in Melbourne, and you in Geelong, and never
come out to us country people at all'. Not long before, Love had ridden
ninety miles to baptize this settler's children. Forbes also was 'a real
riding parson'; and another, the Reverend Peter Gunn, was 'probably
the most indefatigable of them all', yet Gunn also suffered the same
accusation of not visiting the outlying settlers.[53]

Squatters, therefore, were not always easy to please. It was less than
just to complain of ministerial neglect when landowners refused to call
a minister, believing they could not provide for him.[54] And, once they
had one in their midst they could be unreasonable in their demands.
J. D. Mereweather found that the clergyman in the bush

> must not expect a very high appreciation of the sacrifices he makes in
> coming into such a country. Many of the squatters are not gentlemen,
> but rather people who will broadly hint that, having paid a certain sum
> towards a clergyman's support, they expect to get something for their
> money in the shape of so many visits a-year, be the weather what it
> might.[55]

Sometimes the squatters may have been right; sometimes they may

[52] G. Goodman, *The Church in Victoria during the Episcopate of the Right Reverend Charles Perry* . . . (London, 1892), pp. 64-5.
[53] Aeneas MacDonald, *One Hundred Years of Presbyterianism in Victoria* (Melbourne, 1937), p. 21.   [54] M. Kiddle, op. cit., p. 172.
[55] J. D. Mereweather, *Diary* . . . , pp. 210-11.

have been querulously unfair; sometimes they may have been enjoying
a joke at the parson's expense. Certainly the squatters' word is not to
be taken as being beyond question. In particular, when they said that
only Catholics went to the bush, or that Catholics went most often,
they were falsely generalizing from a particular instance, or talking
outright nonsense, or were trying to get something—as W. C. Wentworth was trying to get a general system of education in opposition
to Bishop Broughton, its most dangerous single enemy.

Rather than saying that the Catholic religion was relatively respected
by the sceptical bushmen because priests were most often seen,[56] it
would be less misleading (though not altogether true) to say that priests
were more consistently around the men's huts both because Catholicism usually retained a stronger hold on its adherents there than
other creeds, and also because Catholics were more often to be found
in the huts than in the homesteads.[57] There was often a greater barrier
between the station-hand and the status-conscious Anglican parson than
there was between the hand and some other clergymen—especially the
Irish hand and Irish priest. Mereweather's complaint that many of
the squatters themselves were 'not gentlemen' is vastly suggestive. One
layman's dissatisfaction with the situation as he saw it—that the
'clergy of the Church of England . . . [did] not go so much amongst
the lower class of people as those of other sects'—was quite explicit.[58]
His further question, 'Is this from their having generally received a
better education?', was in line with a Governor's opinion that the
'liberal University education' of the typical Anglican minister was a
hindrance rather than a help in dealing with the Australian population.[59] Too much weight should not be put on the 'University education'
mentioned by Arthur, for many of the colonial Anglican clergy were
not, at any rate, the finished products of universities. Archdeacon William Cowper had an honorary doctorate, no other degree and very
little learning;[60] and a good number of the clergymen's degrees were
honours conferred by the Archbishop of Canterbury: Thomas Hassall,
Robert Forrest, H. T. Stiles, and W. H. Walsh, for instance, received
the Master of Arts degree in this way in 1843, none of them previously
having a degree of any kind.[61] But the accent could certainly be placed

[56] R. Ward, op. cit., pp. 87-8.
[57] M. Kiddle, op. cit., pp. 111, 301; *The Church in Australia, Part II* . . . , pp. 25-6, 28.
[58] G. Mackaness (ed.), *The Correspondence of John Cotton, Victorian Pioneer,
1842-9* (Sydney, 1953), pt. III, p. 45.
[59] Arthur to Bathurst, 21 April 1826, *H.R.A.*, Series III, vol. v, p. 151.
[60] Broughton to Coleridge, 14 February 1842, B.P.; W. M. Cowper, *Autobiography
and Reminiscences* (Sydney, 1902), p. 8.
[61] *Acts and Procedings of the Bishop of Australia*, I, p. 259. For one of the certifi-
cates, see Stiles Papers, p. 53 (A269 ML).

on the 'liberal' training and 'liberal' outlook of the clergy, in Arthur's sense of 'gentlemanly'; they knew where they belonged or intended to belong, and the people sometimes complained of Anglican parsonic airs. 'I fear that the humbler classes of the people are accustomed to look towards the clergy as a kind of high Brahminical caste, rather than as their pastors and spiritual advisers', wrote a newspaper correspondent, 'And this may chiefly arise from the fact, that the clergy have not mingled more with their people'.[62] Another writer accused an Anglican clergyman of accepting ferrymen's coats as a cushion without thanks, and without speaking to his parishioners—boatmen and passengers—while the ferry was pulled across.[63]

Yet this tendency can also be grossly exaggerated, and is not to be substituted for the myth already exposed. For one thing, superior education was not always a barrier or any disadvantage; Broughton, indeed, was sure that, though the people often had little learning, they were 'mighty quick in detecting the want of it in their clergy' and apt to 'despise them accordingly'.[64] Nor is there any lack of illustration to support a claim that Anglican parsons were often kindly, courteous and conscientious regardless of class. The Reverend Samuel Marsden, whose name is almost a byword for harshness as an early clerical magistrate, is an unlikely witness in the case for Anglican tenderness towards the distressed poor; yet even he can be successfully called. In a letter to a neighbouring chaplain, he wrote concerning twenty-years-old Jane Smith, who had been put into the Windsor lock-up fourteen days after giving birth to a child, where she was unable to sleep for fear that the rats, which overran the place, would eat the baby. After a week of this, she was marched (as the custom was) from Windsor to Parramatta, and there she died. A cow and some clothes belonging to the dead girl were still at Windsor, and Marsden asked that the property be claimed for the benefit of the baby. He ended simply, 'I felt much for her'.[65] If Marsden, of all the parsons, could feel and act like this, the many gentler clergy must have felt and done much more for their poor parishioners. The pages of the Reverend Thomas Sharpe's journal bear eloquent testimony to his genuine pity for the convicts, both on Norfolk Island and also when assigned to settlers in the interior.[66] The itinerant chaplains themselves were far from inattentive to the lowest people on the stations. The Reverend J. Gregor in the Moreton Bay district, and the Reverend J. H. Gregory in the Maneroo district, were men who were in the huts both consistently and cour-

---

[62] *Courier,* 24 February 1837, p. 3.   [63] *True Colonist,* 4 October 1839, p. 7.
[64] Broughton to Coleridge, 19 October 1837, B.P.
[65] Marsden to Stiles, 9 December 1834, Stiles Papers (ML).
[66] T. Sharpe, op. cit., pp. 31-2, 63-5.

teously.[67] F. T. C. Russell's name 'became a legend for humanity and kindness far beyond the confines of his own large district, and amongst many not of the Anglican persuasion'.[68] James Hassall reminisced in this vein about his own tours:

> I never hurried away from the stations, often stayed a day or two to visit the shepherds and other station people, and when I called would have a pot of tea and some beef and damper and, I hope, a profitable chat with the lonely shepherd or hutkeeper . . . Often I would sleep at a shepherd's hut and the man would divide his blankets with me and give me his own bed if I had been willing to take it.

Shepherd's huts were notoriously dirty (in contrast to stockmen's), and Hassall's practice should be noted with that in mind. The spirit in which he performed this ministry is revealed in his further comment:

> Even if it were a hardship to rough it in such places there is no greater privilege on earth than for a minister to be able to go to such people as these simple-minded old shepherds and teach them of the love of Christ.

When the Reverend Thomas Hassall was buried, a man was seen standing quietly in his best clothes twenty miles from the place of burial; he explained that, while he could not go to the funeral, he was keeping the day all the same.[69] These things are to go on record, as well as complaints about the Anglican ministers. While they may have often been rather more self-conscious than some other clergy when roughing it in the bush, some of them were used to life in the bush from their birth (James Hassall for one, his superior schooling notwithstanding), and Anglicans from all backgrounds did much faithful and effective work in the outback. The barrier, when there was one between the itinerating cleric and the isolated bushman, was not necessarily from the clergyman's side. As the Presbyterian, the Reverend James Forbes, wrote to one young squatter:

> Private Christians can do a great deal for the Lord's cause, perhaps in some respects they can do more than ministers. The ungodly and profane regard religion as 'the parson's *trade*', and treat his admonitions as very much in the way of business.[70]

What the bushman wanted, or did not want, determined religion in the bush quite as much as what the parsons did or did not do.

[67] *The Church in Australia, Part II* . . . , pp. 18-28; G. Goodman, op. cit., pp. 132-3.
[68] M. Kiddle, op. cit., p. 301.
[69] J. S. Hassall, op. cit., pp. 73, 197.
[70] C. S. Ross, *Colonization and Church Work in Victoria* (Melbourne, 1891), p. 78.

Extensions to the Parochial Ministry

Zealous laymen, the leaven in the mass of indifference, supported many societies which extended the outreach of the Churches. Religion normally loomed large in the constitutions of even the benevolent societies; and one of these groups even went so far as to include the declared aim of giving to the needy 'religious instruction and con-solation in their distress'.[71] More directly connected with the Churches were the organizations active in disseminating religious literature, which might be passed from hand to hand in the interior or in the town slums, where the representatives of the Churches found it hard to make close personal contact. Foremost among these bodies was the Australian Religious Tract Society. Through this society thousands of the pamphlets produced by the English Nonconformists and Evangelicals were distributed each year until, in 1850, no less than twelve and a half thousand were issued free, as well as those which were sold cheaply (for a total of £120). Nor was the work without effect. One city missionary used to leave a tract at houses to which he could not gain admission, and, after repeating this procedure a number of times, he often found that he was invited in, sometimes to be successful in persuading parents to go to church or to send their children to school. The tracts which were sent out to prisoners, labourers and stockmen in the interior were not always wasted, either. Of those issued in the Port Stephens area it was once reported:

> They frequently supply some of the overseers with means of pleasing and instructing their men after the toils of the day, and likewise an inducement to assemble as many as they can on the Sabbath to read to them. We cannot tell what may result from these little beginnings, for they break the monotony of the bush, and in solitude induce many to think of eternal things. Some of the men have said to me, 'They put some strange thoughts into our heads at times, Sir', meaning thoughts of spiritual things.[72]

Not always, therefore, were the bush and the Sabbath unassailed by the gospel. What is more, when the writers were artful enough to ignore the common evangelical disapproval of the novel, and to put their message in story form, the tracts were extremely popular. Hence, in Redfern in 1850, Legh Richmond's *The Dairyman's Daughter* was a favourite, and C. B. Tayler's *The Bar of Iron* was in great demand, though it made the readers weep.[73]

[71] *Report of the Benevolent Society of N.S.W.*, 1836, p. 6.
[72] *Report of the Australian Religious Tract Society*, 1850, p. 11; ibid., 1835, pp. 6-7.
[73] Ibid., 1850, pp. 12-13. See also M. Maison, *Search Your Soul, Eustace: a Survey of the Religious Novel in the Victorian Age* (London, 1961), pp. 72, 89-95.

In addition, the Bible Societies in both colonies steadily put copies of the scriptures into circulation. Some they sold; many more they issued free. A typical early report was of 168 Bibles and 175 Testaments sold in New South Wales, compared with 233 Bibles and 322 Testaments given away. Later, in 1848, the Van Diemen's Land society issued nearly three thousand Bibles and New Testaments, and more than two and a half thousand copies of the scriptures passed through the sister society's hands in New South Wales in 1849. This was not, perhaps, a large number when the colonies' population amounted to about seventy-five thousand and two hundred and twenty thousand respectively; but, taken over the years, and with such other sources of supply as the issues made by surgeon superintendents on migrant ships, Bibles must have been fairly readily available. In 1837 one clergyman was not only reporting that the district of New Norfolk, in the southern colony, was well supplied, but was expressing his anxious desire to have something done for the neighbouring district of Hamilton, which was short of Bibles. This was precisely the kind of call which the Bible societies answered. Free copies had been distributed, according to one typical report, among the poor in Sydney, poor children at a Windsor school, stockmen in the Wellington Valley, convicts at Norfolk Island and poor settlers at Cook's River. One other practice adopted by the societies was that of sending Bibles home with patients returning to the interior after having been in hospital. Local agencies were also established in outlying towns, and even the sale of Bibles by the employment of hawkers was attempted.[74] There must have been more religious literature scattered about the colonies than anything written by the likes of Tom Paine.

These valiant attempts to let the written word reach persons who might seldom hear the spoken word were largely made by Dissenters and evangelical Anglicans. The high churchmen, and the bodies they controlled (S.P.G., S.P.C.K. and some diocesan societies), gave religious literature a lower priority, for they were sceptical of religious notions acquired without clerical safeguards, distrustful of private interpretation and, as Broughton had pointed out to John Robinson, firm believers in the necessity of the 'proper means', by which they meant the pastor, the sacraments, the church and the church school. Hence they gave most attention to supplying settlers with religious buildings and ordained men.

High churchmen also kept aloof from what was the most striking, and the newest, organized effort at moral reform—the temperance

[74] See the printed annual reports of the Auxiliary Bible Societies of New South Wales and of Van Diemen's Land between 1835 and 1850.

movement. Beginning in the United States of America and the British Isles earlier in the century, the movement was speedily introduced into Australia in the thirties. Here it found enough support and had sufficient religious associations to allow it to be hyperbolically described by one historian as 'a sizeable religious sect'.[75] The high churchmen, and some other Christians as well, rejected the total abstinence—and even the temperance—societies through a combination of moderate views about alcohol, jealous regard for their own Church's reforming power and a dislike of groups which could be suspected of relying on man's effort rather more than on divine grace, or which seemed to be frankly substituting the gospel of teetotalism for that of Christ. But the Catholic priests were often fervent supporters of the cause, and so were ministers from every Church in the colonies. Often, in fact, the members of these societies saw their task of calling the drink-sodden colonies to sobriety or teetotalism as a holy task, since drunkenness was not only a social problem but was also a positive sin against God. Reliance on God's grace was sometimes written into the constitution of the groups, which bitterly repudiated the charges that they were offering a substitute religion, and pointed to men who were reclaimed and worshipping in the churches through their work. The societies were very realistic and imaginative in their methods. Halls, libraries, brass bands, tea-meetings, picnics and children's 'Cold Water Armies' all came within their scope; and one illustration of the success they sometimes enjoyed is that, in one month, forty stockholders in a southern New South Wales district pledged themselves to ban spirits from their stations. They had succumbed to the societies' logic that to give men waterproof pants before the sheep-washing was more effective than giving them spirits afterwards, and to the correctness of the societies' claims that many sheep-washings were done without spirits anyway, either because the bullockies tapped the kegs on the road, or because the men impatiently drained the kegs as soon as they arrived. Yet the work of the temperance and total abstinence societies, though a valuable adjunct to the Churches' efforts to reform colonial life, was not successful enough—as the societies were the first to admit. Too many colonials continued to prefer their old associations and their drunkenness.

This was much the same as the final result of every other effort made

[75] M. Roe, 'Society and Thought in Eastern Australia, 1835-51' (Ph.D. thesis, A.N.U., 1960), p. 585. Roe discusses the temperance movement in considerable detail in his thesis. The introduction of the movement into Australia is described in *The Australian Temperance Magazine,* 1 July 1837, p. 3; following numbers of this journal and the printed annual reports of the various societies are the main sources upon which this paragraph is based.

by the Churches and moral reformers. There was success, but not overwhelming success. The lost who were sought were by no means anxious to be found, and the Churches improved society without radically changing it. The limited result, however, does not mean that the Christian influences were an insignificant part of Australian society. Christians, individually and in their denominations, applied their pressure early and maintained it consistently through the years. If a great number of the colonials paid no heed to religion, it was not because a majority of them had no churches and clergymen close to them. If many colonists bothered very little about questions of social morality, it was not because of any lack of improving societies in their main areas of settlement. Australians have always been subjected to fairly strong and very steady religious and moral pressures, even where they have resisted them. Nor has the resistance of most Australians been entirely successful; one way or another, nearly all of them have been touched, if lightly, by something emanating from the Churches. It is fallacious to think of early Australian society as being deeply or even formally religious; it is equally fallacious to dismiss Christianity as of no account in the development of the Australian and his way of life. The society of *de facto* marriages, for instance, did not continue, and did not develop into a nation whose weddings were preeminently civil. Australians soon knuckled under, and still continue to be married mostly in a church. When they come to be married, their notions about God may be hazy, but they do not deny that God exists. Something has kept these practical atheists from going the next step: and it has to do with the persistence of the minority in the Churches.

12

PEW AND PULPIT

Religious Observance

THE COLONIAL CLERGYMEN persisted, not because they were saints and martyrs, but because a sufficiently large number of people wanted them to persist. The immediate response among Anglicans to the Van Diemen's Land Church Act was proof to their archdeacon that the people had a great desire for religious instruction. Bishop Broughton was surprised and pleased to learn that in the Tumut River district, 'far beyond the limits of location', there were over three hundred adults wanting to subscribe between them the £300 needed to qualify for aid towards building a church; and, whatever he had to say on occasion about the unwillingness of squatters to build churches, he had to admit on other occasions that there seemed to be an eagerness to have churches built, to subscribe towards them and to fill them when they were finished. At the beginning of the forties the bishop was sure that there was an increasing respect for Christian teaching, that more people were practising their religion, and that proper marriages were replacing the old *de facto* alliances. One of the leading Wesleyan ministers also noticed a change for the better in the class of migrant and in religious observance in the colonies. A Presbyterian observer, widely acquainted with Australian churches and congregations, expressed the opinion that colonial church-goers gave very marked attention to the service, being far less given to yawning, sleeping and general listlessness than Scottish congregations were. The colonies were not all stony ground where the seed of the Word could not grow to the harvest.[1]

Church-going involved much the same proportion of the population in the colonies around the middle of the nineteenth century as in Australia today. Australian Gallup Polls in 1947, 1961 and 1962

[1] W. Hutchins, *A Sermon on behalf of the V.D.L. Committee of the Societies for Promoting Christian Knowledge, and Propagating the Gospel* . . . (Hobart, 1839), p. 3; *S.P.G. Report* (N.S.W.), 1840, pp. 22-3, 28, 32; J. McKenny, quoted in *Wesleyan Missionary Report* (London, 1840), pp. 28-9; D. Mackenzie, *The Emigrant's Guide* . . . (London, 1845), p. 54.

found that, on an average, about thirty per cent of Australians had attended church in the last two Sundays; and this presumably means that something like twenty per cent attend each week. From the approximate and sometimes ambiguous figures listed for New South Wales in 1850 it seems that the average number at worship on a typical Sunday was in the vicinity of forty-one thousand, again about twenty per cent of the population.[2] In Melbourne, on a Sunday, the people were 'dressed in their best clothes, the shops shut, the streets . . . quiet', and in the Port Phillip District nearly nine and a half thousand people almost filled the twenty-seven churches.[3] This only meant, however, that the existing churches, accommodating thirteen per cent of the population, were well attended; it did not mean that church-going in this newer settlement was as great as in New South Wales proper. Van Diemen's Land naturally came out better in this regard; there, in 1849, almost seventeen thousand—about one-quarter of the population—attended church on Sunday.[4] The highest attendance in the three areas was at Anglican churches, though the percentage of the Anglican population attending was low. Catholics contributed large numbers of worshippers to the New South Wales total (twelve and a half thousand compared with the Anglican fifteen and a half) and a smaller proportion in the Port Phillip District and Van Diemen's Land. Other Protestant denominations attracted some thirteen thousand Sunday worshippers in New South Wales, about half the total attendants in Van Diemen's Land and well over half in the Port Phillip District, the Wesleyan Methodists being the leaders everywhere.

No churchman could pretend that he was satisfied with this attendance. According to the religious census taken in England and Wales in 1851, about forty per cent of that population attended church on Sunday;[5] and, to take another standard of comparison, some forty-seven per cent of adult Americans attend church every week in our own times.[6] That from one-fifth to one-quarter of the Australian colonists went fairly regularly to church, therefore, does not mark them as a church-going people. On the other hand, they were much better attenders than the English are today, for the period has to be extended to one month to allow twenty-eight per cent of them to claim that they have attended church recently[7]—a fact which probably

[2] N.S.W. Blue Book, 1850, p. 611.
[3] D. Mackenzie, op. cit., p. 30; *Statistics of the Port Phillip District . . . 1850* (Melbourne, 1852), p. 6.
[4] *Statistics of V.D.L. for 1849* (Hobart, 1850), Tables 44-50.
[5] *P.P.* (H.C.), 1852-3, vol. LXXXIX, p. 1. See also K. S. Inglis, 'Patterns of Religious Worship in 1851', *Journal of Ecclesiastical History*, vol. 11, no. 1, pp. 74-86.
[6] American Institute of Public Opinion Surveys, 1957-61.
[7] Gallup Poll, London, 1957.

means that no more than fifteen per cent attend weekly.[8] Taking this
as a standard, and allowing for all the colonial difficulties in the way
of church attendance, the colonists do not emerge badly as church-
goers. Sufficient numbers of them went sufficiently often to give their
clergymen solid encouragement and support, and to make worship
a noticeable, though not the dominant, feature of the colonial Sunday.
In this respect, Australians have changed very little from the middle
of one century to the middle of the next.

Candidates for Confirmation flocked to the Anglican churches in
hundreds each year, and the sacrament of Baptism was widely administered. In 1849 the Van Diemen's Land Churches between them
baptized at least two thousand persons, most of whom would have
been young children. Since there were three and a half thousand
children under two years of age in that colony in 1848, and only about
four thousand in 1850, the rate of baptism was sufficient to keep up
with the births. In 1851, in fact, when the Reverend John Mereweather
visited the extremity of the White Hills district—'quite in the bush'—
he found 'a great many children, dirty, untidy, ignorant and healthy.
They had all been baptized'.[9] From the Australian bush have emerged
famous stories of visiting clergymen being told that they could christen
the settlers' offspring if they could catch them, and the fact that the
rites had been administered did not necessarily mean that they had
been sought by people with a proper appreciation of their significance;
yet it would be unreasonable to dismiss these external evidences of
religion in the colonies, for where the rite is, there the spirit may be
also.

Where the spirit of religion is, however, the practice of religion may
be restricted and prejudiced at some points. Colonists who were of
'the same religion as the Queen' often followed her example in making
their communion only twice a year, while others did not bother about
that sacrament at all, so that Van Diemen's Land Anglican churches
with average attendances at worship of three hundred, one hundred
and fifty, or one hundred and fifteen, were accustomed to only forty-
five, twenty-five or nine communicants at the monthly celebrations.
The Wesleyan Methodists, with over three thousand attending their
preaching services, had a little over one-sixth of that number at their
communion services, and the same was true of the other Protestant
Churches. Catholics made their communion more often, a comparison

[8] See also B. S. Rowntree, and G. R. Lavers, *English Life and Leisure* (London,
1951), p. 343.
[9] W. Hutchins, op. cit., pp. 3-4; Acts and Proceedings of the Bishop of Australia,
passim; Statistics for V.D.L. for 1849; J. D. Mereweather, *Diary of a Working Clergyman in Australia . . .* (London, 1859), p. 78.

being possible between the weekly average of one hundred at the
Eucharist in St Joseph's, Hobart, and the average of sixty-five communicants in the Anglican St David's, both churches claiming an
attendance of eight hundred worshippers—either as non-communicants
or at non-sacramental services.[10] This comparatively infrequent communion did not, of course, necessarily point to wilful neglect or to
sheer indifference. It could result from a high appreciation of the
sacrament (as in the Presbyterian tradition), or from an inhibiting dread
of taking it unworthily, for this was a fear which was as real for a
respectable schoolmaster in a state of spiritual depression as it was for
superstitiously ignorant soldiers and convicts on Norfolk Island.[11]

Forms and formality certainly found many critics in the colonies.
Resentful ex-convicts were among them, for they had their memories.

> But there we were, helpless, and forced to submit to it all, and compelled
> to endure the purgatory of two and three long doleful hours—rising,
> kneeling, and sitting, according to the most precise formula, all the
> while holding our faces as grave as an owl, and for all the world look-
> ing, perhaps, about as wise.[12]

There were many others, too, who preferred a different type of service.
An old Methodist woman on Mereweather's ship, who complained that
there were no prayer meetings on board, and that the chaplain's prayers
were 'only parson's prayers', was giving vent to feelings which were
neither irreligious nor likely to be lost in the colonies.[13] After hearing
Morning Prayer read in a small settlement, James Backhouse remarked
that 'this sort of mechanical religious service does not seem to be very
attractive to the people, either here or in other places'.[14] Launceston
Wesleyans vigorously resisted their ministers' attempts to use the Order
for Morning Prayer (though it was used elsewhere),[15] and an incident
in the ministry of the Reverend J. C. Symons, first Wesleyan minister
in Gippsland, is equally revealing. Symons allowed himself to be persuaded to 'don a pair of moles' so that he would not appal his bush
congregation by 'the terrors of a black suit', and was greeted en-
thusiastically as a 'right good fellow in fustian, instead of a mere
formal parson'.[16] Bishop Polding, apparently placing a good deal of

---

[10] *Statistics of V.D.L. for 1849.*
[11] J. F. Castle, Private Journal 1838-52, 2 December 1838 (A.N.U. Archives);
T. Sharpe, Journal Kept at Norfolk Island, 1839-40, p. 37 (ML).
[12] W. Gates, *Recollections of Life in Van Dieman's [sic] Land* (Lockport, 1850),
pp. 93-4.
[13] J. D. Mereweather, *Life on Board an Emigrant Ship* . . . (London, 1852), p. 18.
[14] J. Backhouse, *Narrative of a Visit to the Australian Colonies* . . . (London, 1843),
p. 189.   [15] V.D.L. Wes. Dist. Min., 5 June 1837; ibid., 1 November 1838.
[16] W. L. Blamires and J. B. Smith, *The Early Story of the Wesleyan Methodist
Church in Victoria* (Melbourne, 1886), p. 251.

faith in the visual drama of Catholic services, once remarked confidently, 'to suppose that the cold forms of Protestantism can ever have effect on our abandoned population is absurd. . . . So long as Methodism does not come in, we have no rival to fear.'[17] The Anglican clergymen revealed their awareness of this critical spirit, even among worshipping members of the Church of England, by making frequent defences of their Church's practices and by a proud insistence that it did not attempt to allure men by 'novelty or excitement'.[18]

Anglicans, however, were doubly and painfully conscious of the two approaches to worship because many of their clergy had adopted the high church principles then being stressed by the new Tractarian party. This emphasis was very much considered to be a novelty, and one to be resisted, by the low churchmen. At home, at the beginning of the century, the dominant party in Anglicanism had been low church, and the most important minority party—the fervent Evangelicals—was also low church. The early Australian chaplains reflected this dominance, but men of high church views, such as W. G. Broughton himself, arrived in the colonies in later years. Their principles were developed and their numbers were enlarged after 1833, when the Tractarians, headed by the Oxford men, J. H. Newman, John Keble and E. B. Pusey, became influential. Old chaplains like William Cowper and Philip Palmer were happy in 'scattering the tracts of the Religious Tract Society', which were Evangelical and Dissenting productions, and they were shocked by the Anglo-Catholicism of the *Tracts for the Times* coming out of the Oxford Movement.[19] For them, their fellow Evangelicals and the other low churchmen, the priestly office, sacramental grace and the corporate nature of the Church, could be minimized in favour of individual conversion and faith. But what they relegated to the background, the Tractarians brought to the forefront, a move which struck answering chords in the hearts of the colonial bishops (Charles Perry excluded) and many of the newer clergymen.[20] This led to conflicts within the Church of England, and to a widening of the breach between Anglicanism and other forms of Protestantism.

[17] H. N. Birt, *Benedictine Pioneers in Australia* (London, 1911), I, p. 306.
[18] *Proceedings of the Paramatta [sic] District Committee of the Societies for Promoting Christian Knowledge and the Propagation of the Gospel . . . and the Anniversary Sermon . . . by the Rev. Robert Allwood . . .* (Parramatta, 1840), pp. 18, 23; F. H. Cox, *Perseverance and Endurance . . .* (Hobart, 1851), pp. 12-13; A. Stackhouse, *The Christian's Encouragement in well doing . . .* (Launceston, 1845), p. 5; G. E. Turner, *A Sermon, preached on Whit-Sunday, May 27th, 1849* (Sydney, n.d.), p. 3.
[19] F. R. Nixon to Woodcock, 24 February 1844, N. Nixon (ed.), *The Pioneer Bishop in Van Diemen's Land, 1843-63* (Hobart, 1953), p. 22; Broughton to Coleridge, 14 February 1842, 14 January 1846, B.P.
[20] Compare W. Cowper, *A Sermon preached in St. Philip's Church, Sydney . . . October 14, 1849* (Sydney, n.d.), pp. 3-4, with W. G. Broughton, *The Nature and Intent of the Holy Communion . . .* (Sydney, 1841), pp. 12, 15.

There was considerable unrest in the Church in 1848 after the Reverend R. K. Sconce and the Reverend T. C. Makinson had renounced Anglicanism and joined the Catholic Church. Although twenty of the clergy, including the Evangelicals, William Cowper, P. T. Beamish and F. T. C. Russell, and the Church of England Lay Association signed addresses to Bishop Broughton sympathizing with him in his embarrassment, and pledging their own loyalty, some of the evangelical country parsons, among them James Hassall and G. E. Turner, joined with some low church landed gentry in condemning Tractarianism. They suggested that their bishop should do more to stamp out the movement which was having this bad effect on their Church. Broughton was here at his most astute in steering the controversy into channels where it could die down.[21] It did not, however, die out. A year later the two young deacons, Beamish and Russell, being low church, disgruntled and impulsively indiscreet, publicly criticized the 'popish' invasion of the Church of England in a way which led to their licences being revoked by Broughton, an action which called forth a protest from a good many laymen who sided with the deacons.[22] Bishop Broughton's force of character, his ruthlessness in the face of opposition, his own hatred of Roman Catholicism and consequent mistrust of the less moderate Tractarians,[23] and the common bond of the liturgy among his clergy, damped down the fires of controversy— at least temporarily—and promoted the Anglican virtue of accommodation. But the underlying differences and tension remained to be revealed again in the subsequent history of the Diocese of Sydney, in more serious clashes between Van Diemen's Land clergymen and Bishop Nixon (who was a less commanding person and a more dedicated Tractarian than Broughton), in dissent by the evangelical Bishop Perry from the doctrine of baptismal regeneration accepted by his fellow bishops, and in the relations between the Church of England and the other Protestant Churches.

When the Wesleyans at Windsor built a new chapel in 1840, and approached the public for donations, the Anglican incumbent launched a bitter attack on them as being in no true Church. It not only drew an immediate retort, but also left a legacy of resentment against 'the

[21] *Herald*, 24 February 1848, p. 2; 4 March 1848, p. 2. See also K. J. Cable, 'Religious Controversies in New South Wales in the Mid-Nineteenth Century', *J.R.A.H.S.*, vol. 49, part 1, pp. 64-5.

[22] *Herald*, 5 June 1849, p. 1, and following issues; Acts and Proceedings of the Bishop of Australia, II, p. 57; *Statement by the Rev. F. T. C. Russell* . . . (Sydney, 1849).

[23] Broughton to Coleridge, 14 October 1839, 20 September 1843, 10 July 1844, B.P.; W. G. Broughton, *A Charge to the Clergy of the Diocese of Australia* . . . (Sydney, 1844), pp. 39-40, 51. Compare with the comment on Nixon in Broughton to Coleridge, 9 April 1845.

vaunting apostolic successionists' in the very denomination which was closest to the Church of England in history and in some continuing practices.[24] Nonconformists asked sarcastic questions about 'the precise line of demarcation' between Anglicanism and 'a more ancient communion', and put forward their proud defence that they did 'not pretend to be lineal successors of the apostles' but did desire 'to imitate the piety and preach the doctrines taught by the apostles'.[25] But the high church Anglicans continued to scoff at *'Ministers of Religion* (socalled)', and to condemn the Protestantism of Evangelicals and Dissenters as the 'spurious' product of the eighteenth century, from which the original reformers' respect for 'the rational veneration for the Teaching and Witness of Antiquity' had been sloughed off.[26]

While the Churches tried to score off each other, the colonial mission field waited and the colonists who were inclined to piety simply went to church with the denomination which had done most for them, or into which they had been born. On the whole, they were indifferent to the controversy. Sometimes they expressed regret and resentment:

> A generation has passed since this colony was formed; forty years long were we without a bishop; then all classes assisted each other, and every good man approved without suspicion the labours of his neighbours . . . Now we see attempts to drive every good feeling into denominational channels, and to struggle for ascendency.[27]

Occasionally the laymen rose up in vigorous protest, but never for long or in great numbers. A broad acceptance of religion kept them loyal to their denominations, but it was too broad to turn them into crusaders. In the late forties there was talk in Sydney and Melbourne of forming a 'free' Church of England, but nothing emerged of any significance, and other dissident groups, like the Wroeites and the Wesleyan Methodist Association, either remained small or collapsed completely. Prophets who had seen visions were not warmly welcomed; one named Westwood toured the Western District of Victoria only to be politely heard or sternly rebuffed; no big following was gathered by him or any other.[28] Broughton was not indulging in mere wishful thinking when he wrote of Geelong, 'There has never been a clergyman

---

[24] H. T. Stiles, *A Sermon preached . . . previously to the opening of a new Wesleyan Chapel . . .* (Sydney, 1840): 'A Friend to Truth and Peace', *A Letter to the Rev. Henry Tarlton Stiles . . .* (Sydney, 1840); N.S.W. Wes. Dist. Min., 1849, Appendix 1.

[25] *Examiner*, 14 October 1843, p. 641; *The Eighth Report of the V.D.L. Colonial Missionary . . . Society . . .* (Hobart, 1844), p. 7.

[26] Archdeacon Hutchin's petition, *V. & P.* (V.D.L.), 1840; *S.P.G. Report* (Parramatta), 1840, pp. 12, 14.

[27] *Examiner*, 8 November 1843, p. 697.

[28] M. Kiddle, *Men of Yesterday* (Melbourne, 1961), p. 301.

here before; and yet they have a presbyterian minister, a wesleyan preacher, and a Romish priest: and yet more remarkable, the Church of England feeling still pervades the great number, and the most intelligent'.[29] A tolerant support of the orthodox denominations was the positive characteristic of the Australian colonist, just as his negative qualities were scepticism of exclusive denominational claims and phlegmatic moderation in spiritual things generally. A very accurate summary of colonial religion was given by two Wesleyan ministers in Victoria, fifty years after their colony's foundation, when they said of the colonists that religion had a home and a welcome among them, and toned down the 'rough asperities' while developing the 'better elements', but that 'it assumed not the stern type of the Puritan in New England'.[30] The colonists were certainly not puritanical, and not religious enthusiasts; on the contrary, they seem to have shown, almost always and everywhere, a resistance to fervently revivalistic religion. Wesleyans occasionally reported small local revivals—thirty persons won at Dapto, New South Wales, and a few persons gathered in from the world at Back River, Van Diemen's Land; but the general situation was described by the Reverend Nathaniel Turner in the words, 'We have at times appeared just on the eve of revival amongst the people, and then something has transpired that has appeared to put an extinguisher upon the gracious flame'.[31] The devout Mrs Sarah Hopkins, of Hobart, recorded in her diary the prayerful hope of a revival among Independents and those they could reach, but this did not come either.[32] The later, and noteworthy, revival which swept through the United States of America in 1858, and crossed the Atlantic into the British Isles in 1859, did not much influence Australians. In 1859-60 it was supposed to have 'visited also these shores', but it 'came in lessened energy', according to commentators who thus exaggerated the faint ripple.[33] The colonists were well proofed against revivals, a fact which is not only significant for the modern sociologist of religion, but which also meant that few of the colonists who were outside the Churches were persuaded to come into them.

Yet the church leaders were inclined to over-state the case against the tolerant and the partially committed, relegating them too readily to the legions of the damned. Broughton was alarmed at 'a spirit of self-

[29] Broughton to Coleridge, 20, 29 September 1843, B.P.
[30] W. L. Blamires and J. B. Smith, op. cit., p. 11.
[31] N. Turner, Journal, 14 August 1840 (MS. ML).
[32] J. West, *The Hope of Life Eternal. A Sermon: occasioned by the death of Mrs. Sarah Hopkins . . . [with] . . . extracts from the memoranda of the deceased* (Launceston, 1850, pp. 92-4.
[33] Blamires and Smith, op. cit., p. 89. See also J. C. Robinson, *The Free Presbyterian Church of Australia* (Melbourne, 1947), pp. 85-8; M. Kiddle, op. cit., p. 446.

will' amounting 'practically to atheism' among the leading men. Nixon, in his bitter remark that he was 'old fashioned enough' to believe that a country needed God's blessing, implied that the Legislative Councillors in his diocese did not think so. Hutchins condemned the readiness of ostensibly Christian legislators to support 'acknowledged error'. The Catholic Bishop Davis complained that the New South Wales Legislative Council was 'chiefly composed of a fearful set of infidels'.[34] The liberal opinions condemned by these churchmen did sometimes lead to the rejection of revealed religion, and constantly led to the rejection of some of the Churches' demands; but the official debates and decisions rebut the idea that the councillors, and their social peers, were characteristically atheists or agnostics or on the road to spiritual ruin. So far were they from this, that all affirmed their belief in the necessity for religion, backing their talk by large grants of money and by strenuous efforts to find acceptable methods of religious instruction in State schools. No doubt the religion of many leading men, and of other respectable citizens, sat comparatively lightly on their shoulders; but the real cause of the frustrated annoyance among leading churchmen was not that the prominent citizens were 'infidels', but that they, like many of the colonial church-goers, lacked denominational exclusiveness and doctrinal rigidity. They knew the many areas in which all ministers were welcomed and 'controversial divinity was excluded by common consent', and they were very sympathetic to the view that it was wrong to dwell on 'differences in the forms and modes of worship . . . till in the heat of controversy and bigotry, they forgot that they were Christians'.[35] Against the claims that the colonies were seething oceans of irreligion may be set the fact that the true religious extremists usually expected small support for their views. G. M. C. Bowen, in 1836, anticipated not only 'expressions of surprise' from his friends, but also their 'strong disapproval'. In the next decade, Henry Melville was not willing to risk putting his printed rejection of Christianity on the market, but presented it to friends with the request that they should not allow it out of their possession.[36] There were, therefore, big islands and long peninsulas of orthodox belief in the colonial sea of unbelief. The story of religion in the Australian colonies is not just a tale without significance; it is a vital chapter in the history of the making of Australia.

[34] Broughton to Coleridge, 6 March 1847, B.P.; *Courier*, 3 November 1843, p. 2; W. Hutchins, op. cit., p. 26; Davis to Heptonstall, 22 August 1850, in H. N. Birt, op. cit., II, p. 166.
[35] J. West, *The History of Tasmania* (Launceston, 1852), I, pp. 85-6, 196; *Herald*, 10 October 1846, p. 2.
[36] Bowen to Broughton, 24 November 1836, Stiles Papers (A1323 ML); Melville's *Exposition . . .* —the copy presented to H. S. Thomson, now in the Mitchell Library.

What the Parsons Preached

When men believed in hell and possession by Satan, and had never heard of psychoneurosis and release by Dr Freud, it was easy for preachers to play upon men's fears. Warnings of God's judgment were seldom absent from the colonies' sermons, and were sometimes very strong. Bishop Broughton and the Dissenter, Barzillai Quaife, preaching diverse doctrines of the Holy Communion, came together at the end to warn of punishment for its neglect. The Catholic Vicar-General and a motley group of total abstainers agreed that the drunkard had 'a doom appointed for all eternity'. Wesleyans might hear of 'endless burnings', and Presbyterians of 'misery inconceivable and eternal'.[37] Yet the remarkable thing about the preaching in the second quarter of the nineteenth century is not how much, but how little fire and brimstone there was in the typical sermon. Judgment and damnation were unquestioningly accepted, but they were usually mentioned with brevity and restraint. As likely as not, the congregation would simply be reminded that they were in need of salvation in words like these: 'Spend your Christmas with a true Christian joy, but remember that there is no true Christian joy apart from repentance'. The common appeal was to the better nature of the hearers. 'But are you not weary of this evil doing?', asked the Reverend Alfred Stackhouse. 'You have a great trust', the Reverend William Yate told parents and masters, warning them that children, born in sin, would grow up in sin unless their elders corrected them. To the young people themselves he addressed words of understanding and encouragement, not of grim foreboding. Bishop Polding's 'bitter grief' over his people's neglect of their religion, and the 'affectionate' nature of his exhortation, did not remain mere words for the reader: they breathed in the document.[38] The clergy kept the hard doctrines before their people, but not usually in a harsh manner.

The doctrine of the predestination of all but the elect to damnation does not seem to have been firmly accepted even by the Presbyterian preachers. J. D. Lang declared that 'eternal life is wholly and solely the gift of God', but went on to put in italics, *'Look unto me, and be*

---

[37] W. G. Broughton, *The Nature and Intent of the Holy Communion* . . . (Sydney, 1841); B. Quaife, *A condensed view of the proper design and uses of the Lord's Supper* (Parramatta, 1845); W. Ullathorne, *Substance of a Sermon against Drunkenness* . . . (Sydney, n.d. [1834]); *Annual Report of V.D.L. Total Abstinence Society*, 1850, p. 2; 'A Friend to Truth and Peace', op. cit., p. 22: J. D. Lang, 'Sketch of a Sermon in the Bush in Australia', *An Historical and Statistical Account of New South Wales* . . . (Sydney, 3rd ed., 1852), II, p. 588.

[38] W. Dry, *Sermons* (Launceston, 1850), Sermon II; A. Stackhouse, op. cit., p. 23; W. Yate, *To the Parishioners of St. James' Church* . . . (Sydney, 1836), pp. 4-11; J. B. Polding, *Pastoral Instruction for Lent* . . . (Sydney, 1837), pp. 4, 8.

ye saved, all ye ends of the earth'. The Reverend John McGarvie, though a Presbyterian whom Lang accused of being 'a Minister of the gospel which he never preached', in truth spoke no differently. He believed, indeed, that not all men would be saved, but in preaching on John 3:16 he pronounced that 'the term *world* . . . denotes the human family, all of whom are loved by the gift of Christ', and he offered salvation to any who were willing to accept 'the easy terms on which it is bestowed—faith in the only begotten Son of God'. He was even prepared to say, 'Whether faith is first, and grace succeeds, or whether grace prepares the heart for the reception of faith, the same consequence follows'.[39] This was an impossible statement for a rigid Calvinist who accepted the Westminster Confession's dogma that the natural spirit must be passive and incapable of moral response until grace was bestowed upon it; but it was in line with those Calvinists who rejected the notion of deterministic predestination and, following the idea of the covenant between God and man, allowed that man could make some spontaneous response and prepare himself for the reception of grace—with the implication that any man who did this would almost certainly be granted it.[40] Such modification of the Calvinistic doctrine was also common among Anglican Evangelicals. Hence, though it cannot be said that the absence of revival was due to the absence of hell from the sermons, it can be said that the preaching emphasized the offer of salvation rather than the threat of hell.

To some extent the clergymen preached a hell on earth, for they firmly believed that God intervened in men's affairs to punish them. Parodies of religion sometimes came to life in all piety in this connection. The Reverend Christopher Eipper (a continental reformed pastor working with the Presbyterians) referred to the venereal disease raging among the aboriginal women near Moreton Bay as 'that shocking malady which Divine Providence has wisely ordained as the due reward of profligacy'.[41] All these preachers were at all times in the hand of God, the God who could test them through illness, warn them through the death of one close to them, and show himself in the devastation of a storm as the one whose 'judicial procedure' went on 'even in the present life'.[42] The clergy took very seriously an invitation

[39] J. McGarvie, *Sermons* . . . (Sydney, 1842), pp. 268, 258-9, 270-1.
[40] See Perry Miller, 'Preparation for Salvation in Seventeenth Century New England', *Journal of the History of Ideas*, vol. IV, no. 3, pp. 253-86.
[41] C. Eipper, *Statement of the Origins, Condition, and Prospects of the German Mission to the Aborigines* . . . (Sydney, 1841), p. 10.
[42] G. E. Turner, *A Few Words from a Minister to his Flock* . . . (Sydney, 1844), p. 3; S. Leigh, *Journal from England to New South Wales, 1815*, B.T.Miss., Box 50, 188-9 (ML); A. M. Ramsay, *The Voice of the Storm . . . Preached in the Protestant Hall, Stephen Street, Melbourne* . . . (Melbourne, 1850), p. 3.

from the Governor of New South Wales in 1838 to observe a day of fast and to pray for the ending of a severe drought, and duly held the services. Nine days afterwards, a week of heavy rain began, and penitence gave place to thanksgiving. The Reverend John McGarvie, in his sermon on the day of fasting, explained that God, while not infringing upon his own laws for slight causes, did use physical evils as chastisement for moral guilt, and had to use this means for the punishment of guilty nations, since nations did not have immortal souls to be punished in the world to come. The breaking of the drought was followed by an epidemic, the seriousness of which can be gathered from an entry in the diary of Frederick Castle, the schoolmaster: 'Heard that 10,000 in Sydney are ill of this Influenza or Catarrh & 2,000 in bed—not a family exempt—had scarcely any pupils last week—one Day pupil dead'. McGarvie had a ready explanation of this also: it was not a judgment but proof that man's mind could not fathom the inscrutable wisdom of Providence.[43] Fortunately, God's ways with men were not always reduced to the simplest interpretations: Samuel Leigh, first Wesleyan minister to come to Australia, rejected the notion that the loss of a gunner overboard meant a judgment on him for sin; and a later preacher, influenced by Archbishop Trench's book on the parables (published 1841), maintained that Christ did not deny the connection between sin and suffering, but did deny man's power to trace the connection and interpret a man's character by his afflictions.[44]

That the advancement or decline of races and nations was determined by God, and a people's response to God, was a common and emphasized theme. To some, the selection of the British people was 'clearly revealed on the page of inspired prophecy', though others stressed that this depended upon what the British people continued to do.[45] As the various missions to the aborigines struggled on or were given up, the decline of the aboriginal people was sometimes attributed to the decree of Providence—'God shall enlarge Japheth, and she shall dwell in the tents of Shem'. Others, though close to despair, kept hoping that the gospel might yet be received by the blacks, and some were sensible enough to see in the aboriginal decline 'the fatal influence of profligate whites' rather than any divinely predestined extinction.[46] Most common of all was the warning typified by some words of the Reverend W. B. Clarke, geologist and Evangelical:

[43] J. McGarvie, op. cit., pp. 77, 84; J. F. Castle, op. cit., 2-20 November 1838.
[44] T. McK. Fraser, *Calamities Not Judgements* . . . (Geelong, 1866), pp. 3-4.
[45] *Report of V.D.L. Colonial Missionary . . . Society*, 1844, p. 4; *Courier*, 3 November 1843, p. 2.
[46] *Annual Report of the Aboriginal Protection Society* (London, 1847), pp. 23-4; Marsden to Coates, 23 February 1836, B.T.Miss., Box 54 (ML).

And shall the nation to which we belong . . . this highly favoured nation escape; if, contented with the blessings she enjoys, she shuts up her sympathies in shameless selfishness, forgetful of the office to which she has been called . . . as the defender of the Faith, as the guardian of the ark of liberty 'wherewith Christ hath made us free'?[47]

One part of the obedience to God which determined a people's greatness was the proper observance of Sunday. The day of rest was the one institution to survive the Fall, and its observance was a protection for religion, a bulwark against ungodliness, and a test of men's loyalty or enmity to God:

In proportion as nations, churches, or individuals have risen in the scale of religion and morality, they have improved this holy day, commemorative of the world's redemption by our Lord Jesus Christ, and prefiguring that 'rest which remains for the people of God'.[48]

This day's rest did not mean a day's play, so the clergy came out in strong support of such things as the New South Wales Bill to prevent shooting on Sunday, a Bill which Bishop Broughton wanted to have extended to prohibit boxing, cricket, fishing, cock-fighting, the opening of shops (except butchers' shops, to 8 a.m.) and the loading and packing of goods for markets within forty miles distance.[49] Commonsense was to the fore in the last two suggestions, and the Council's committee, appointed at Broughton's suggestion, showed a like realism in its recommendation that hay-making should be permitted on Sunday when a magistrate declared that weather conditions made it necessary. The preachers were practical about this world's goods; but, at the same time, they were very conscious of the snares of riches.

However much the spirit of Protestantism may have helped the growth of capitalism as an economic system, as distinct from the presence of capitalists in other systems, it is wrong to hold that this was anything other than an unintended accompaniment of the Protestant appreciation of industry, sobriety and frugality. Greed and the individualism which replaced community responsibilities did not cease to be sins for the Reformers, and warnings to this effect were repeatedly given from colonial pulpits. Both riches and poverty, indeed, were crosses laid on men's shoulders, according to the Reverend William Dry; it was hard to have wealth and to use it as God's steward, and it was hard to be poor and not to rail against God.[50] The Reverend

[47] *S.P.G. Report* (N.S.W.), 1840, p. 6.
[48] J. D. Lang, *Lectures on the Sabbath . . . by Ministers of the Presbyterian Church* (Sydney, 1841), Lecture 1: *Report of the Wesleyan Methodist Sunday Schools in the Hobart Town Circuit* (Hobart, 1843), p. 5.
[49] *V. & P.* (N.S.W.), 1841.   [50] W. Dry, op. cit., Sermon v.

W. B. Clarke had serious misgivings on his own account when he took two years' leave of absence to conduct a geological survey of the gold fields in the service of the Government. He secured from Broughton a licence to minister within the whole diocese, and, after preaching to one group of settlers, wrote to a friend, 'It is to be hoped that I may never be reproached with forsaking my calling to seek the gold that perisheth, for the judgements of the Lord, which I proclaimed amidst the mountains are more to be desired than gold, yea, than fine gold!'[51] Bishop Broughton's surrender of a large part of his salary to help establish the other bishoprics, and the Reverend J. Jennings Smith's *coup de grâce* to any hope of educating one of his sons for the ministry by giving £600 to build and furnish a church,[52] were applied sermons on those things which are to be preferred to personal gain, and financial sacrifices were often made by the ministers of religion simply in remaining true to their calling.

Yet there were ministers with a standard of living which left them open to a critic's sneer that 'their outward appearance' did not 'proclaim them as belonging to Pharaoh's lean kine'.[53] As a class, the ministers lived as much like gentlemen as they could, and often lived very much like gentlemen indeed. This was a natural class alignment which, in turn, determined their attitude to the structure of society, making them disinclined to support any radical change in it. Catholic clergymen, often Irish and always standing with their typically poor parishioners against Protestant wealth and power, were frequently radical in their politics, and in this they were joined by a few Protestant clergymen, such as Charles Price and Dr Lang. But the latter damned the social conservatism of the clergy generally, saying scornfully:

> the clergy of all communions, especially if supported by the State, are almost uniformly on the side of wealth, and rank, and power, and real, although perhaps disguised injustice and oppression. . . . And, oh, how they hate universal suffrage, and vote by ballot, equal electoral districts, popular election and the rights of men![54]

Charity rather than social reform, benevolent paternalism rather than democracy, were what most ministers believed and preached. Broughton condemned, as evil, the 'levelling spirit in politics'. Dry taught that the Lord fixed men's stations. Stiles called for acts of mercy, but

[51] W. B. Clarke, *Researches in the Southern Goldfields of New South Wales* (Sydney, 1860), p. 119n.
[52] Smith to Broughton, 29 January 1846; Broughton to Coleridge, 3 October 1846, B.P.
[53] J. O. Balfour, *A Sketch of New South Wales . . .* (London, 1845), p. 114.
[54] J. D. Lang, *Freedom and Independence for the Golden Lands of Australia . . .* (Sydney, 1857), pp. 365-6.

gave no hint that anything more than an offering for the poor might be considered.[55] And these were the typical clerical attitudes. The social organization was attributed to God, and men were told to be content with it. Government was established by God to have a parental regard for its subjects, who were to be obedient children. Church leaders offered much criticism of government policy on education, State aid, revenue from liquor duties, and many other issues; but the basic structure of State and society they did not wish to alter.

Radical political threats to the established order were, in fact, far more alarming to the conservative majority among the clergy than were the new discoveries trickling out from scientific experiments, though these were becoming numerous and were ultimately to have an important bearing on Christian belief.[56] Colonial clergymen could not possibly recognize that such contemporary events as Dalton's atomic theory and Faraday's experiments in electro-chemistry were the foundation for a new atomic science, or that science was soon to change men's ways of thinking and topple many old theories. The very word 'scientist' was newly-coined (by the Reverend William Whewell, who was one of them himself) in 1840, and their discoveries were at first merely interesting. Even when they were noticed by men at large, it was not at all obvious where they, and the scientific method itself, were leading. There was only one, and even this not an unqualified, exception.

The immensely popular science of geology was then in its 'heroic age', enjoying a prestige similar to that held by nuclear physics today, but offering the far greater attraction of permitting the amateur, and even the lady, to participate actively in its researches.[57] All the more serious was it, therefore, that some geological theories were iconolastic. The 'Vulcanist' school argued that heat, not the flood, had been crucial in forming the earth's surface; James Hutton declared that he could find in the earth no mark of a beginning or prospect of an end; and Sir Charles Lyell denied any catastrophic divine intervention in the creation of man, insisting upon an unbroken operation of uniform law from remotest antiquity. To cap it all, in anticipation of Darwin, Robert Chambers argued in his intuitive *Vestiges of the Natural History of Creation* (1844) for the slow development of species. The situation was saved—or, rather, the final reckoning was delayed until after 1850—by two facts. First, the geologists themselves were usually divided

[55] Broughton to Coleridge, 14 January 1843, B.P.; W. Dry, op. cit., Sermon ix; H. T. Stiles, *A Sermon Preached at St. Matthew's Church, Windsor . . . before the . . . United Loyal Hawkesbury Lodge . . .* (Sydney, 1845), pp. 13-15.
[56] See W. C. Dampier, *A History of Science and its Relations with Philosophy and Religion* (Cambridge, 4th ed., 1948), pp. 200 ff.
[57] C. C. Gillispie, *Genesis and Geology* (New York, Torchbook ed., 1959), pp. 41, 87-8. The whole of this paragraph is based on this work.

about each new claim and, anyway, did not see the full implications
of the steps they were taking. Secondly, most of them did not wish to
overthrow the book of Genesis or break absolutely with the old Paleyist
teleology which, indeed, was widely accepted right up to the middle
of the century. Though the Vulcanist theory had won general support
in Britain by 1825, the Reverend John Playfair was arguing, as geologist
as well as clergyman, that the contemplation of natural order led to
greater reverence for the Designer than did the idea of sudden con-
vulsions. The Reverend Professor William Buckland likewise declared
that geology tended to confirm the evidences of natural religion, and
also that its discoveries were consistent with the Mosaic account of
creation. Despite some earlier flutterings, by 1830 the descriptive
sciences—zoology and paleontology, as well as geology—simply seemed
to offer 'new and specific evidence for the recent creation of mankind
and for the historical reality of the flood', which were the 'essential
points, both in Genesis and geology'; and, as late as 1850, few scientists
of any repute gave any support to Chambers' idea of the gradual
development of species. On the whole, therefore, the new science did
not seem about to storm the ramparts of the old religious proofs.
Rather, the deposits of iron, coal and limestone in England revealed
'the most clear design of Providence to make the inhabitants of the
British Isles, by means of this gift, the most powerful and the richest
nation on earth'. If the English leisured classes collected fossils, if
crowds were regularly drawn to Sir Humphry Davy's brilliant lectures
in London, and other crowds heard Buckland and his fellow scientists
speak in caves and Mechanics' Institutes, they were only learning that
the psa'mist's 'how beautiful is thy dwelling place' could be as happily
rendered 'how useful is they dwelling place', and the Bishop of Bath
and Wells urged the universities to take up the teaching of science
for the masses.

Colonial clergymen probably enjoyed the *Sydney Morning Herald*'s
joke that some people contended that Australia came into existence
'late on the first Saturday evening', while others maintained that it had
appeared 'early on the first Monday morning', in the course of its
editorial on fossil bones in 1842. Australians were more interested in
manufactures, mechanics and anaesthetics, than in materialistic theories
of the universe. While there were the odd men out, like Henry Melville, the true colonial scientists, such as W. S. Macleay, the zoologist,
found only greater wonder at 'the work of an all-wise, all-powerful
Deity' in their researches.[58] Many of the best scientists in the colonies

[58] J. J. Fletcher, 'The Society's Heritage from the Macleays', *Proceedings of the
Linnean Society, N.S.W.*, vol. XLV, pp. 593-4.

were, in fact, clergymen. The Reverend W. B. Clarke, scientific adviser to the New South Wales Government, was the first university-trained geologist to come to Australia; the Reverend William Woolls was a botanist; the Reverend R. L. King was an entomologist; and other clergymen with at least an informed interest in scientific matters included James Walker, T. B. Naylor, C. P. N. Wilton, R. R. Davies, T. Dove, T. J. Ewing and Dr John Lillie. They did more than address Mechanics' Institutes and support the Tasmanian Natural History Society (founded by Sir John Franklin in 1838). Clarke, for instance, laid a basis for the accurate correlation of the Australian rock series with those of Europe. These were not the men to be frightened by scientific murmurings. On the contrary, they were happy in the union of science and religion. Lillie told his working men that '*Chance* had been demonstrated to have no place and no office in the unlimited range of universal nature'.[59] Dr Lang, though realizing that his biblical exegesis had to be subtle in the light of the new science, found no difficulty in reconciling the geology of the Port Phillip District with the chronology of Genesis. Remarking on the extremely remote origin of the area, suggested by the signs of volcanic activity, Lang explained that the biblical sentence, 'And the Spirit of God moved upon the face of the waters', was 'a general description of the long series of changes that subsequently passed upon the face of our planet in the course, it may be, of millions of years'.[60] Clarke also had no doubts about religion and science complementing each other, though he saw that men might have to revise a few bad theories. 'But', he wrote, 'this much do speculation and theorizing avail for good, that no man, with a simple-minded aim, can explore any of the beautiful fields of science which are spread out so magnificently above him, and not find himself a *better man,* even if he have to acknowledge himself a worse philosopher than he imagined.'[61] Clarke did not mean to suggest that the study of science might turn a man from the philosophy of Archdeacon Paley to that of Tom Paine; rather, fallible man, by the study of science, would have his unbelief rebuked or his reverence deepened. Thus far, science was religion's obedient handmaid; if she stamped her foot now and then, she had not yet dismayed the household of faith by brazenly walking out of morning prayers. And most who had much to do with her did not dream that she ever would.

It was not, of course, that the clergy paid much heed to science in

[59] J. Lillie, *Opening Lecture . . . upon the Subserviency of the Works of Nature to Religion, delivered at the V.D.L. Mechanics' Institution . . .* (Hobart, 1841), p. 27.
[60] A. C. Gilchrist, *John Dunmore Lang, an Assembling of Contemporary Documents* (Melbourne, 1951), II, p. 393.
[61] *Magazine of Natural History*, vol. VII, p. 615.

the pulpit. Theirs was a revealed religion, not one established by reason
or based upon the argument of design in the universe. The Reverend
John West frankly discounted philosophical and scientific proofs of
Christian truth, saying, 'The external evidences of Christianity were
rarely dwelt upon by the Apostle Paul. It was from the substance and
effects of the gospel, that he usually argued its truth'.[62] Archdeacon
Hutchins, though a mathematician and former Cambridge Fellow,
believed that there was 'no room for discovery' in Christianity, since
its doctrine was 'not discovered by the wit of man, but given by the
inspiration of God'.[63] The Wesleyan, W. B. Boyce, simply ignored the
new geology in his school book on ancient history; the only remarks
he passed on the creation of the world were on the different dates given
by Ussher (4,004 B.C., based on the Hebrew text of the Old Testament) and Hale (5,441 B.C., calculated from the Septuagint).[64] Bishop
Broughton was most insistent that the role of science should not be
exaggerated, lest men be encouraged to think that they could dispense
with revelation. Broughton pointed to two dangers which the more
alert clergy could see in the scientific vogue—the glorification of man's
intellect, and an obsession with material things and demonstrable
proofs. Men's confidence in their own powers had waxed, and men's
faith in God had consequently waned, because of the 'incessant aim
at mechanical perfection, and almost successful attainment of it'.
The remedy was not in hostility to science, in 'casting anchor amidst
the shoals of ignorance', but in following the example of Robert
Boyle and showing that science was 'not deteriorated by an union with
devotion', and that all things were not to be 'brought down to the
level of the senses'.[65] This was the real fear: that science and mechanics
would distract men from the things of the spirit. For the colonial
clergy the possibility of some of their people becoming absorbed in such
pursuits was yet one more materialistic preoccupation to add to the
flocks, herds and commerce which already obsessed so many colonists.
But there was one consolation for them at this point: the universe
at large still seemed to be marked by law and order, even if the
squatting districts were not.

Many of the colonial preachers put their points of view with considerable homiletic skill. It was a day of carefully prepared preaching,
extempore utterances being unusual, and many sermon manuscripts
were passed on to the printers. Though the sermons were long, running

[62] J. West, *The Hope of Life Eternal* . . . , p. 6.
[63] W. Hutchins, op. cit., pp. 24-5.
[64] W. B. Boyce, *Brief Grammar of Ancient History* (Sydney, 1850), p. iv, n.(1), (2).
[65] W. G. Broughton, *The Present Position and Duties of the Church of England* . . .
September the 17th, 1835 . . . (Canterbury, n.d.), pp. 11-13.

to fifteen or even thirty printed pages, and taking forty or more minutes
to read aloud with effect, they were often far from being tedious.[66]
Granted the preachers' premisses, they were logical; within the frame-
work of an uncritical social philosophy, they were bold; shadowed by
a stern eschatology, they were none the less compassionate; and the
appeal and force of their sermons can still be felt in those which are
preserved in manuscript or printed form. If the clergy accepted unquestioningly some ideas which were not to survive the questions of
the next generation, they were only doing what all men do. As preachers
and teachers they had no need to be ashamed, and if the sheep looked
up they were fed.

[66] Compare with D. Mackenzie, op. cit., pp. 51-3.

13

ON BALANCE

'Is there much vital religion in the Church in Australia?', asked the Reverend Thomas Braim in 1846. Though he raised the point boldly, he had to deal with it awkwardly, for he confessed that 'in proportion to the importance of this question is the difficulty of coming to a satisfactory conclusion respecting it'. He was content to conclude on a note of agnosticism:

> The public feeling is all on the side of the form of religion, how much of the power exists among us, the searcher of hearts alone can tell.[1]

The passing of another hundred years of history hardly makes the question any simpler to answer. It is easy to amass contemporary evidence of 'little practical Christianity', of 'fearfully low' moral standards and 'intense selfishness' in the colonial community, and of a people who 'for the most part quitted their native country principally intent on the acquisition of wealth, and with little thought . . . of those durable riches, and of that better country'.[2] Religious carelessness was greater, indeed, than religious zeal in the colonies. Yet the zeal was also there, and was felt as a very real force. New South Wales legislators were not just indulging in wishful thinking when they asserted that many colonists regarded 'the advancement of Virtue and Religion . . . with becoming solicitude',[3] for the history of the Church Acts and of the Churches' growth gives substance to the claim; and the extant private diaries and letters of ordinary lay colonists repeatedly reveal genuine spiritual wrestlings and ecstacies. One contemporary observer, therefore, dismissed the religious aspect of colonial life too peremptorily when he said, 'Appearances are all in favour of religion in the Colony, it would be well if there were the reality'.[4] The view of the Reverend Thomas Braim is to be preferred. Too acute and cautious to claim

---

[1] T. H. Braim, *History of New South Wales from its Settlement to . . . 1844* (London, 1846), II, pp. 168-9.
[2] J. Backhouse, *Narrative of a Visit to the Australain Colonies . . .* (London, 1843), p. cxii; Denison to Grey, 25 April 1848, G.O. 33/63 (TA); *Report of V.D.L. Colonial Missionary . . . Society*, 1843, p. 4.   [3] 10 July, *V. & P.* (N.S.W.), 1838.
[4] J. C. Byrne, *Emigrant's Guide to New South Wales . . .* (London, 1848), p. 48.

overmuch, he rightly allowed the possibility of religion being vital to a significant number of colonials. The most, and the least, that can be said is that many ignored religion, many supported it for conventional and utilitarian reasons, and not a few were deeply religious people.

This calls for caution in assessing the role of religion in the colonies, for that role can easily be exaggerated, and as easily discounted. If it be argued that there was, in the 1835-50 era, an 'essential, if not fully acknowledged, antipathy between moral liberalism and traditional Christianity',[5] great weight should be placed on the qualification that the antipathy was not fully acknowledged; and it may be added that it is possible to be deeply impressed by the place occupied by traditional Christianity in the thinking and legislating of the colonists, even in an age when old Church prerogatives were being taken over by a State which defended liberty of conscience rather than one of several faiths. The later history of Australia has also been described in terms of religious decline, so that the 'wealth of love which used to be lavished on Him is turned upon the whole of nature'.[6] Yet there is much to be said to the contrary. The second quarter of the nineteenth century was, if anything, an improvement upon the years of serious religious neglect which had preceded it. To be sure, the churchmen were appalled by the unbelief and scepticism about them. But they had always been appalled by this. Men and women were maintaining continuity with the past when they lived for land and sheep and pleasure, for money and lust and rum, for their children and their new country, seldom troubling over God's existence, quite absorbed in their own. This was not new. What was new, and what heartened the churchmen in this era of deeper and wider attention to religious needs, was a readier response among rather more people. There was no mighty revival, but, far from declining, religion distinctly gained ground. A decline in religion is not a necessary deduction from the 'free, secular and compulsory' education Acts of the sixties and seventies. These neither removed religious teaching entirely from the schools, nor indicated a new scorn of religion in private and community life. Independency, after all, has a long history in Christianity, going somewhat farther back than the day, which some would call ill-fated, when the Roman State adopted the Christian religion. There are too many intangibles in the history of religion to allow of any easy conclusions regarding its role in any period, its rise or decline.

Perhaps the least risky generalization from the Churches' story in

---

[5] M. Roe, 'Society and Thought in Eastern Australia, 1835-51' (Ph.D. Thesis, A.N.U., 1960), p. vi.
[6] C. M. H. Clark, *A History of Australia* (Melbourne, 1962), I, p. 380.

Australia is that the basic situation has remained much the same, though the scenes have altered in each successive chapter. The Church which hoped to be established was emphatically denied that privilege in the eighteen thirties, yet it is still among the strongest of Churches. Church extension was boosted by State aid, but the Churches spread and built their sanctuaries no less when government assistance was withdrawn. The voice of the Churches is faint in twentieth-century Australian education, but that voice was not convincing in the nineteenth century either. Secular systems of State education came in to dominate the schools before 1850, yet the question of State aid to church schools is still being raised, though a century has passed. Many Australians now prefer the sun and the beach to the interior of a church, yet as high a proportion of them attend worship as in colonial days. Most Australians seldom go to church, but most attach a denominational label to themselves. The Churches have neither fully consolidated their victories, nor completely succumbed to their defeats. In winning, the Churches have often lost; in losing, they have still held much ground. The Churches are always on the decline, but never fade away. Revival is often round the corner, but has never turned it yet.

The interpreter of Australian religious history must balance two facts. One is that at no time has the striving for a secular Utopia replaced the striving for the Kingdom of Heaven among a substantial minority of the people. The other is that the Australian Churches have never been able to claim the dedicated allegiance of more than a minority of the people. Perhaps the Churches would have done better if they had been more liberal towards the middle of the nineteenth century. At any rate they have not done better, and they do not seem to have done worse. The position of the Churches in the Australian community has been constantly changing yet essentially the same. There is little drama here for the historian. Its absence may lead him to talk of religious decline. If so, he must first justify the implication that religion in the Australian colonies was ever on a sufficiently high level to make it reasonable to speak of a later decline. This would be extremely difficult, and the voices heard again in these pages would not agree with him. More often, the historian is inclined simply to ignore the role of religion in Australia. This is no less wrong. Colonial legislatures do not wrangle for decades over State aid and church schools without some impact on community life and thinking; and churches and ministers have not appeared in every Australian town and hamlet without cause and effect. He who would rightly interpret Australian history must remember the religious aspect.

INDEX OF CONTEMPORARY
AUSTRALIAN HISTORIANS

GENERAL INDEX

Aborigines, 43, 176, 195, 196
Allen, George, 109
Allwood, Rev. Robert, 108, 142
Allyn River (N.S.W.), 173
Anstey, Thomas, 121
Antill family, 155
Argyle county (N.S.W.), 26, 78
Arnold of Rugby, 31
Arnold, Thomas, 147
Arthur, Col. George, 27, 37, 115, 178
Atlas, 65, 113-14
Australian, 93
Australian School Society, 91

Backhouse, James, 13, 188
Back River (V.D.L.), 192
Baptists, 13, 36, 78, 106, 117, 120, 126,
  158, 175
Bathurst (N.S.W.): county, 26, 41, 78;
  town, 52, 173, 174, 175
Beamish, Rev. P. T., 58, 190
Beazley, Rev. Joseph, 27-8, 175
Bell, Rev. Andrew, 97, 115
Benevolent societies, 181
Bentham, Jeremy, 31
Bernard, W. D., 130
Bible in schools, 91, 94, 95, 118, 121,
  137-9
Bible societies, 182
Bishton, Rev. Henry, 124n., 125
Blaxland family, 155
Bligh, Capt. William, 87
Blomfield, Rt Rev. C. J., 5
Bonwick, James, 125, 128 139, 145
Bothwell (V.D.L.), 120
Bourke, Sir Richard: Church and State,
  2, 33-4, 45; critic of Broughton, 88, 96;
  on education, 88-9, 153
Bowden, Thomas, 87
Bowen, G. M. C., 168, 193
Bowman, J., 70
Boyce, Rev. W. B., 202
Braidwood (N.S.W.), 62, 75, 172
Braim, Rev. T. H., 120, 124
Brisbane, Sir Thomas, 87
Broad Marsh (V.D.L.), 27
Brodribb family, 156
Broken River (Vic.), 176
Broughton, Rt Rev. W. G.: Anglican
  bishop, 12, 25; conservative in politics,
29, 140-1, 198; control of diocese, 58,
  190; critic of Church Act, 34-5, 49-50,
  62; defends Church and School Corporation, 33; demands more religious
  provision, 18, 25, 46, 143, 182; excluded
  from Legislative Council, 105; forgoes
  part of stipend, 56-7, 72, 198; high
  churchman, 189; introduces offertory,
  65; opinions (Bible reading) 139, 143,
  (clerical education) 179, (family prayers) 25, 144, (land policy) 69, (religion
  in England) 18, 19, 143, (Roman
  Catholics) 190, (science) 142, 202, (Sunday observance) 197, (Tractarians) 190;
  pastoral tours, 77-8, 172-3; people's
  support, 66, 67-8, 71, 95, 100, 191; re-
  signs from Executive Council, 50;
  school campaign (addresses) 95-6, 100,
  (Chairman, General Committee of
  Protestants) 92, (charged with inconsistency) 98, (critic of Arthur) 116,
  (critic of Bourke) 88, (final stand) 113
Bungadore (N.S.W.), 173
Bungonia (N.S.W.), 176
Bunting, Rev. Jabez, 99
Buntingdale aboriginal mission, 43
Burrows (N.S.W.), 174
Buxton family, 156

Cambridge (V.D.L.), 128
Camden (N.S.W.): county, 78; town, 70,
  78
Campaspe River (Vic.), 176
Campbell, Robert, 70
Campbelltown (N.S.W.), 155
Campbell Town (V.D.L.), 161
Cape Colony, 119
Cape, W. T., 110
Carlyle, Thomas, 4-5
Carmichael, Rev. Henry, 159
Cartwright, Rev. Robert, 174
Casterton (Vic.), 176
Castle, J. F., 157, 170, 196
Castle Hill (N.S.W.), 169
Catholic emancipation, 32
Catholics, Roman: anti-catholicism, 91-
  3, 100, 108; arrival of clergy, 13, 46;
  early difficulties, 11-13, 26; erection of
  Hierarchy, 57; in U.K., 21, 23-4; in-
  cluded in Church Acts, 34, 38; re-

Society of Christian Brothers, 110
Society of Friends, *see* Quakers
South Australia, 66
Sowerby, Rev. W., 160-1
Spurr, Rev. T., 125
Squatters: defined, 67; religious atti-
tudes, 68-71, 169-70, 171-2, 177-8, 180;
see also Land Policies
Stackhouse, Rev. Alfred, 194
Stanley district (N.S.W.), 78
Stanley, Lord, fourteenth Earl, 48, 89,
105, 130
State aid abolished, 52, 55-6n., 112n.
Steel, Peter, 110, 148, 149
Stiles, Rev. H. T., 178, 190, 191n.
Strauss, D. F., 167
Sunday observance, 168-9, 181, 197
Suttor, W. H., 70; family, 155
Swan Port (V.D.L.), 28
Swanston, Charles, 54
Sydney (N.S.W.): Anglican diocese, 190;
in the 1840s, 2; population centre, 28;
on Sundays, 169; school petitions,
106-7
Sydney Gazette, 93
Sydney [Morning] Herald, 2, 35, 67, 93,
98, 108, 200
Symons, Rev. J. C., 188

Tasmanian, 39, 116, 117
Tasmanian Natural History Society, 201
Temperance societies, 151, 182-3
Therry, Rev. J. J., 13, 33, 122
Therry, Roger, 102
Thomson, James, 120
Thrupp family, 156
Tory Party, 30, 31-2
Tractarians, 6, 31, 65, 128-9, 189-91
Tracts for the Times, 6, 189
True Colonist, 120, 121, 130
Tumut (N.S.W.), 172
Turner, Rev. G. E., 190
Turner, Rev. Nathaniel, 160, 192

Twofold Bay (Vic.), 176
Tyrrell, Rt Rev. William, 57, 113

Ullathorne, Rev. Dr W. B., 101, 103,
103-4, 194
United States of America, 83, 183, 186,
192
Utilitarianism, 140

Voyages to Australia, 170-1

Walker, Rev. James, 201
Walker, J. J., 25
Walsh, Rev. R., 176
Walsh, Rev. W. H., 178
Waterfield, Rev. William, 72, 175
Wellington Valley (N.S.W.), 182
Wentworth, W. C., 105, 114, 172, 178
West, Rev. John, 45, 120, 159, 175, 202
Western Australia, 172
Western District (Vic.), 70, 109, 170, 191
Westwood, J. J., 191
Whewell, Rev. William, 199
Whig Party, 30, 89, 91, 97
White Hills District (V.D.L.), 187
Wilberforce, William, 4
Wilkins, W., 145, 147
Wilkinson, Thomas, 120
William's River (N.S.W.), 26
Willson, Rt Rev. R. W., 57
Wilton, Rev. C. P. N., 201
Wimmera (Vic.), 176
Windsor (N.S.W.), 179, 182, 190
Wiseman, Solomon, 69, 109
Wollongong (N.S.W.), 78, 90, 101, 172,
175
Women, religious influence, 25, 70-1,
170
Woolls, Rev. William, 156, 201
Wroeites, 83n., 191

Yass (N.S.W.), 169, 172, 173, 174
Yate, Rev. William, 194